# MUSIC

## Is the Answer

# MUSIC
# Is the Answer

Practical Ways to ***Manage Stress***, ***Sleep Better***, and ***Live Brighter***

ROB STEPHENSON

WILEY

Published by John Wiley & Sons, Inc., Hoboken, New Jersey.



For general information on our other products and services or for technical support, please contact our Customer Care Department within the United States at (800) 762-2974, outside the United States at (317) 572-3993 or fax (317) 572-4002.

Wiley also publishes its books in a variety of electronic formats. Some content that appears in print may not be available in electronic formats. For more information about Wiley products, visit our web site at www.wiley.com.

***Library of Congress Cataloging-in-Publication Data:***

Names: Stephenson, Rob (Writer of Music is the answer) author
Title: Music is the answer / Rob Stephenson.
Description: First edition. | Hoboken, New Jersey : John Wiley & Sons, Inc, 2026. | Includes bibliographical references and index.
Identifiers: LCCN 2026021507 (print) | LCCN 2026021508 (ebook) | ISBN 9781394419609 cloth | ISBN 9781394419623 adobe pdf | ISBN 9781394419616 epub
Subjects: LCSH: Music therapy | Music—Psychological aspects | Music, Influence of | Self-help techniques
Classification: LCC ML3920 .S814 2026 (print) | LCC ML3920 (ebook) | DDC 615.8/5154—dc23/eng/20260428
LC record available at https://lccn.loc.gov/2026021507
LC ebook record available at https://lccn.loc.gov/2026021508

Cover Design: Jon Boylan
Cover Image: PNG Lab/stock.adobe.com
Author Photo: Courtesy of Rob Stephenson

# Generative AI Disclosure

ChatGPT-5.1 was used across Parts I and II to assist with research and concept development and Parts I, II, and III to assist with editing and reviewing content for spelling, grammar, clarity, and conciseness.

The human review process included careful line-by-line editing, fact checking, and style adjustments to ensure the final text was authentic, warm, and aligned with the author's voice. The influence on the conclusion was to enhance accessibility and readability, while maintaining the personal and emotional resonance that is central to the book's message.

*For Gabby and Noah. Thank you for always inspiring me.*

# Contents

# Introduction – The Universal Language

There's a moment just before the drop in your favorite song when the world seems to hold its breath – shoulders soften, your chest opens a little, and for a second you remember what ease feels like.

It's not magic. It's music.

Music is one of the few things that reaches us before language ever can. Long before we know how to form sentences, we know how to respond to melody. A lullaby can settle a crying baby; a chorus can lift a roomful of strangers. Music can stabilize, energize, soothe, and shift us because it is built into our biology.

And crucially, the science backs this up. Throughout the book, you'll see research and references that show just how deeply music influences the systems that shape our mood, stress, energy, and well-being.

When we hear a track we love, our brain releases dopamine – the same chemical that powers motivation and delight. Music also boosts endorphins, which naturally soften pain and increase a sense of lightness. These chemical changes aren't abstract: they're why a favorite track can steady anxious thoughts, lift a low mood, or help us reconnect with ourselves when we feel disconnected.

Research shows that music can support stress recovery, improve sleep, reduce perceived pain, enhance memory, and boost performance. It's far more than background noise – it's a portable well-being tool we all have access to.

Why does it hold such power? Because music bypasses the part of our brain that tries to analyze everything. It goes straight to feeling. It reaches the emotional center directly, without requiring us to explain or justify anything.

In a world obsessed with speed, optimization, and constant output, music gives us something rare: a genuine pause. A recalibration. A reminder that we're human long before we're productive.

So, what if we started using music on purpose – not just as something that happens around us, but as something that actively supports us? A way to shift your stress levels, restore calm, boost your energy, or steady your mind.

Picture using a playlist to get into the right headspace before a big meeting. Or to unwind when the day has taken more from you than you expected. Or to lift you through the last stretch of a workout. Music can be coach, companion, and grounding force all at once.

This book will show you how. We'll explore the science, translate it into simple practices, and help you build playlists that support different moments of your life. By the end, music will feel like a trusted ally – one that helps you rest more deeply, focus more clearly, and live more intentionally.

The best part? You don't need to be a musician or a DJ. You just need to listen – and trust that music is, and always has been, the answer.

## Last Night a DJ Saved My Life

I've always known that music was more than just background noise for me – it's been a lifeline. From the goosebumps on my arms when a favorite song plays to the unexpected tears certain melodies bring – music has always moved me deeply and viscerally. As someone who lives with bipolar disorder, I've relied on music to help keep my mood balanced, to ground me through the highs and the lows. Before the pandemic, cycling was the most important pillar of my well-being. The open road, the rhythm of the pedals, the rush of endorphins – all played a vital role in keeping my mind healthy.

Then COVID hit, a sudden shift that left me vulnerable and uncertain, and with it came long COVID. Lack of energy, chronic fatigue, headaches, and nausea were all symptoms of this mysterious post-viral condition. However, crucially, my ability to exercise was suddenly taken from me, and I worried deeply about the impact this would have on my mental health. The threat of falling into depression felt real and close. But rather than give in, I turned to the other constant in my life: music. I threw myself back into DJing, creating new mixes, streaming online, and even started producing my own tracks.

DJing became a deeply mindful practice – completely present, absorbed in the music and crowd. A 10-hour set at a friend's wedding in Formentera tested my resilience but gave me a profound sense of connection. Playing "We Are Your Friends" by Justice & Simian was a special moment, with everyone surrounding the bride and groom in pure joy.

**Guided Listening**

Scan the QR code to listen to "We Are Your Friends." If you are reading digitally, you may find it easier to click the hyperlink in the song title and look out for links whenever you see a QR code.

DJing clears my mind and lifts my spirit, creating experiences that boost my own well-being as much as the audience's. You might not be a DJ, but you've probably felt that same spark – dancing in your kitchen, singing in the shower, or swaying at a gig. This book is about helping you capture and harness that feeling as a tool for your own well-being.

For me, music doesn't just fill a gap – it is my primary source of strength, helping me stay well and connected when I need it most. This powerful realization inspired me to create two music and mental health performances: Harmonizing the Mind and Life Lyrics. It also ultimately sparked the idea for this book, because I want you to discover the same joy and healing that I found – to realize that music can truly be the answer to many of our problems.

Are you with me on this journey?

Together, we'll discover how you can create your own soundtrack for well-being – and let music become your most loyal guide.

## Your Guide to This Journey

Think of this book as a musical journey, not a textbook. You don't have to read it all in one go, and you certainly don't have to follow every suggestion perfectly. Each chapter helps you explore a different way music can support your well-being – whether that's boosting your energy, helping you sleep better, or lifting your mood on a tough day. The book has a special approach: blending personal stories, science, and practical tools to give you a well-rounded perspective.

Throughout, you'll find mantras, guided listening exercises, and QR code links to Spotify for songs and playlists to make the experience immersive and interactive. (There are also hyperlinks for those reading digitally.) Listen along as you read or return to them whenever you need a boost. You might not love every track – our music tastes are as unique and personal as our well-being journeys. But don't worry, we'll explore a wide range of genres and styles, so there's something to inspire everyone.

You'll also come across reflection prompts. For example: "What song matches your mood today?," "What do you need right now?," or "What memory does this song bring up?" These help you pause and check in with yourself. They are gentle invitations to notice how you're feeling, connect with your emotions, and explore how music might support you in that moment. You can jot your thoughts down in a journal, share them with a friend, or simply reflect quietly. Some prompts are short and focused, and others are longer and more open. Either way, don't overthink them – just use the prompts as a chance to deepen your self-awareness and make the experience more personal. Revisit these prompts as often as you'd like – they're not just one-off exercises, but ongoing tools to help you tune into yourself over time.

Most importantly, this book invites you to experiment in a supportive, non-judgmental space. Think of it as your personal invitation to play – to explore, to tune in to what you need, and to find the songs and pieces that resonate with you. There's no right or wrong way to use music for your well-being – only your way.

By the end of the book, you'll have a toolkit of musical strategies to help you manage stress, improve sleep, and feel more alive.

## Time to Check-In

Music has the power to move us – but first, we need to understand where we're at. Let's start with a gentle invitation to connect inward before we press play.

Before we go any further, let's pause for a moment and check in with ourselves – because music works best when we know how we feel first. Taking the time to check in on our well-being is essential; it helps us stay connected to ourselves, notice early signs of stress or imbalance, and make choices that support our mental and emotional health.

Take a deep breath. Ask yourself, how am I feeling today, really? There's no judgment here – the goal is simply to notice and become aware. As part of this check-in, also reflect on some key drivers of your well-being: How has your sleep been? Are you moving your body and getting exercise? How are your connections with friends and family? What are your stress levels, energy, and motivation like today? Taking a moment to consider these factors can give you a fuller picture of where you are right now.

You might even rate your overall well-being on a scale of 1–10, where 10 represents feeling your best and 1 reflects being in crisis. I developed this approach into a tool called FormScore, designed to help you build self-awareness and track your well-being over time (see Figure I.1).

**Figure I.1 The FormScore Scale.**

We recommend reflecting on your well-being daily or weekly. You don't need to dedicate much time to it – simply asking yourself, "How am I today?" over a coffee or while brushing your teeth can be enough. Anchoring this check-in to an existing habit makes it more likely to stick and be more impactful.

Now, here's a little experiment to consider. What song best represents your well-being today? It might be an energizing anthem, a slow ballad, an old favorite, or even something you've never shared with anyone before.

At the time of writing, my choice would be the beautiful "Fast Car" by Tracy Chapman. My FormScore is 5/10 – reflecting a lower mood, but I'm feeling resolute and motivated. The feeling of the song captures this balance of struggle and hope perfectly for me today.

How about you? Write down your choice. Listen to it. Feel it. This simple act of matching a song to your current state can help you understand your emotions more clearly – and give you a musical snapshot of where you are right now. If you feel comfortable, share your choice with a friend or loved one – and ask them what theirs would be. This is an exercise in trust and vulnerability that can spark a moment of real and meaningful connection. By opening up about your inner world through music, you invite deeper conversations and strengthen your relationships.

Throughout this book, we'll keep coming back to the idea of checking in, choosing intentionally, and letting music guide us back to ourselves.

Now, are you ready to press play?

Let's go.

# PART I
# The Power of Music

Music is, and always has been, the answer.

# 1 Music and the Brain

I've always loved music for as long as I can remember – way before I ever thought about the science behind it. As a teenager, I'd blast motivational tracks through cheap headphones before a basketball game, hoping the right beat would switch something on inside me. Late at night, I'd sit in my room pretending to be a radio DJ, introducing songs to an imaginary audience while everyone else slept. In my twenties, I threw myself into learning to DJ properly – a process that involved as much frustration as it did joy. Beat-matching, mixing, starting again when it all fell apart. . .but when it worked, it felt like magic.

Yet, for all those years of loving music, depending on it, shaping my identity around it – I'd never really stopped to think about what music *is*. What actually happens between a vibrating string or a kick drum and your ears along with the feeling it creates inside us.

## What Is Music?

Music, at its simplest, is organized sound (Varèse & Wen-Chung, 1966). But what does that really mean? Before we can explore how music shapes our mood and brain, we need to understand what sound is – and how our brain transforms it into the rich emotional experiences we call music.

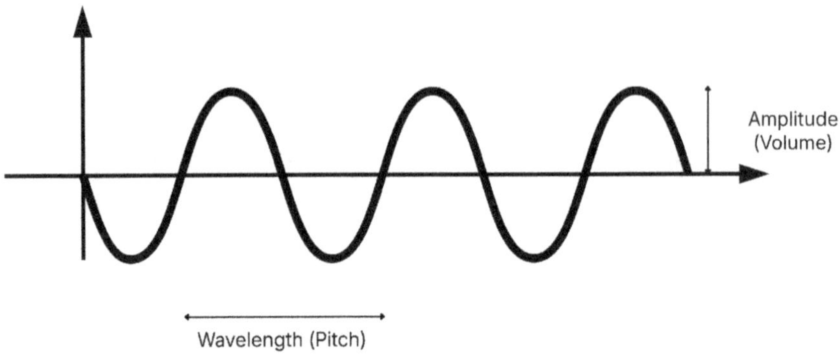


**Figure 1.1 Music begins as physics – but it ends as feeling.**

Sound begins as vibration, with waves moving through the air (or another medium) that enter our ears. (See Figure 1.1.) The ear picks these waves up and converts them into electrical signals that travel to the brain. Only then do they become what we recognize as sound – and, ultimately, music.

However, this raises a key question. Why should something purely governed by the rules of physics have the power to feel like a warm wave washing over you on a summer day, or bring tears to your eyes with a single note? This mystery lies at the heart of music's emotional magic – it is the way the brain transforms simple vibrations into deeply felt human experiences, turning raw sound into moments of meaning and connection.

The brain interprets these vibrations in several essential ways – a bit like how you instinctively tell the difference between a friend's voice and a stranger's, or why a single off-beat note can make you smile, flinch, or stop what you're doing. Even if we don't consciously notice each element, they still shape our emotional response at a deep level. Here's a list of the various elements of music:

- **Pitch:** the perceived highness or lowness of a sound, created by the frequency of the waves. (Think of the different sounds from the keys on a piano.)
- **Volume:** the loudness or softness of a sound, tied to the amplitude of the waves.

- **Timbre:** the unique texture or color of a sound that helps us distinguish between instruments or voices.
- **Rhythm:** patterns of sound and silence that create a sense of movement or groove.
- **Harmony:** the combination of different pitches that create chords and emotional depth.
- **Contour:** the shape or direction of a melody as it rises and falls.
- **Tempo:** the overall speed or pace of a piece of music.
- **Key:** the "home base" or tonal center that gives a piece of music its mood.
- **Spatial position:** how we perceive where a sound is coming from – left or right, near or far – which creates a sense of space and immersion when listening.
- **Reverberation:** how sound reflects and decays in a space, creating a sense of depth or atmosphere. A spacious, echoing reverb can feel dreamy or ethereal, while a dry sound feels intimate and direct.

Our brain doesn't just receive these signals passively – it actively organizes, interprets, and assigns emotional meaning to them. In this way, the brain itself becomes the true instrument. This is why music can make us cry, dance, reflect, or feel energized. The same piece of music can bring comfort to one person and nostalgia or sadness to another. Music is both universal and deeply personal; it connects us to each other and to ourselves.

Across all cultures and throughout human history, music has served as a tool for communication, healing, ritual, and storytelling. From drum circles to lullabies, anthems to chants, music helps us process joy and grief, mark transitions, and create community.

Importantly, music is not reserved for the skilled or the elite – it belongs to everyone, and you have the power to use it as your own personal well-being tool. Using music intentionally is a skill anyone can learn and develop over time, and you're encouraged to experiment without worrying about "getting it wrong." Let's have a go, together.

**Guided Listening**

Scan the QR code to listen to ABBA's "Gimme! Gimme! Gimme! (A Man After Midnight)."

As you listen, focus on just a few elements such as the driving tempo, the rise and fall of the main melody, and the contrast between the bass line and the string stabs. Notice how these layers work together to lift your energy and shift your mood. Keep it simple – pay attention to what you feel and what changes as the song unfolds. Enjoy this joyful exploration – focus on how it makes you move and feel, without worrying about "getting it right."

You might even repeat this exercise with different songs to deepen your understanding and discover new layers each time.

## The Science of Music and the Brain

Ever wondered why your favorite song can make your heart race, bring tears to your eyes, or give you goosebumps, as if someone has flipped a secret emotional switch inside you? The answer lies in the beautifully complex way our brain processes music – a process that feels almost like magic, but is deeply rooted in science.

When we listen to music, a symphony of brain regions lights up and starts working together, just like different sections of an orchestra coming together to create a powerful performance. Let's meet these players who all contribute to the overall harmony, working together like an orchestra in perfect sync – each with its own instrument and role, harmonizing to shape our emotional experience.

### *The Concert Hall – Auditory System*

Before the orchestra starts, the auditory system acts like the concert hall itself – the space that receives and shapes sound before it reaches the players. Sound waves enter our ears, travel through the auditory pathways – the series of neural routes that sound information follows from the ear to the brain's higher processing centers. This sets the stage for the emotional symphony that follows.

### *The Conductor – Prefrontal Cortex*

The prefrontal cortex acts like the conductor of our brain's orchestra. It sits at the front of your brain and is responsible for higher-order functions like decision-making, planning, self-control, and interpreting complex emotions. It helps us focus on the music, interpret its emotional meaning, and decide how we respond – whether we sing along, dance, or simply close our eyes and feel every note. This region weaves together all the different sections into a unified, meaningful experience, giving music its personal significance and depth.

### *The Percussion Section – Amygdala*

The amygdala is our brain's emotional alarm system and one of its oldest evolutionary structures. Think of it like the percussion section. This part of the brain evolved long before our rational thinking abilities, which is why it can react so instantly and instinctively to music's emotional cues. Quick, powerful, and impossible to ignore, it sets the emotional tone in an instant, just as a dramatic drumroll or cymbal crash can electrify an audience. It helps us process the feelings that music stirs up, whether it's excitement, nostalgia, or pure joy. This ancient part of the brain rapidly scans our environment for emotional cues and plays a central role in triggering immediate emotional reactions, making music feel intensely moving and deeply instinctual.

On a personal note, when I'm auditioning new tracks for a DJ set, I can often tell within a few seconds which ones will work – not because I've analyzed them, but because of how they make me feel almost immediately. That flash of excitement or tension? That's the amygdala at work.

### *The Strings – Hippocampus*

The hippocampus, known for its role in memory, acts like the string section, weaving rich, emotive melodies that connect us to our memories and past experiences. It ties certain songs to specific moments in our lives, making them feel deeply personal and powerful. Maybe singing "Wonderwall" with friends in a park, jumping around to "House of Pain" at a wedding, or the song you listened to on repeat as you grieved for a loved one.

> ***Reflection prompt:*** *What song instantly transports you back in time? Write it down and notice what feelings arise.*

### *The Metronome – Cerebellum*

The cerebellum, sometimes called the brain's rhythm keeper, acts like our internal metronome. While in an actual orchestra this timing role would be performed by the conductor waving their baton to keep every section in time, in our brain, the cerebellum works behind the scenes to ensure that all movements and timing are precisely coordinated, supporting our ability to move and dance smoothly in sync with the music. It's why your foot starts tapping without you thinking, why you can clap along at a concert, and why a beat drop can make your whole body respond before your mind has caught up.

### *The Audience – Sensory Cortex*

The sensory cortex receives and processes sensory information from the body – like touch, temperature, and body position. In the context of music, it helps us physically feel the vibrations through the floor or a speaker, the tingling sensation from loud bass, or the goosebumps that spread across our skin when we hear an especially moving passage. Here, it acts as the attentive audience, fully experiencing and interpreting the final emotional performance crafted by all the other sections.

### *The Brass Section – Nucleus Accumbens*

Meanwhile, the nucleus accumbens, a core part of our brain's reward system, acts like the brass section – bold, thrilling, and deeply satisfying. It is responsible for that rush of pleasure we feel when the orchestral crescendo hits or a beautiful melody soars. It helps us crave and anticipate musical moments, amplifying our emotional response and making us want to keep coming back for more. This region is also closely tied to motivation and reinforcement, explaining why music can feel so rewarding and even addictive in the best possible way.

### *The Chemistry of Joy*

Beyond the individual players in our brain's orchestra, we have the chemistry that floods the concert hall. Music triggers the almost instant release of feel-good chemicals, showing how quickly it can uplift and energize us. Dopamine is actually often called the "feel-good" neurotransmitter – it's the same chemical released when we eat delicious food, achieve a goal, or fall in love. In today's world, many of us chase dopamine through endless "doom scrolling" on social media, hunting for likes and external validation. These spikes are often shallow and short-lived, leaving us feeling empty and craving more. Music, however, offers a healthier, more natural way to get our dopamine fix – one that provides deeper, longer-lasting emotional rewards and truly nourishes us rather than drains us.

Endorphins, on the other hand, act like natural painkillers and stress relievers, helping us feel calm and even euphoric. They are released by the pituitary gland and the central nervous system, especially during activities like exercise, where they help reduce pain and create a sense of well-being often known as a "runner's high." Music, much like exercise, can stimulate the release of endorphins, providing a natural boost to our mood and helping us manage stress more effectively.

Just like the roaring applause and cheers from a captivated audience, dopamine and endorphins represent the waves of joy, excitement, and relief that flood through us when all these sections play in harmony. They don't play instruments themselves – instead, they amplify the entire experience, making us want more and helping us feel connected and alive.

### *Neuroplasticity – The Ongoing Rehearsal*

Over time, listening to music doesn't just spark these momentary bursts of happiness – it can actually help reshape our brain. This is down to neuroplasticity: the brain's amazing ability to reorganize itself and form new connections. For example, learning a new instrument or practicing a challenging piece can strengthen and create new neural pathways, supporting lifelong brain health by keeping the mind adaptable and resilient. In this orchestra metaphor, neuroplasticity is like the ongoing rehearsals and refinements that help each section play better together over time. By engaging with music regularly, we can strengthen the neural pathways that support positive moods, resilience, and emotional balance. This all makes your inner orchestra more skilled and expressive with every practice.

I experienced this firsthand when I was learning to beat-match on vinyl in my twenties. At first it felt impossible. The tiny pitch-fader adjustments, listening for minute timing differences, nudging the record at exactly the right moment. My brain had no idea what to do with all that sensory information. But with repetition, something clicked. My ears learned to detect micro-differences in tempo, my hands learned how much pressure to apply, and my brain built a whole new network of timing, coordination, and feel. That's neuroplasticity in action.

Music isn't just entertainment – it's a powerful tool that shapes our emotions, memories, and even the very wiring of our brains. And that's something truly worth turning up the volume for. So next time you press play, remember – you're conducting a symphony within your own mind.

## Further Reading

For a deeper dive into these fascinating concepts, check out *This Is Your Brain on Music* by Daniel J. Levitin (2006) – a brilliant exploration of the science behind our emotional and cognitive responses to music.

# 2 Music and Mood

Have you ever noticed how certain songs can instantly lift you up, calm you down, or help you process a heartbreak? Music is like a remote control for our emotions.

Understanding and regulating our mood is essential for overall well-being, and music offers a powerful, accessible way to support this.

Music has an incredible power to shift our emotional state. And importantly, these effects aren't just anecdotal – they're supported by a growing body of scientific research, which we'll reference throughout. Whether we need an energy boost to tackle a workout, a calming influence to unwind after a stressful day, or a comforting presence to navigate difficult emotions, music can help us get there.

In this chapter, we explore these ideas – and we'll be delving deeper into these concepts later in the book, exploring practical strategies, playlists, and real-life stories to help you harness music's full power for mood and well-being.

## Different Types of Music and Their Emotional Influence

We relate emotionally to different songs and styles. Here are some examples:

- Uplifting and energizing music: These are the tracks that feel like a shot of sunlight – fast tempos, bright major keys, and strong beats that naturally pull your energy upward. Think of the songs that make you want to move before you've even realized it.

- Calming and soothing music: Rather than focusing on tempo alone, these tracks invite you to slow down. Gentle melodies, spacious arrangements, and softer textures help the nervous system settle.
- Melancholic or reflective music: Instead of simply being "sad songs," this kind of music can help us sit with our emotions. For many people, reflective tracks offer companionship – a sense of being understood.
- Empowering or motivational music: Some songs feel like a pep talk – bold vocals, strong builds, or lyrics that speak to resilience. These are the tracks people reach for before big moments.
- Groovy or rhythmic music: Music with a strong groove – funk, Afrobeat, certain electronic genres – often works on the body first. You feel it before you think it, which is why it so often boosts mood and social connection – like funk or certain electronic genres can encourage movement and connection, lifting energy levels and enhancing feelings of joy and social bonding.

## Types of Listening

We engage with music in different ways, and each one affects us slightly differently. Sometimes we choose a song with a clear purpose – to lift our mood, to calm down, or to help us focus. Other times, music simply sits in the background while we go about our day. And in more intentional settings, music can even be used in a guided or therapeutic way to support healing or emotional regulation. You don't need to memorize categories – just notice how you're listening, and how each approach makes you feel.

## Practical Ideas for Using Music to Regulate Your Mood

Imagine that you've had a long day. You walk through the door feeling drained, and before you even think about what you need, you hit play on a favorite song. Within seconds, your shoulders drop, your breath deepens, and the tension begins to soften. This is where mood-shifting with music really begins. Not with perfect playlists or a five-step plan, but with small, human moments like this.

With that in mind, here are some gentle approaches you can play with:

- Instead of creating rigid playlists, think of broad emotional "zones," such as comfort, clarity, or activation – and drop songs into them over time. Let them evolve naturally.
- Use music as a bridge between parts of your day. For example, a grounding track on your commute home can help you shed the workday before you walk through your front door.
- When you feel stuck, try pausing for a moment and asking yourself, "What do I need right now?" A lift, a slowdown, a release? Let your answer guide your choice.
- If singing, moving, or playing an instrument feels good, let yourself lean into it. Sometimes humming along while you make dinner does more for your mood than a perfectly curated playlist.
- Pair music with small rituals, such as a warm drink, a stretch, or dimming the lights to help the emotional shift land more fully.

Above all, approach this as an experiment. There's no right or wrong – only what works for you.

## Additional Dimensions of Music and Mood

Music shapes our emotional world in more ways than we often realize. It can transport us back to a specific memory, deepen our sense of connection with others, help us express who we are, or even steady our breathing and calm our nervous system. Music can sharpen our focus, fuel our creativity, or offer a safe space to explore emotions we find difficult to name. And in the quieter moments, music – or even intentional silence – can help us reset and reconnect with ourselves.

You'll see these ideas woven throughout the rest of the book – each chapter picking up one of these threads and exploring it more deeply. For example, how music links to memory and identity, how it supports focus and rest, how it strengthens relationships and communities, and how it can act as a companion through joy, uncertainty, or healing. Think of this chapter as a starting point – a first look at the many ways music touches our inner world.

## Illustrative Examples

Listening to a soft piano playlist while journaling can help you process emotions and calm your mind, just as an empowering anthem before an important meeting can boost confidence and sharpen your focus. In the evenings, nature sounds blended with ambient music can ease you into rest, while upbeat Latin or Afrobeat rhythms can lift your spirits or add energy to a workout on low-motivation days. And for moments of stillness, traditional chanting or spiritual music can help deepen meditation or create a sense of grounding and connection.

> ***Reflection prompt:*** *Take a few minutes to reflect: What type of music have you turned to lately? Was it intentional, or just in the background? How did it make you feel – and what do you need next? You might also journal about this or discuss it with someone close to you to deepen your reflection.*

# 3 Intentional Listening and Building Playlists

Music can be so much more than a background soundtrack to our daily lives. While passive listening can still bring us joy, intentional listening transforms music into a powerful tool for well-being. Intentional listening means choosing music with a specific purpose in mind: to shift your mood, energize your body, soothe your mind, or help you focus. When we approach music this way, we actively participate in our emotional and mental states rather than simply reacting to them.

On a scientific level, this matters because intentional listening engages our brain's reward system more fully. It increases the release of dopamine (the "feel-good" chemical) and endorphins (our natural painkillers and mood boosters). This targeted engagement can help us manage stress, boost motivation, and deepen our emotional resilience (Chanda & Levitin, 2013).

## The Science Behind Intentional Listening

Why does intention make such a difference? Research shows that music is significantly more effective when we listen with a clear goal. For example, studies have shown that people who deliberately try to improve their mood while listening to upbeat music experience greater increases in happiness compared to those who listen passively (Ferguson & Sheldon, 2013).

Curated playlists designed for emotion regulation can help reduce self-stigma and encourage individuals to seek further mental health support (Krause et al., 2020). Deep absorption in music – fully immersing yourself rather than treating it as background noise – is strongly linked to more powerful mood effects and better emotional regulation (Saarikallio & Erkkilä, 2007). In clinical settings, guided playlists have been shown to support stress reduction and help relieve anxiety more effectively than general music listening (Thoma et al., 2013).

Beyond mood shifts, engaging intentionally with music can strengthen our sense of agency and emotional self-efficacy – in simple terms, the feeling that *"I can influence how I feel, and I have tools that help me do that."* At the same time, it's worth staying mindful. Certain songs can sometimes reinforce sadness or negative patterns, so it's important to notice what truly supports you and adjust as needed.

This practice gives us a tangible way to influence our internal world, reinforcing that we are not merely at the mercy of our feelings but can actively guide them. This deepens the sense of empowerment and personal growth.

These benefits tie directly into the brain mechanisms we explored in Chapter 1, "Music and the Brain." The reward system (nucleus accumbens), emotional processing centers (amygdala), and executive functions (prefrontal cortex) all work together when we intentionally engage with music (Chanda & Levitin, 2013).

## The Power of Curated Playlists

Playlists allow us to harness the power of intention in a tangible, structured way. By creating playlists for specific emotional states or activities – like energy, relaxation, focus, or comfort – we build a personal well-being toolkit that we can reach for whenever we need support.

Because everyone's emotional and musical responses are unique, playlists offer an opportunity for deep personalization. You're not just choosing songs; you're crafting an emotional journey that reflects your needs and helps you move toward the state you want to be in.

## Practical Guidance on Creating Playlists

Start by asking yourself how you want to feel. Once you've identified your desired state, choose songs that evoke that feeling for you. Be open to experimenting and refining your selections over time.

Example playlists might include "Morning Motivation" for starting the day strong, "Stress Soother" for unwinding after work, or "Sleep Sanctuary" for easing into restful sleep. Don't be afraid to try new genres or artists – you might discover unexpected sources of comfort or inspiration.

## How to Integrate Playlists into Daily Life

One of the most consistent ways I use music intentionally is during my morning cold plunge. I'm usually in the water for 5 or 10 minutes, and I have a dedicated playlist for it – songs that give me energy, determination, and just enough attitude to override the instinct to get straight back out. At the time of writing, one of my go-to tracks is "Electric Feel (Justice Remix)" by MGMT and Justice. The moment the beat drops, something in me switches on. It becomes less about enduring the cold and more about riding the rhythm. This is a perfect example of how music can shape a daily ritual, turning something challenging into something empowering.

Think about the natural rhythms of your day and where music might support you. Use energizing playlists as part of your morning routine or calming playlists to transition into your evening. Playlists can boost focus before important meetings, provide a sense of ritual during workouts, or help signal to your brain that it's time to relax and prepare for sleep.

Building these habits makes music a reliable ally in your self-care practice, turning it into an intentional and empowering ritual rather than a passive experience.

---

### Example Mood Boosting Playlist and Guided Listening

Here's a playlist I turn to whenever I'm feeling flat and need a genuine boost. It features tracks across different genres and energy levels – from high-energy dance anthems to uplifting indie pop and soulful classics.

Scan the QR code to listen to Rob's Mood Boosting Playlist.

I often choose which song to start with, depending on my mood in that moment, and let the music guide me from there. "Eye of the Tiger" by Survivor is always a winning choice! It's also fun to put it on shuffle and see what pops up.

This playlist serves as a flexible emotional toolkit, offering options to match subtle shifts in how I feel and helping me move toward a more positive, energized state. As you explore, think about creating your own playlists too – they're a powerful way to personalize your emotional toolkit and make music work uniquely for you.

---

## Reflection and Personalization Exercise

Take a moment to check in with yourself. What do you need most right now? How do you feel today, and what music might support or shift that feeling? What playlists could you create to help guide you through different moments of your life?

Consider journaling about your experiences or sharing your reflections with a friend. The act of choosing, listening, and reflecting deepens your connection with both the music and with yourself.

## Connect to the Broader Journey

In later chapters, we'll explore more practical exercises, stories, and curated playlists to inspire and guide you further. Remember, music can be a lifelong companion – a reliable, ever-present ally for nurturing your emotional and mental well-being.

# 4 Stress, Recovery, and Rhythm

Picture yourself moments before stepping on stage to deliver a talk to a thousand people. Your palms are slick with sweat, your heart pounds against your chest, and each breath feels too shallow to steady you. I know this feeling well. I've been there. Stress is right beside you, humming like background noise that refuses to fade. In this moment, stress is both ally and adversary. It's a signal preparing your body for action, yet a force that can tip into overwhelm if left unchecked. Think of it like rhythm – when it's steady, it powers you forward; when it's chaotic, it drowns everything else out. Music, as we'll see, can be the reset button that restores harmony.

That racing heart before a keynote – and let's be honest, we've all had that split-second of "why am I doing this again?" – isn't so different from what our ancestors felt when survival was on the line. Stress has always been part of the human story – the real question is whether it helps us adapt, or whether it pushes us past the point of balance.

## What Is Stress?

Stress is not the enemy. And it doesn't show up the same way for everyone. Some feel it as a racing mind, others as a knot in the stomach or a burst of restless energy. It is an ancient survival system built into our bodies to keep us alive. When our ancestors faced a threat – like a sabre-tooth tiger emerging from the bushes – the body's fight-or-flight response kicked in. In an instant, your amygdala sounded the alarm, and the stress hormones of adrenaline and cortisol flooded the bloodstream. Your body shifted into survival mode. Heart rate and blood pressure spiked, breathing quickened, and focus narrowed to a razor-sharp point. Blood was diverted away from nonessential systems like digestion so that muscles had every ounce of fuel they needed to either fight or flee. This automatic response was lifesaving when danger was real and immediate.

That same mechanism is still at work today. The trouble is, the "tigers" we face aren't predators but looming deadlines, back-to-back meetings, or the relentless ping of notifications. Our bodies react just as if our life were at stake, but because the threats don't pass quickly, the stress response stays switched on. What once helped us survive can now leave us depleted, anxious, and burnt out.

In most of my keynotes, I like to make the point – and I often say this with a smile – that not all stress is bad. Acute stress – the kind that sharpens your focus before a big presentation – can actually improve performance. It gives you energy, alertness, and drive. Chronic stress, however, is when the system becomes overloaded. Without recovery, your stress hormone, cortisol, remains high, sleep and mood suffer, and the very system that once protected us begins to work against us.

That's why recovery is such an essential part of the stress cycle. The body is designed to ramp up under threat and then return to balance. Without that return, stress accumulates like static noise in the background, never letting the mind rest. Music offers one of the simplest ways to complete the cycle. A slow tempo track can bring your heart rate down, a steady rhythm can regulate your breath, and familiar melodies can soothe the amygdala's alarm. Later in this chapter, we'll explore how rhythm and music can help us release tension and restore harmony.

## Why Stress Is Such a Problem Today

Stress has always been part of human life – and here's the thing, it still is, but the way we experience it today is fundamentally different from our ancestors. Instead of rare, life-threatening encounters, we now live in an "always on" world. Emails, deadlines, and back-to-back meetings mean the body's alarm system is triggered far more often than it was designed for, and the recovery periods that used to follow are missing.

The World Health Organization has called stress "the health epidemic of the 21st century," and the evidence is stark. Two-thirds of employees report feeling burned out (Robinson, 2025) – the highest levels ever recorded – and surveys show that more than 9 out of 10 adults in the United Kingdom experienced high or extreme pressure in the past year, with a third feeling this way often or always (Mental Health UK, 2025). Stress is no longer an occasional spike; for many, it is a constant state. In all of my keynotes, I run a well-being check-in that captures the drivers behind how people are feeling. Stress is consistently one of the top three factors pulling scores down across every organization I work with.

The costs are immense. The World Health Organization and International Labour Organization estimate that depression and anxiety, much of it stress-related, result in 12 billion lost working days every year, costing the global economy around $1 trillion (WHO, 2024). Stress also directly affects health. Long working hours and chronic strain are linked to hundreds of thousands of deaths annually from heart disease and stroke. What starts as a racing heart before a presentation can, if repeated without recovery, translate into lasting damage to the body.

Psychologists often illustrate this with the Yerkes-Dodson curve, shown in Figure 4.1 (Yerkes & Dodson, 1908).

The curve itself is a simple inverted-U graph showing how a little stress can improve performance, but too much sends it crashing down. The problem in modern life is not stress itself, but under-recovery. We spend too much time on the far right of the curve, where performance falters and well-being collapses. The challenge – and the opportunity – is to find strategies we actually recognize in real life: catching ourselves mid-spiral and thinking, *Right, pause . . . what's one thing I can shift here?* – and using that moment to bring ourselves back to the center, where stress energizes without being overwhelming. This is where rhythm and music become powerful tools, helping us adjust our internal tempo and step back into balance.

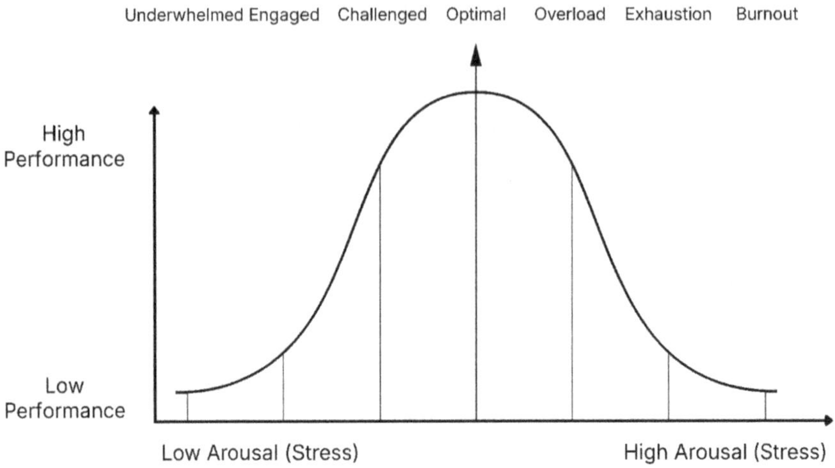


**Figure 4.1 The sweet spot: how optimal stress boosts performance.**

> Here's a fun fact. Back in 1908, Mr. Yerkes and Mr. Dodson demonstrated this by giving dancing mice what they called a "disagreeable electric shock." Performances certainly dropped under those conditions – proof that too much stress isn't good for anyone, dancing mouse or human.

## How Music Helps (the Science)

If stress is the body's alarm system – the kind that sometimes blares like an oversensitive smoke detector when you've just made toast – it's no wonder our bodies feel on edge.

Music is one of the simplest ways to hit the reset button. Over the past two decades, research has shown that listening to music can calm the autonomic nervous system (your body's fight or flight response), reduce levels of cortisol, and speed up recovery after stressful events (Thoma et al., 2013).

One of the most powerful effects of music lies in rhythm. Just as stress speeds up the heart and quickens the breath, steady, predictable rhythms in music can help bring them back down. Scientists call this *entrainment* – the process by which biological rhythms sync with the beat of the music. Studies show that listening to music with a slow tempo can lower heart rate and blood pressure, while rhythmic breathing exercises paired with calming sounds can restore balance to the nervous system (Bernadi et al., 2006).

Brain imaging studies also show how music influences emotional circuits. I remember seeing one brain scan that stopped me in my tracks, the amygdala visibly quietening as the music swelled. Just as in an orchestra, different brain regions play their part. The amygdala, our emotional percussion section, reacts strongly to stress – but it also quiets when by music, dampening its threat signals (Koelsch, 2014). The memory part of the brain (called the hippocampus), like the string section, ties songs to calming or positive memories, offering comfort during moments of tension. And the brain's reward center (nucleus accumbens), our brass section, blasts out reward signals, releasing dopamine when we listen to music we love and creating a sense of pleasure and relief. As we explored in Chapter 1, this brain orchestra plays in harmony – and music can change the score from chaos to calm.

Chemistry plays its part too. Dopamine and endorphins – the same "feel-good" chemicals released during exercise – are triggered by music. Oxytocin, often called the "bonding hormone," that helps us feel connected, can also be stimulated by singing or making music together, deepening connection and reducing feelings of isolation. Together, these chemicals ease tension, improve mood, and even reduce physical pain (Onieva-Zafra et al., 2013). In fact, some studies suggest that listening to music before or after surgery can lower anxiety and support faster recovery.

The beauty of music is that it works quickly. And what soothes one person might do very little for someone else – our calming tracks are as individual as our stress triggers. Within minutes of intentional listening, the body begins to shift. Muscles unclench, breathing slows, and thoughts become clearer. Unlike medication, music has no side effects, and unlike many well-being practices, it is always accessible – in your headphones, in the car, or even humming to yourself. In fact, try listening to the opening bars of "Three Little Birds" by Bob Marley. I can feel my shoulders drop almost instantly – there's something about that light, skipping drum groove that tells my whole system, "You're safe. Breathe."

Stress may be unavoidable – it sneaks into our days whether we invite it or not – but science shows that music offers a direct line to the systems it disrupts. By calming the alarm, syncing our rhythm, and rewarding the brain, music helps us reset the beat from chaos back to calm. In the next section, we'll explore how to turn this science into practical tools you can use every day.

## Practical Applications and Guided Listening

The science tells us that music can calm our bodies and minds – but honestly, most of us forget to reach for it when we need it most. So how do we use that knowledge in daily life? The key is to turn listening into a deliberate practice, one that helps us reset during moments of tension and build recovery into the fabric of our days. It is, therefore helpful to set up a dedicated stress management playlist.

### *The Stress Reset Playlist*

Creating your own Stress Reset Playlist is one of the simplest and most effective tools. It's worth noting that what feels calming varies hugely across cultures and genres. A track that soothes someone raised on Indian classical music might be totally different from what works for someone who grew up with folk, gospel, ambient, or reggae. This diversity is a strength – your playlist should reflect *your* roots, tastes, and cultural moments of comfort. Choose some tracks with a slower tempo (around 60–80 beats per minute), predictable rhythms, and soothing textures. These qualities help slow heart rate and steady breathing. You probably already have a calming track that works for you. For me, "Breathe" by Anna Phoebe, Klara Schumann, and Jake Downs is always a winner. Let's also think about a few scenarios:

- *Commute reset* – Imagine stepping onto the train after a long day and pressing play on a calming instrumental. As the landscape rolls past, the music helps you let go of work thoughts and arrive home more present and relaxed.

- *Bedtime wind-down* – Picture yourself lying in bed with the lights low, ambient music playing softly. The slow tempo lowers your breathing rate, and the reflective tone prepares both mind and body to drift into sleep.
- *Workday micro-break* – Between back-to-back meetings or during your break from the shop floor, you put on headphones and play a three-minute rhythmic track. With each beat, tension releases from your shoulders, and you return to your tasks with clearer focus and a lighter mood.

### *Habit Stacking and Anchoring*

Music is more powerful when tied to existing routines. Drawing on insights from behavioral science, try stacking a musical ritual onto a habit you already do – for example, pairing your morning coffee with an uplifting track. Anchoring works similarly, where you choose a specific song as a cue to shift state. Over time, hearing that song will signal your body it's time to calm down or refocus.

### *Integration with Other Pillars*

Music combines naturally with other well-being practices. Pair energizing music with exercise to boost motivation, or calming music with sleep rituals to prepare your mind for rest. You might also journal while listening to a reflective track (try "*Ayni*" by ANNA), or meditate with soft instrumentals in the background. In the next chapter, we'll look more closely at how music supports sleep and recovery in particular.

---

**Guided Listening**

Let's make this real for a moment – here are three very different tracks that capture different stress-relief effects. These are also included as the first three tracks in my Stress Reset Playlist.

Scan the QR code for Rob's Stress Rest Playlist.

**DJ Koze** – "The Universe in a Nutshell" brings gentle rhythmic grounding. Its steady percussion provides a sense of stability, while subtle chants and uplifting keys create a gentle sense of expansion and lightness.

**Jacqueline du Pré** – "Elgar: Cello Concerto in E Minor, Op. 85: I. Adagio – Moderato" provides reflective, emotional release. The rich cello lines balance sorrow and beauty, expressing vulnerability while also offering catharsis. This performance is widely celebrated as one of the most moving interpretations of Elgar's concerto.

**Brian Eno** – "An Ending (Ascent)" offers ambient calm through slow-moving choral textures that create a sense of awe and serenity. Originally written for the 1983 film *For All Mankind*, it has become a classic of ambient music, often used to evoke spaciousness and stillness.

You may not like all of these tracks, which is why I've included a broader selection in the full playlist. The real magic, though, comes from the joy of building your own – discovering the songs that resonate most with you, and noticing how each one shifts your state in a different way.

---

### *Reflection and Action*

Spend 10 minutes adding a few of your own songs to your Stress Reset Playlist – tracks that calm you, ground you, or give you release. This makes it truly yours. Use the *suggested songs* in your streaming service to discover fresh tracks that resonate for you. Pick a five-minute slot later today to try it out. Notice how your body and mind feel afterwards. Could this become a regular ritual? Jot down how you felt before and after – you might be surprised at the difference.

Think about trying to grow your playlist to 50+ tracks across different genres that really resonate with you, then hit shuffle. The mix keeps things fresh – and the surprise of what drops next adds to the fun.

## Perspectives

After an intense week of travel, deadlines, and back-to-back conversations, I can feel the tension stacking up in my body. My mind is still racing, even when the laptop snaps shut. That's when I turn to the decks. It's become my Friday night ritual – a personal transition zone between "doing" and "being."

The moment I cue up the first track, something in me shifts. My breath falls into step with the beat. The music starts gently taking over the mental chatter, replacing it with rhythm, color, and flow. As the low-end bass rolls in, my shoulders drop. My thoughts – which felt like speeding cars only minutes before – begin to fall into a calmer, more spacious rhythm.

Track by track, I feel myself returning to center. Mixing becomes a form of active meditation with my hands moving instinctively, my ears tuning into texture, my attention narrowing into the present moment. The stress of the week quietly dissolves into the background, replaced by a sense of grounding and ease.

By the time I pack away the headphones and turn off the lights, I feel lighter. More connected. Ready for the weekend, rather than dragging the week behind me. DJing has become my ritual buffer – the space where I release the pressure of work and ease into the softer rhythms of home life.

Do you have something similar? What ritual helps *you* switch gears from work to rest? What activity signals to your nervous system that it's safe to let go?

### *Workplace Reset*

I recently spoke with someone who works in a London office who told me about a small but powerful practice their manager uses at the start of meetings. Before anyone speaks, they play 30 seconds of calming music. The first time it happens, people look around, unsure what to make of it. But then – something subtle shifts. Shoulders relax. The room settles. Conversations begin with less tension and a noticeably more human tone.

In another workplace, a team has created a "Friday Reset" ritual. Every week, just before people head home, colleagues gather for 10 minutes and play a shared playlist – sometimes uplifting, sometimes reflective, sometimes just fun. It's not formal or forced. People simply come together, breathe, listen, reset, and then head into the weekend with a sense of closure and connection.

These small collective moments matter. They mark a transition. They help teams move from scattered to centered, from tense to attuned. Music becomes the shared rhythm that aligns people before they begin – or before they pause. Consider how your team could use music to transition together – into meetings, into focus, or into the weekend? What small ritual would make the biggest difference?

## Reflection Prompt

Before we shift gears, take a moment to gather the stories we've just explored – each one a reminder that stress shows up differently for all of us.

How we experience stress is as individual as our music tastes. Sometimes it shows up as a racing mind, sometimes as physical tension, and sometimes as a constant low-level hum in the background. The stories in this chapter illustrate that while the causes may vary, the rhythms of stress are something we all share.

Music gives us a way to listen more closely, not only to songs but to ourselves. When we slow down long enough to notice how a track changes our breathing or shifts our mood, we begin to understand our own stress rhythm.

> ***Reflection:*** *What's your current stress rhythm? Racing? Flat? Somewhere in between? How might music help restore balance?*

**Action**

Take five minutes today to pause and notice your stress rhythm across the day. When does it typically peak? Then choose one track – from the playlist or your own – to see how it shifts your state. Jot down a few words before and after to capture the change.

## Chapter Takeaway

Stress is unavoidable and it often feels messy. It's a bit like trying to untangle your headphones in a hurry. However, stress is a part of being human. But we need to remember that recovery is essential. Without it, stress builds and builds until it erodes our health, performance, and sense of balance.

Music offers one of the simplest and most powerful recovery tools we have. It can calm the body's alarm system, steady the breath, lift our mood, and create rituals that help us transition from pressure to calm. From DJ sets to cello concertos to ambient soundscapes, music reminds us that recovery isn't a luxury – it's non-negotiable. Stress is rhythm gone awry. Music helps us reset the beat.

***Mantra:*** *Find your rhythm, find your calm.*

# 5 Music, Sleep, and Restoration

It's late. You switch off the light, sink into the pillow, and wait for the day to release its grip. But instead of slipping into calm, your mind begins to wander. Thoughts replay like a stuck record – the presentation tomorrow, the unanswered email, the conversation you wish had gone differently. And the harder you chase sleep, the more it slips through your fingers. Hours later, you find yourself staring at the ceiling, caught between frustration and fatigue.

For many people, this scene feels all too familiar. Sleep should move like a tide, drawing us gently toward shore – but most nights, it feels more like weather you can't predict. Modern life often whips up storms that keep the waters unsettled. The blue glow of screens, the pressures of work, and the weight of daily responsibilities keep our bodies on alert long after the world goes quiet. Instead of surrendering to night, we find ourselves restless, half-awake, and running on empty.

Sleep is meant to be restoration – a sanctuary for body and mind. But in a world that rarely slows down, that sanctuary can feel fragile, and without it, our whole system suffers.

## What Is Sleep?

Sleep is our built-in repair system – the time when the body restores energy, files memories away, and quietly fixes what the day has worn down. From an evolutionary perspective, it's essential for survival – regulating metabolism, boosting immune defenses, balancing mood, and protecting cardiovascular health. Even a few nights of broken sleep can knock us off balance, reducing resilience.

When we finally reach deep sleep, the body gets to work. Heart rate and blood pressure settle, the brain clears out waste, and muscles rebuild. At the same time, sleep restores energy and motivation. It also sharpens our ability to handle risk and decision-making. Sleep even influences the food choices we make by regulating hormones such as ghrelin, the hormone that stimulates hunger. Have you ever noticed eating a lot of junk food after poor sleep?

One of the things I love about sleep is that its benefits can be immediate: a single good night's rest can lift mood, restore clarity, and improve self-control the very next day. Unlike exercise plans or nutrition programs, which take patience, sleep pays you back straight away. In this way, sleep acts like nature's reset button – clearing the slate, refreshing the mind, and allowing us to begin again with energy and focus. Without this restoration, focus, mood, and physical well-being quickly decline.

---

Scan the QR code to watch Rob's quick guide on why sleep is so important.

---

## Challenges to Sleep Today

Modern life hasn't been kind to our sleep. Surveys show that roughly a third of adults struggle with sleep, with many averaging fewer than six hours per night. Research links insufficient sleep to obesity, diabetes, cardiovascular disease, and depression (Institute of Medicine, 2006).

Blue light from devices, caffeine, late-night stress, alcohol consumption, and 24/7 connectivity keep our bodies wired when they should be winding down. Alcohol, in particular, fragments sleep and delays the restorative recovery processes, meaning that even if you fall asleep quickly, the quality of rest is reduced. That extra glass of wine might make you drowsy, but it prevents your body from entering the deep stages of recovery sleep, leaving you more fatigued the next day (Roehrs & Roth, 2001).

The result? Many of us are running on empty without realizing it. You can feel it on those mornings when your eyes sting and the day feels heavier before it even starts. Surveys suggest over 10% of adults admit to using alcohol as a sleep aid (National Sleep Foundation, 2005). This underlines how common, yet counterproductive, the practice has become – in fact, alcohol remains the most frequently self-administered sleep aid despite its disruptive effects on sleep quality.

## How Music Helps (the Science)

Music can act like a gentle signal, guiding body and mind into rhythms of rest. One way this happens is through *entrainment*, where our heart rate and breathing begin to sync with an external rhythm – something we already explored in Chapter 2, "Music and Mood," when looking at how rhythm supports recovery from stress. Slow tempos – roughly 60–80 BPM – sit close to a resting heartbeat and help nudge the body toward calm.

Inside the brain, the effect is just as real. The amygdala, our emotional alarm system, softens its reactions in the presence of soothing music, like percussion easing its beat. The hippocampus plays a quieter but important role. It ties sound to memory – our string section in the brain's orchestra – helping certain melodies carry emotional weight. And the hypothalamus, the body's metronome for cycles like sleep and wake, takes cues from gentle rhythms to regulate rest more effectively.

And then there's the chemistry. Put simply, music can lower cortisol, the stress hormone. For example, in one controlled study, people who listened to relaxing music before being exposed to a stressful task recovered faster, with their autonomic nervous system returning to baseline more quickly (Thoma et al., 2013). It can also increase melatonin, the hormone that signals "night mode" to the body and prepares us for sleep. In a clinical study with Alzheimer's patients, daily music therapy was linked to measurable increases in melatonin, suggesting that music can directly influence hormonal pathways connected to sleep regulation (Kumar et al., 1999). And music boosts serotonin, the neurotransmitter that stabilizes mood and supports regular sleep cycles (Chanda & Levitin, 2013). Put together, these responses make it easier for the body to settle.

### *Sound Frequencies and Sleep*

Of course, not all sounds help us wind down. Research highlights certain frequencies that support the transition into sleep. Delta waves (0.5–4 Hz) are associated with deep, restorative rest. They create a kind of heavy, sinking feeling when your whole body finally lets go. Theta waves (4–8 Hz) emerge during drowsiness and the moments just before sleep. These are types of brain activity, or brainwaves, that scientists measure when studying sleep. Low-frequency tones under 250 Hz are often experienced as calming and grounding. I've always found that these deep, rumbling tones feel a bit like someone placing a warm hand on your back – steady, reassuring, and surprisingly soothing.

Even the pitch of music can matter. While 440 Hz is the modern concert standard, some people swear by 432 Hz tuning, and early research suggests it may feel more relaxing to some listeners. A pilot study found that participants listening to 432 Hz reported lower anxiety and a greater sense of calm compared to those exposed to 440 Hz (Calamassi & Pomponi, 2019). Listeners rated their mood and anxiety levels after sessions and consistently preferred the 432 Hz tuning, though the authors emphasized the findings were preliminary. Other studies have explored brainwave entrainment, where sounds are used to nudge the brain into different states. A pilot trial with young elite soccer players explored whether binaural beats during rest could support recovery (Abeln et al., 2014). Players reported better subjective sleep quality and showed small improvements in morning alertness, suggesting potential benefits beyond placebo. It's still early days for this research and I'm both curious and a little skeptical about how much of it will hold up as the evidence base grows.

These insights explain why binaural beats, ambient tracks, and low-frequency soundscapes are increasingly featured in well-being apps like Calm and Headspace. The science may still be developing, but the practice is already part of many people's bedtime routines.

## Practical Applications and Guided Listening

So how can we put all of this into practice? It's time to get intentional and create a playlist designed specifically to help us sleep better. The qualities that matter most are a slow tempo (no faster than 80 beats per minute), gentle textures such as acoustic guitar or soft strings, and a consistent volume without sudden shifts. This kind of playlist acts almost like a sonic blanket, wrapping you in familiarity and calm.

### *Evening Wind-Down*

Soft strings or ambient tones can help signal to the body that it's time to shift gears. Imagine dimming the lights, closing the laptop, and letting a slow string piece create the sense of evening drawing to a close. The music becomes a cue that the day is ending and rest is on its way.

### *Bedtime Transition*

At the moment of bedtime, acoustic guitar or lullaby-like melodies can pair beautifully with journaling, allowing worries to be released before sleep. Picture writing down tomorrow's to-do list while a simple guitar melody flows in the background. The act of writing provides closure, and the sound creates a bridge into sleep.

### *Night-Time Reset*

If you wake in the night, ambient tones mixed with ocean waves or gentle piano can help ease you back toward sleep, offering a reassuring soundscape to settle the mind. Think of these tracks as companions that stand guard through the night, ready to settle your mind again. Hearing the same familiar tones can reduce anxiety and signal safety, making the return to sleep quicker.

---

## Designing Your Sleep Playlist and Guided Listening

Intentional listening can turn music from background noise into a deliberate tool to promote rest. Here are three simple exercises to try, each paired with a suggested soundscape.

Scan the QR code for Rob's Sleep Playlist.

## Slow Strings for Deep Breathing

Choose a piece of gentle classical music with sustained string notes. For example, Max Richter's "On the Nature of Daylight" is widely loved for its slow, enveloping string textures – it's a track that almost seems to breathe with you. As you listen, notice how your breath begins to lengthen and your shoulders start to drop. Allow the sound to act like a signal, cueing your body to release tension. Remember: personal preference matters. If another string piece resonates more strongly for you, use that instead.

### Ambient Waves for Letting Go

Play an ambient track that blends tones with the sound of the ocean. Sigur Rós's "*Varðeldur*" offers this kind of atmosphere, with its drifting textures and meditative quality. As the waves rise and fall, imagine yourself floating on the surface, carried by the rhythm. Let the water wash away lingering thoughts from the day. There's no right answer here – the key is choosing sounds that feel right for you.

### Acoustic Guitar for Night Journaling

Put on a simple acoustic guitar piece – something steady, soft, and uncluttered. Andy McKee's "Rylynn" is a beautiful example, with warm tones and a soothing flow. While it plays, jot down tomorrow's tasks or any thoughts keeping you awake. The act of writing, combined with the calming tones, helps clear your mind for sleep.

---

> ***Reflection:*** *What sounds help you drift off most easily? How can you bring more of them into your evenings?*

## Perspectives

Music's effect on sleep isn't just theoretical – it is lived, nightly, in countless homes, hospitals, and bedrooms around the world. One of the clearest examples for me came just after my daughter was born. In those early weeks, sleep felt like something we were constantly negotiating with a tiny, unpredictable human. I tried the usual lullabies at first, but they didn't feel quite *me*. Without realizing it, I slipped into something far more familiar – "Ring Ring Ring" by De La Soul.

Night after night, I found myself softly singing the opening line. "Hey, how ya doin'. . . sorry you can't get through. . ."

It wasn't exactly "Twinkle, Twinkle," but it became ours.

At first it was just a melody I loved. But slowly, something beautiful happened. As she got older, she recognized it instantly. Her eyes softened, her body relaxed, and she would smile in that half-asleep way only babies can. The familiar cadence slowed her breathing – and mine. In an otherwise chaotic season of new parenthood, that song became an anchor.

It worked not because it was traditionally soothing, but because it was *consistent*. It became a cue – *we're safe, we're together, it's time for rest now.* That's the real magic of bedtime music. Whether it's a whispered hum, a childhood favorite, or an old-school hip-hop hook lovingly repurposed as a lullaby, these rituals soothe both parent and child. They connect us to a tradition as old as humanity itself – using rhythm, voice, and familiarity to guide tired bodies toward sleep.

## Reflection Prompt

Pause here for a moment. Think about your own bedtime rituals. Is music part of them? If not, what would it feel like to make sound as important as silence in your evenings?

Take a few minutes to journal or simply reflect. Picture the last time you slept deeply and woke refreshed – the weight of the duvet, the softness of the morning light, or the quiet around you – what contributed to that? Was it the sounds around you, the absence of noise, or perhaps a song that soothed you? Consider what gets in the way of that same rest now. Is it stress, screens, or racing thoughts? Writing these down can help you see patterns more clearly.

Then imagine experimenting with music as part of your evening rhythm. You might start with one piece of gentle music, pairing it with dimmed lights or a warm cup of tea. Reflect on how it changes your state. Over time, these small experiments can grow into rituals that support you night after night.

### Action

Create your own starter sleep playlist with 20+ calming tracks that make you feel safe, relaxed, and ready for rest. Build on it gradually and don't be afraid of overlap with your stress-recovery playlist. Try committing to this for a week and notice how your body and mood respond.

## Chapter Takeaway

Sleep is one of our most powerful forms of restoration, yet it is fragile in modern life. Music can be a gentle anchor – slowing our rhythms, softening our stress, and guiding us into rest. We've all felt how one good night's sleep can reset the body and mind almost instantly, like pressing nature's reset button. Just as lullabies soothe children, music can serve as a lullaby for adults – a gentle guide into restoration. The right sounds transform bedtime from a struggle into a ritual, and each night offers a chance to clear the slate and begin again with energy and clarity.

> ***Mantra:*** *Let music be the tide that carries you to sleep.*

# 6 Music, Focus, Work, and Learning

Picture yourself sitting down to tackle an important task – maybe drafting a report you've been putting off or untangling a tricky spreadsheet. Your inbox pings, your phone lights up and the room buzzes with background noise. Each small distraction chips away at your concentration, leaving you feeling scattered before you've even begun. You straighten a crooked stack of papers, sigh at the cold coffee you meant to drink an hour ago, and notice how your desk has somehow become a museum of half-finished thoughts. For a moment, you wonder if you should give up before you've even started.

Then you press play on the right track – and something shifts. The distractions soften, as if someone has gently turned the world down a notch. A steady rhythm anchors your breathing. A warm, familiar melody pulls your attention inward in a way that feels almost physical, like your mind is settling into its chair at last. The buzzing in your head loosens. Time doesn't dissolve so much as it stops tugging at you – it just sits beside you, quietly. You notice yourself leaning into the work without forcing it. A few minutes pass. Then a few more. You look up and realize you've actually made progress.

This is the hidden power of music for work and learning. Its ability to turn a scattered, overstimulated moment into one where deep attention can finally take hold – even in a world designed to pull us in every direction.

## What Is Focus?

Focus is the capacity of your brain to direct limited mental resources toward one goal while filtering out the rest. In real life, that might look like trying to finish a report while someone in the next room is on a loud Zoom call or attempting to learn something new while your phone vibrates with notifications you're trying very hard to ignore. Even the sound of the air-conditioning or the flicker of a hallway light can tug at your attention. It's not just about turning *toward* one thing – it's also about turning *away* from everything else. When this selective filtering breaks down, your attention scatters and even simple tasks can feel strangely unmanageable.

Psychologist Daniel Kahneman described attention as a *finite pool of effort* that becomes depleted with every competing demand (Kahneman, 1973). Neuroscientists Michael Posner and Steven Petersen later mapped the brain's three key attention networks – the alerting system (which keeps you ready), the orienting system (which helps you select information), and the executive system (which manages conflicts and goals) (Posner & Petersen, 1990). A more everyday analogy might be this: you're at your desk, highlighter in hand, leaning closer to the sentence you're trying to understand – not because the text changed, but because *you* shifted your mental beam.

But that beam flickers easily. Research shows that constant interruptions don't just slow us down – they push us to work faster to compensate, raising stress, frustration, and time pressure along the way (Mark et al., 2008). When our focus fractures repeatedly, our cognitive resources drain faster, and we finish the day feeling more wrung out than productive.

So rather than calling focus a "mental superpower," it's more accurate – and more helpful – to think of it as a fragile capacity that thrives under the right conditions and falters under the wrong ones. On the days it wobbles, that's not a personal failing – it's just your brain trying to cope. Our job is to create the environment where it can hold steady.

## Why Focus Is a Problem Today

We live in what's often called the "attention economy." Competing demands pull at us from every direction – email, instant messages, team chats, social media, shifting deadlines, and a steady drip of notifications. Office workers are interrupted every 11 minutes on average, and it can take more than 20 minutes to return to the original task (Mark et al., 2005). A 2022 King's College London survey found that nearly half of people (49%) feel their attention span is shorter than it used to be. Distraction isn't a quirk of modern life; for many, it's become the soundtrack of the working day.

In workplaces, interruption has become almost structural. A 2018 Udemy report found that 70% of workers feel distracted at work, with 16% saying they are *almost always* distracted. Hybrid working adds another layer with the blurred boundaries between home and office meaning your "workday" can feel like it never truly starts or ends. You answer a message while loading the dishwasher or switch between spreadsheets and family logistics without noticing the mental whiplash. If you've had days where your focus seems to evaporate the moment you sit down – where even the sound of your own Slack notification makes your shoulders tighten – you're in good company. The data simply confirms what you've already felt.

The cost of this scattered attention is enormous. Gallup's 2023 *State of the Global Workplace* report found that only 23% of employees worldwide are engaged at work, with low engagement draining an estimated $8.8 trillion from the global economy each year. But beyond productivity, the emotional toll matters too. Chronic distraction drives overwhelm, decreases satisfaction, and contributes to burnout – recognized by the World Health Organization as an occupational phenomenon since 2019.

In this climate, focus isn't simply a performance skill; it's a well-being necessity. And rather than relying solely on willpower in an environment designed to fracture attention, we need tools that help steady the mind. Music can be one of the simplest, most adaptable, and most effective of those tools.

## How Music Helps (the Science)

Music doesn't simply fill the silence; sometimes it slips into the room almost unnoticed – the low thrum of a lo-fi beat, the soft pulse of a synth – and your breathing begins to follow its lead. Music becomes an active partner in shaping how your brain works. Think about the moment you put on a track while you're struggling to settle into work – your breathing shifts, your shoulders loosen a little, and the world feels less intrusive. That's not imagined. Music is a multi-sensory stimulus that engages a number of brain networks at once. Rhythms can steady your internal timing, harmonies can regulate emotional tone, and melodies can give your thoughts something to grip onto. In other words, music isn't passive background – it's a tool that influences how you focus, learn, and create. Here's how:

### *Memory Boost*

Picture yourself trying to memorize a list for an exam – dry, repetitive, and instantly forgettable. But turn the same list into a simple tune and recall suddenly improves. Studies show that singing foreign-language words significantly boosts memory compared with reading or speaking alone (Ludke et al., 2014). Other research finds that pairing names or phrases with a melody creates a kind of mental anchor, helping information stick (Rainey & Larsen, 2002). The lesson? If you need to remember something, try giving it a tune.

### *Verbal Learning*

This isn't just for musicians. Reviews show that music consistently supports verbal learning across age groups – from rehearsing presentations to revising study notes. Music provides a structure that words can attach to (Ferrari & Verga, 2016). Think of melody as the shelf your ideas rest on, making them easier to retrieve later.

### *Dopamine Reward*

If you've ever put on a favorite track to get through a boring task, you've used dopamine to your advantage. Music increases dopamine release in the brain's reward circuits (Salimpoor et al., 2011). This boosts motivation and persistence, helping repetitive or low-energy tasks feel more manageable – even slightly enjoyable.

### *Creativity*

When you hit a creative block, the right track can loosen things up. Experiments show that certain types of music increase divergent thinking – the ability to generate multiple ideas (Ritter et al., 2012). It's a bit like cracking open a window in a stuffy room – not a dramatic breeze, just a small shift that lets your thinking loosen and move again.

### *Performance*

Tempo matters too. Research shows that faster music boosts physical performance and elevates mood (Karageorghis & Priest, 2012). For focus work, it's about choosing a pace that supports steady momentum without tipping into overstimulation.

Think back to our "orchestra in the brain" metaphor from Chapter 1. When you play music, it's like giving your internal orchestra a new score designed for focus – but not everything lines up neatly, and that's the point. The **prefrontal cortex (the conductor)** steadies attention. The **hippocampus (strings)** binds new information to melody. The **amygdala (percussion)** helps regulate arousal so stress doesn't hijack your thinking. The **nucleus accumbens (brass)** boosts motivation through dopamine. And the **cerebellum (metronome)** keeps time – though, like any metronome, it sometimes clicks a fraction ahead or behind, and that human wobble is part of the mix. Sometimes one section comes in a beat early or late – but together, these regions create the conditions for concentration.

Not all music works for everyone. Positively valenced (uplifting) music improves memory more than neutral tracks (Gold et al., 2019). Musical training also influences what helps vs. what distracts. Musicians may benefit more from complex music – or find it more distracting – because their brains instinctively tune into nuance. In the end, the real skill is experimentation. *What helps one person lock in can pull another person off track entirely.*

Taken together, music isn't just decorative background – and it doesn't need to be perfect to work. It's a practical, accessible cognitive tool – one that can help us focus, learn, and perform more effectively on the days when attention feels steady – and especially on the days when it doesn't.

## Practical Applications and Guided Listening

Let's bring this into the real world for a moment. The best focus playlists are usually instrumental and moderate in tempo – but rather than treating that as a rule, think of it as a starting point. Lyrics can compete with verbal processing, but everyone's brain is wired a little differently. The real goal is to find music that makes the work in front of you feel just a bit more doable.

If you want to explore different textures for focus, it can help to think in terms of how each sound world shapes attention and emotional tone. Classical and string-led music offers a sense of steadiness and structure. "Infra 1" by Max Richter is a beautiful example: minimalist string layers shift almost imperceptibly over time, creating a calm framework that gently steadies the mind. If you listen closely, you can hear faint effects and electronic beeps woven into the fabric of the piece – small traces of digital noise repurposed as texture. The first time I noticed that detail it genuinely surprised me, and it makes the track a powerful opener for a focus playlist, symbolically turning distraction into something intentional and artful.

Lo-fi beats and soft electronic textures offer a different kind of support. "Controlla" by Idealism is purely instrumental, built around dreamy piano loops and understated beats that provide gentle momentum without demanding attention. The rhythm feels like a quiet heartbeat ticking away in the background, wrapping the space in a slightly blurred, comforting atmosphere. There is just enough shape to help you move forward, but never so much that it pulls your focus away from the task at hand.

For moments when you need maximum spaciousness and minimal distraction, nature-inspired ambient music can be especially effective. "Weightless" by Marconi Union has become an ambient classic for good reason. Its slow-moving, evolving textures and wide-open sonic field reduce arousal and help calm the nervous system. It is particularly well suited to long stretches of deep work where you want to sink in and stay there. I often reach for it when facing a wall of emails, as it seems to soften the edges of the task and make sustained focus feel more manageable.

**Guided Listening**

Scan the QR code for Rob's Focus Playlist.

## Micro-Scenarios

For a deep work session, it helps to choose longer ambient pieces or minimalist string compositions that stretch gently across time without sudden shifts or surprises. This kind of music is designed to almost disappear into the background, creating a steady sonic bed that keeps you grounded without pulling attention away from the task itself.

When you're learning a new skill, steady lo fi beats or repeating piano loops tend to work particularly well. They provide a consistent sense of momentum and can support both encoding and recall, with the underlying rhythm acting like a form of structural scaffolding that helps the brain organize and retain new information.

For brainstorming or creative thinking, slightly more upbeat instrumental tracks can be useful. A touch of energy can encourage more divergent thinking and idea generation, as long as the music stays instrumental and doesn't tip into being distracting. The balance to aim for is stimulation without overwhelm – enough lift to spark ideas, but not so much that it steals the spotlight.

### *Pro Tips*

Aim to build your playlist out to at least 50 tracks so you can use shuffle without constantly hearing the same pieces on repeat. A longer playlist helps the music fade into the background, which is exactly what you want for sustained focus.

Don't hesitate to borrow tracks from your stress or sleep playlists. Music is highly contextual, and the same piece can calm you in one moment and support concentration in another, depending on what you need and how you're listening.

It's also worth letting your streaming service's recommendations do some of the work for you. Many people discover their most effective focus tracks this way, as the algorithms can surface similar sounds and textures that naturally fit with their listening patterns.

**What about binaural beats and tuned frequencies?**

Experiment with curiosity rather than certainty. Some studies suggest binaural beats may support attention or reduce anxiety, and that 432 Hz tuning can feel calmer than the standard 440 Hz. Some people notice a real difference; others barely feel anything at all. But the science is mixed, and responses vary widely. If you're curious, try it out – no expectations needed. The playlist from Chapter 5, "Music, Sleep, and Restoration," includes some tuned and binaural tracks you can experiment with.

## Perspectives

I often lean on a focus playlist when I'm drafting a keynote, shaping a chapter, or trying to push through a stubborn batch of admin. It's become an almost automatic part of my working rhythm. Most days you'll find me at my desk – or traveling between meetings – with headphones on, creating a small sonic bubble that helps me shut out the noise of the world.

In fact, this very chapter was written with a playlist droning quietly in the background. Nothing dramatic, just steady, atmospheric tracks with enough texture to hold my attention without hijacking it. As soon as I hit play, my brain gets the message: *right – time to get on with it now.* Within a few minutes, the conversations around me blur into nothing, my nervous system settles, and the words begin to land with more ease.

I'm not alone in this. A senior executive assistant once told me – with a small laugh as she nudged her headphones into place – "When I need to get into my zone, headphones go on, music plays, and I become laser-focused. Sometimes it's classical, sometimes it's one track on repeat, sometimes it's a whole album." Over time, her colleagues learned the pattern. Headphones meant *please don't interrupt unless the building is on fire.*

For her, music wasn't just supporting concentration. It was quietly drawing a boundary in a hectic open-plan office. A signal to herself – and to everyone around her – that she was entering deep-work mode. A simple ritual that shifted the atmosphere of her day from scattered to intentional.

These cues matter. Music doesn't only nudge the brain into focus; it marks the moment when you choose to direct your attention. It's a way of reclaiming a pocket of control in environments full of noise, demands, and distraction.

## Reflection Prompt

Think about your own working or studying rituals. Is music part of them? If not, what would it feel like to make sound as important as silence in your daily routine?

Take a few minutes to journal or simply reflect. Picture the last time you entered a state of deep concentration where the hours seemed to slip away – what contributed to that? Was it the sounds around you, the absence of noise, or perhaps a particular piece of music that carried you along? Consider what gets in the way of that same focus now. Is it constant notifications, background chatter, or racing thoughts? Writing these down can help you see patterns more clearly.

Then imagine experimenting with music as part of your focus ritual. You might start with one piece of instrumental music, pairing it with clearing your desk or silencing your phone. Reflect on how it changes your state. Over time, these small experiments can grow into rituals that support you day after day.

**Action**

Create your own starter focus playlist with 20+ tracks that make you feel steady, alert, and absorbed in the task. Build on it gradually and don't be afraid of overlap with your stress-recovery or sleep playlists. Use this playlist whenever you feel a need to focus. Try committing to this for a week and notice how your attention and productivity respond.

## Chapter Takeaway

Music can cut through distraction and help us focus, learn, and perform at our best. Think of it as the lighthouse in the fog of distraction – guiding your attention back to where it matters. Press play, and you can find flow again, even in the middle of chaos. This is not about following rigid rules or chasing the perfect playlist; it's about discovering, through trial and error, what sounds steady your mind and what rhythms unlock your flow. The beauty lies in experimenting, because what works for one person may not work for another.

The more you explore and refine, the more your playlists become tools – not just background noise, but active partners in your ability to think deeply, learn more effectively, and create with greater freedom.

***Mantra:*** *Press Play, find flow.*

# 7 Music, Energy, Movement, and Motivation

It's a cold, grey Monday morning in November. Summer seems like a long way in the past. The alarm feels too early, your body is heavy, and your mind is already cycling through the long to-do list ahead. You'd rather stay curled under the covers, cocooned in warmth. But then, after your shower, you press play on "Titanium" by David Guetta and Sia. Within seconds, the soaring vocals and pounding beat fill the kitchen. You start to sway, then dance, laughing at yourself as energy ripples through your body. By the end of the track, you're standing taller, breathing deeper, and ready to face the challenges of the day.

Music can kick-start your brain in ways little else can. With the possible exception of coffee of course! A single track can shift you from foggy to focused. Like when I witnessed Coldplay taking the Pyramid Stage at Glastonbury – the cold air, the lights, the whole field moving as one organism. Or a stadium of soccer fans chanting in perfect rhythm, their voices blending into one unstoppable force. The right song is like someone quietly lighting the fuse inside you. It doesn't just add energy – it transforms effort into momentum.

And it's not just the big moments that matter. Sometimes it's the small shifts that save the day, such as a three-minute song that saves your morning or a chorus sung aloud in the car that lifts your mood before a difficult meeting. These are the sparks music gives us – like the little jolt you feel when a bass line vibrates through your chest or a familiar harmony brushes the back of your neck, available any time we need to reignite.

For me, this shows up in so many moments personally. I remember vividly my basketball team playing the theme tune from *The A-Team* as we traveled in the bus to an away game. Imagine too the collective rituals. The national anthem before a game, the drum line leading a parade, or a choir warming up before a concert. These are more than traditions – they are reminders that music doesn't just prepare individuals, it rallies groups. One person may find themselves ready for a workday after a song in the kitchen; thousands can feel unified by a single chant.

## What Are Energy and Motivation?

Energy is more than just calories burned or hours of sleep banked – you can feel it on the mornings when you wake up buzzing for no clear reason, and on the ones when you don't. It's that felt sense of vitality – the physical power in the body and the motivational drive in the mind. Motivation is the spark that turns potential into action. Together, energy and motivation form the engine that powers our daily lives.

If you look back through human history – and even just through the way we instinctively move – rhythm and music have always been tied to energy, from the thump of feet on packed earth to the echo of communal drums. Ancient hunters chanted to coordinate movements. Soldiers marched in step to the beat of drums. Communities danced in circles to summon strength for harvest or ritual. These practices weren't just cultural decoration; they were tools to synchronize bodies, focus minds, and generate collective vitality.

Even today, echoes of this are everywhere. Football chants galvanize crowds and players alike. Protest songs rally movements for justice. Rowing crews and military units use cadence calls to maintain pace and morale. Wherever human beings need energy, music is there as the invisible motivator.

In my own life – and in the experience of most people I speak to – music's motivational power tends to show up most clearly in two areas. The first is exercise and movement, where music helps us move faster, endure for longer, and push a little harder than we might otherwise manage. The second is work, where music supports persistence through demanding tasks, helps us push through mental fatigue, and can even summon a sense of confidence at moments when it's needed most.

Energy fuels both the body and the mind – like the difference between dragging yourself to the gym and suddenly feeling lighter the moment the right track hits. Whether you're lacing up for a run or gearing up for a presentation, music activates the same motivational systems. It is both a spark and sustainer.

To put it simply – in my experience, at least – energy is the fuel, motivation is the ignition, and music is the catalyst that helps them work together.

It is worth considering this too. Energy without motivation can feel restless – like pacing around the house with nowhere to put it; motivation without energy can feel frustrating – like wanting to start but having nothing in the tank. It's only when both are aligned that we move forward smoothly. And music has the power to align them.

## Why It's a Problem Today

Despite knowing we need energy to thrive, many of us feel perpetually drained. The statistics are worrying. According to the World Health Organization, over 30% adults globally do not meet recommended activity guidelines (WHO, 2024). As someone whose exercise has been curtailed by long COVID, I find this to be a worrying statistic. The American Heart Association estimates that adults spend an average of 6–8 hours per day sitting (Tian et al., 2025). And honestly, modern life often feels set up to sap energy more than replenish it.

Fatigue is compounded by the way we live and work. Poor sleep, chronic stress, and digital overload take their toll. I've lived versions of this myself. Picture a "day in the life" for many knowledge workers – you wake up and immediately check emails, spend the morning in back-to-back video calls, scroll social media during breaks, and finish the evening in front of another glowing screen. Your body is restless – maybe you stand up only to sit straight back down again – your eyes ache, and overstimulation dulls your mind. Motivation, once sparked by novelty and connection, sputters under the weight of monotony.

And it's not only adults feeling it. Children and young people face similar challenges. Studies show rising sedentary behavior among teens – long stretches on screens, fewer chances for active play, and more time spent indoors. For both adults and young people, the modern world makes it far easier to sit and scroll than to move and motivate.

Add to this the cultural messages that glorify productivity over rest. We celebrate hustle but neglect recovery – working through lunch, replying to emails late at night, squeezing rest into the gaps. We chase constant output while sacrificing play, movement, and rhythm. So, it's no surprise many of us feel our energy slipping away. Motivation wanes not because we don't care, but because our systems aren't designed to support it.

I often think of it as an energy crisis – not the kind that makes headlines about oil or electricity, but a personal energy deficit that affects mood, productivity, and well-being. This is where music can act as both remedy and ritual.

## How Music Helps (the Science)

The science tells us that music has a strong physical and psychological power. In exercise contexts, tempo and rhythm drive movement, endurance, and cadence. In work contexts, music boosts psychological confidence, momentum, and motivation to persist with challenging tasks.

### *Tempo and Movement*

Faster music increases work rate and endurance in exercise settings. A landmark study tested sub-maximal cycling performance and found that participants cycled harder, reported lower perceived exertion, and enjoyed the exercise more when listening to upbeat, faster-tempo tracks (Karageorghis & Jones, 2009). A separate study also showed that adjusting running cadence to faster beats improved efficiency and step frequency. Today, spin classes synchronize pedaling to the beat, and running apps recommend playlists matching stride cadence – modern applications of these findings (Snyder et al., 2012). I can certainly attest to this. When I used to do hard, high-intensity cycling intervals, I would inevitably turn to something like "One" by the Swedish House Mafia to get through them.

### *Mood and Dopamine*

Uplifting music triggers dopamine – the brain's primary reward chemical. This fuels pleasure, motivation, and the drive to act. That's why an upbeat anthem can transform reluctance into readiness. Dopamine also underpins the so-called "runner's high," a euphoric state often experienced after sustained exercise. For me, examples of dopamine-spiking tracks include "Titanium" by David Guetta & Sia, "Stronger" by Kanye West, and "Can't Stop the Feeling" by Justin Timberlake – songs that reliably deliver that rush of drive and joy.

### *Endorphins*

Singing, dancing, or even clapping along to music can boost endorphins, another feel-good chemical linked to vitality. Everyday moments – like the time I found myself belting out "Don't Stop Believin'" in the car, dancing to "Uptown Funk," chanting with strangers at a festival – mimic the endorphin surge of exercise. In groups, the effect multiplies: choirs, football crowds, and concert audiences experience waves of collective energy that bind people together.

### *Cognitive Drive*

I notice this myself as music activates the brain's reward pathways, making repetitive or difficult tasks feel more engaging. Ferreri & Verga (2016) reviewed studies showing that musical pleasure not only aids memory but also supports motivation and perseverance. In workplaces, upbeat playlists can help people push through spreadsheets or monotonous admin. Music transforms drudgery into something lighter. Personally, I struggle with task repetition, so music is an essential companion to help get me through. For students, background music can turn revision marathons into sessions that feel more bearable, even enjoyable.

### *Intentional Boost*

This is possibly my favorite piece of research on music and well-being. Two studies were run where participants either deliberately tried to feel happier while listening to positive music or simply listened passively. Those who set the intention reported significantly greater increases in motivation and well-being. Intention acts like an amplifier. When we consciously use music as a tool, its effects strengthen. Choosing a pump-up anthem before a workout, or curating a playlist for a demanding workday, primes the brain's reward system for action (Ferguson & Sheldon, 2013).

> Before big keynotes, I often choose one song, listen with full attention, and feel my state shift almost instantly. Think about one song you could play with intention this week – not just as background, but as a deliberate motivator before exercise or work? Before your next workout or important task, choose this song and play it with full attention. Notice how your energy, mood, and motivation shift, then jot down a few reflections on the effect.

### *Workplace Studies*

And it's not just personal experience – workplace research backs this up too. One study found that employees who listened to music at work reported better mood and perceived time-on-task (Lesiuk, 2005). Another study observed that music in offices supported persistence during repetitive tasks (Haake, 2011). Other studies suggest energizing tracks can boost confidence and productivity before presentations. Music doesn't just keep us moving; it keeps us motivated at our desks.

More recently, neuroscientists have started exploring something I find genuinely exciting – how certain kinds of background music can gently influence brainwave patterns. Put simply, your brain produces rhythmic activity – like electrical waves. And when you listen to steady rhythms, your brain can start to "sync up" with the beat. Early studies suggest this kind of entrainment might help people feel more alert, less fatigued, and more focused. The science is evolving, but it points to a fascinating possibility in that the right background rhythms could act like a natural tune-up for the brain – something I've certainly felt on long writing days, keeping us energized in demanding environments. For example, a fascinating study looked at how external rhythmic or periodic sounds can entrain brainwaves to reduce fatigue or maintain alertness (Moessinger et al., 2021).

## Practical Applications and Guided Listening

Now it's time to put the science into practice – and for me, this is where music really comes alive. The most effective way to harness music for motivation is to make it intentional – not just background noise, but playlists built for purpose. In this chapter, we'll separate two main uses: **exercise motivation** and **work motivation**. Each deserves its own playlist, because the demands are different. For exercise, tempo and rhythm push the body to move faster and endure longer. For work, lyrics, groove, or anthemic energy can help you transition between tasks, overcome dips, and summon confidence when it matters. Think of these playlists as tools you can reach for – I certainly do – a gym mix that fires up your muscles and a workday soundtrack that keeps you focused and energized. Over time, they become rituals you can rely on to spark energy exactly when you need it.

### *Designing Your Motivation Playlists*

These playlists become rituals you can rely on to spark energy exactly when you need it. For exercise, I often look for higher tempos (usually around 128 BPM for me), strong rhythmic drive, and tracks that make you want to move. For work, focus on songs with uplifting grooves, lyrical intensity, or anthemic power that helps you feel confident and engaged. Consistency matters too: avoid sudden changes in volume or mood that could disrupt your flow. The aim is to create playlists that feel like reliable companions – your personal spark for energy and motivation.

It is worth noting that hip-hop can serve as both exercise and work motivation music. Even at lower BPMs, the lyrical intensity or groove can energize and drive action.

### Exercise Motivation and Guided Listening

Next time you hit the gym, you might experiment with selecting tracks in the 120–140 BPM range – I often do this myself – to match your cardio pace. Try matching your stride to the beat during a run or syncing push-ups to the rhythm. Imagine pressing play on "Can't Hold Us" by Macklemore & Ryan Lewis – suddenly your tempo quickens and your stamina extends. Or picture yourself in a spin class, the instructor calling out cues just as the drop hits, the entire room moving in synchrony to Calvin Harris's "Feel So Close." The beat doesn't just accompany your workout – it drives it.

Scan the QR code for Rob's Exercise Playlist.

Next time you go for a run or workout, try matching your stride or reps to the beat of a high-tempo track. Notice how it changes your endurance and enjoyment.

### Work Motivation

For mental energy, choose tracks that spark momentum – anthems, upbeat pop, or driving electronic beats. These are ideal for transition rituals, like shifting from commute to office, or gearing up before a big presentation. Picture yourself on the train, headphones on – I often do this on the way into London – listening to Beyoncé's "Run the World (Girls)." By the time you arrive, you're walking taller, ready to perform. Or imagine the mid-afternoon slump where, instead of automatically reaching for caffeine (a trap I fall into too), you hit play on Queen's "Don't Stop Me Now." Within seconds, your energy shifts from sluggish to soaring.

Scan the QR code for Rob's Work Motivation Playlist.

Before your next work sprint or meeting, put on one motivating anthem and fully immerse yourself. Observe whether your energy and confidence shift.

---

### *Mini Motivation Moments*

In practice, this kind of intentional listening often shows up at predictable moments in the day. On mornings when I'm feeling slow or foggy, I'll sometimes swap coffee for an energizing track like "Happy" by Pharrell Williams. There's something about the bounce of that rhythm that reminds the body it's alive and ready to move. When the mid-afternoon slump hits and my eyelids start to droop, I'll cue up "Can't Stop" by Red Hot Chili Peppers or "Get Ur Freak On" by Missy Elliott for a short, sharp burst of vitality.

And just before a presentation or important event, pressing play on "Lose Yourself" by Eminem or "Good as Hell" by Lizzo helps me channel confidence and a sense of personal power.

It's worth experimenting with this yourself by inserting a single three-to-five-minute energizing track into one of these moments. Used consistently, it becomes a ritual – a clear signal to your body and mind that it's time to reset and shift gears. Over time, you can take this further by creating themed playlists for different goals. I have ones called Morning Ignition, Deep Work Energy, and even a slightly chaotic Reset Rituals mix. Simply naming them can make the habit feel more intentional, memorable, and easy to repeat.

## Perspectives

There was a night when I almost skipped my workout after a long day. I remember standing in the hallway, one shoe on, one shoe off, trying to negotiate with myself. The hallway light was buzzing faintly – one of those little annoyances you only really notice when you're tired. Out of habit more than motivation, I pressed play on "Eye of the Tiger" by Survivor. The opening riff gave me a familiar nudge – not dramatic, just enough to get me moving. I climbed onto my Wattbike, legs still heavy, telling myself I'd only spin for five minutes. But as the pedal rhythm synced with the beat, something shifted. The resistance felt less daunting, my breathing steadied, and the day's weight loosened a little. By the time I stepped off the bike, flushed and slightly amused that I'd almost talked myself out of it, the heaviness from earlier had eased. It was a small, very human reminder that mood can shift with the right spark.

Think back to a moment when a song helped you push through – during a run, a deadline, or even a tough morning. Jot down a few details: Where were you? What were you feeling? What changed once the music started? For example: *"I was stuck on a difficult email; after playing that track, I didn't feel braver, just a little less tense – enough to begin."* These details help you spot your own activation tracks. If you feel comfortable, share your activation track with a friend or colleague. These little exchanges often spark connection – and you might discover a new track that gives you a lift.

## Reflection Prompt

What song makes you move – no matter your mood? Could you make it your activation track?

Take a moment to map out your top three motivator tracks. Write them down, then note when in your day you could use each one most effectively – for example, one for mornings, one for slumps, and one for transitions. Think of these as your personal toolkit, ready whenever energy dips.

Go further and note why each song works for you. Is it the lyrics, the beat, the memory attached to it? This helps you understand the ingredients of your motivation and makes it easier to discover new tracks that fit the same formula.

## Chapter Takeaway

Music is an energy multiplier. It fuels both physical vitality and mental drive. The right beat doesn't just accompany effort – it transforms it.

Choose one moment this week – a workout, commute, or work task – and test the impact of a deliberately chosen motivating track. Notice the difference and consider making it part of your regular routine.

Think of music as spark, as octane fuel, as wind in your sails. Just as a single track can lift you from bed to dance floor, music can propel you through life's demands with renewed strength. Energy is not just something we wait for; it's something we can create. And music is one of the most powerful tools we have to generate it.

> ***Mantra:*** *The right beat turns effort into energy.*

# 8 Music, Pain, and Physical Healing

The air in the hospital room felt heavy. A faint chemical smell lingered, the kind you only notice after hours of sitting still. The silence was broken only by the rumble of activity outside the room and the faint hiss of oxygen. I sat beside his bed, watching each shallow breath etched with discomfort, feeling helpless. The sterile light above us casting long shadows, and I caught the sound of his uneven breathing filling the space.

My hand trembled as I pressed play on Ravel's "Piano Concerto in G Major" on my phone, hoping that music could offer some relief. He always liked that piece. The first gentle notes filled the air. They felt strangely out of place in that setting – too full of color and movement for such a quiet, clinical space. At first, nothing changed – the tension held, his brow furrowed – but then I saw small shifts. His shoulders easing, his jaw loosening, his grip on the bedrail relaxing. His body settled bit by bit, the way you only notice when you've learned every sign of discomfort. It wasn't relief – the pain was still there – but it looked a little less sharp, a little less consuming. The music gave him a moment of ease, something softer to rest against.

My own heartbeat slowed as the music settled over us both. For the first time all day, I breathed more easily, the sound offering a small moment of calm that silence never could. And what I witnessed in that room is what science now helps explain.

## What Is Pain?

Pain is both a sensory and emotional experience. It acts as the body's alarm system. Nerves detect a potential threat and send signals to the brain, which then interprets them as pain. This system keeps us safe, alerting us to injury or danger.

Not all pain is the same and understanding the difference matters. Acute pain is typically sharp and short-lived, usually tied to a clear cause such as touching something hot or twisting an ankle. It functions as an urgent warning signal, telling you to stop, pull back, and protect yourself from further harm. Chronic pain, by contrast, persists well beyond the normal healing process and can last for months or even years. In many cases it becomes a condition in its own right, lingering even after the original injury or illness has faded. For people living with arthritis, migraines, or ongoing back pain, it is not an occasional alarm, but a constant presence woven into daily life.

Pain is never purely physical. It is always shaped by mood, attention, memory, and meaning. Athletes often describe this vividly. The sting of tired muscles during training can feel unbearable in isolation, yet in the middle of the London Marathon, that same ache becomes bearable – even empowering – when fueled by roaring crowds, adrenaline, and purpose. A child's scraped knee may hurt less when soothed by a parent's comforting words. By contrast, pain often feels worse when we are anxious, lonely, or focused on it intensely.

Our perception of pain is influenced by context. What we believe it means, who we share it with, and whether we feel safe. A soldier in battle might not notice an injury until the danger has passed, while someone lying awake at night with no distraction may feel every twinge amplified. Pain is not just a mechanical signal from the body; it is shaped by our thoughts, memories, surroundings, and sense of safety. Evolution has developed this system to prioritize protection, even when it sometimes overreacts or continues sounding the alarm after the body has healed.

We also use the language of pain to describe emotional experiences – heartbreak, grief, or loss – reflecting how the brain's circuits for physical and emotional suffering overlap. Clinicians recognize this subjectivity when they ask patients to rate their pain on a simple scale of 1–10, knowing the number tells them as much about context and coping as about tissue damage.

Understanding pain's complexity helps explain why it poses such a widespread modern challenge – and why any meaningful solution must support both the body and the mind.

## Why Pain Is a Problem Today

Chronic pain affects more lives than most people realize. Current estimates suggest that around one in five adults live with some form of chronic pain, with rates even higher in older populations (Breivik et al., 2006; Dahlhamer et al., 2018). Conditions like arthritis, fibromyalgia, migraines, and back pain affect millions, each with its own daily frustrations. For many, pain is a daily companion that impacts sleep, mood, work, and relationships.

The challenge is not only individual suffering but also ripple effects. Families often shoulder emotional and financial burdens, workplaces lose productivity, and healthcare systems face escalating costs. For example, in the United States alone, the economic cost of chronic pain – including healthcare expenses and lost productivity – has been estimated at over $600 billion annually (Institute of Medicine, 2011). In the United Kingdom, back pain alone is one of the leading causes of work absence (Health and Safety Executive, 2021). Beyond statistics, the real weight is carried in small, everyday moments: a parent unable to pick up their child or a loved one withdrawing from social life because pain makes even simple outings unbearable.

Chronic pain is also closely linked to poor mental health. Living with constant discomfort increases the risk of depression and anxiety, creating a cycle where pain worsens mood, and low mood makes pain harder to manage. Social isolation compounds this, leaving many feeling cut off from friends, work, and community.

Recent global analyses highlight the enormous economic and social costs of untreated pain, from lost working days to reductions in GDP and increased reliance on disability benefits (Institute for Health Metrics and Evaluation, 2023). Worldwide, an estimated 1.5 billion adults live with chronic pain, making it one of the leading contributors to disability across regions (Institute for Health Metrics and Evaluation, 2023). This number is greater than those living with diabetes, heart disease, and cancer combined. Prevalence is consistently higher among women, and in many low and middle-income countries the impact is magnified by limited access to effective treatment or rehabilitation services. Chronic pain is not just a medical issue – it has become a public health crisis that touches families, workplaces, and whole communities.

Medical treatments are often imperfect. Painkillers can bring temporary relief but risk side effects and dependency. The global opioid crisis has shown the dangers of relying solely on pharmaceuticals (Volkow & McLellan, 2016). Years of over-prescription have fueled addiction and overdose deaths, hitting some communities especially hard. While opioids can be effective for short-term pain relief, their risks are profound when used long term. This crisis highlights the urgent need for alternative, non-addictive approaches to pain management – tools like music that are safe, inexpensive, and supportive of both body and mind. People need safe, non-invasive tools that help them cope – and this is where music offers hope.

This scale of suffering and cost is why researchers have turned to unexpected allies – like music – in search of relief.

## How Music Helps (the Science)

Music doesn't switch off pain, but it can soften its intensity and change how it feels in the body. It helps in several different ways at the same time:

### *Natural Painkillers*

Listening to music we love releases dopamine, the brain's spark of pleasure and anticipation, and endorphins, our body's own morphine-like chemicals that soothe pain (Salimpoor et al., 2011; NorthShore University HealthSystem, 2020; Cleveland Clinic, 2021).

### *Distraction*

Music redirects attention away from pain signals, lowering perceived intensity. Our brains can only process so much at once. When we become absorbed in melody or lyrics, fewer resources remain for processing pain.

MRI scan evidence demonstrates this clearly, showing how attention modulates pain perception in the brain (Bantick et al., 2002). This helps explain why favorite or personally significant songs often provide greater relief – the deeper the engagement, the stronger the effect.

### *Relaxation Response*

Slow, soothing music reduces muscle tension, heart rate, and cortisol. Cortisol acts like the body's built-in alarm bell. In short bursts it helps mobilize energy, but left ringing for too long it increases inflammation, disrupts sleep, and heightens pain sensitivity. As explored in earlier chapters, lowering cortisol helps the body return to balance. Music provides a gentle signal to the nervous system that it is safe to relax (McEwen, 2007).

### *Positive Mood and Energy*

Happy or upbeat music also plays a role. By lifting mood and boosting dopamine, it not only distracts from pain but can motivate movement. Dancing, tapping, or even nodding along encourages endorphin release. For some in rehabilitation, energizing tracks provide the rhythm to push through exercises that might otherwise feel impossible (Dahlhamer et al., 2018; Martin-Saavedra et al., 2018).

Additionally, a number of clinical studies evidence these effects in practice:

### *Fibromyalgia*

Daily music listening for four weeks reduced both pain and depression (Dahlhamer et al., 2018). For participants who had lived for years with widespread aches, the routine created a structured pause – an emotional reset that gradually built into greater resilience. Many described the music as providing companionship when their condition otherwise felt isolating.

### *Surgical Recovery*

Patients given music reported less pain and anxiety, even under general anesthetic (Hole et al., 2015). Those unconscious needed less medication afterwards, while awake patients found music masked intimidating theater sounds. Several described it as a protective barrier between themselves and the clinical environment.

### *Children in Procedures*

Studies show that when young patients wear headphones with their favorite songs during injections or blood tests, distress and reported pain drop significantly (Nguyen et al., 2010; Uggla et al., 2016). In one trial, children who listened to music during procedures reported pain scores nearly 30% lower than those without music, and parents observed noticeably less anxiety. For children, music offers both distraction and empowerment in situations that might otherwise feel frightening.

### *Palliative Care*

In hospice settings, patients often choose familiar songs that evoke comfort or identity. Reports describe how these tracks reduce the perception of pain and provide emotional relief for families gathered at the bedside (Hilliard, 2005; Dahlhamer et al., 2018). One randomized controlled trial found that patients receiving music therapy reported significantly lower pain scores and reduced need for breakthrough analgesics. Families also described moments of connection, with music creating a shared space of comfort at the end of life.

### *Meta-Analyses*

A large umbrella review found that music meaningfully reduces pain intensity and emotional distress across many conditions (Martin-Saavedra et al., 2018). The Cochrane Review (Bradt et al., 2021) reported similar findings in adults, with some trials showing up to a 30% drop in perceived pain. The takeaway is clear – music reliably reduces both the physical sensation of pain and the emotional load that comes with it.

In essence, music helps the body settle and the mind reinterpret pain, creating just a little more room for ease. Whether in operating rooms, pediatric wards or living rooms at home, the pattern is consistent – music doesn't erase pain, but it changes the way we meet it. And as we'll explore next, the type of music you choose matters.

Try choosing one piece of music you personally find calming and another that feels uplifting or energizing. Put on headphones, close your eyes, and listen to the first track while noticing any shifts in your breathing, muscle tension, or pain sensations. Then switch to the second track and observe how your body and mind respond differently. Which worked best for you in that moment? Jot down a note about the contrast. This exercise can help you shape a playlist that genuinely supports what your body and mood need most.

## Music Preferences and Pain Relief

A recent international study by the International Federation of the Phonographic Industry (IFPI, 2023) explored how people use music for pain relief across 20 countries, drawing on responses from more than 33,000 participants. The findings are striking. An overwhelming majority – 86.5% – said they prefer listening to music when they are experiencing pain, and nearly three quarters (73.1%) said they choose their favorite music rather than a genre prescribed or suggested to them.

What people choose to listen to varies widely across countries and cultures, underlining the importance of a personalized approach. In Latin America, listeners often gravitated toward pop and reggaeton, while in parts of Asia, traditional and folk styles were more commonly chosen. In North America, pop and rock dominated, whereas in many African countries people blended traditional rhythms with contemporary styles. These differences matter, because culture plays a powerful role in shaping what feels soothing, familiar, or empowering in moments of pain.

Despite this, many people still hold on to the idea of the so-called "Mozart effect" – the belief that classical music is uniquely calming or cognitively superior. This belief can be traced back to early 1990s studies that hinted at a short-term boost in spatial reasoning, but later research consistently shows that a person's favorite music, whatever the genre, is far more effective for pain relief. Interestingly, when IFPI participants did choose a genre outside their usual favorites, classical music was the most common choice, selected by 43.3%. This is likely because classical music is culturally associated with relaxation and medical settings, rather than because it works better in itself. Clinically, this distinction is important. Hospitals often default to classical playlists, yet simply asking patients what they actually want to hear leads to far better outcomes.

Why do favorites matter so much? Neuroscience shows that familiar tracks activate not only reward pathways but also memory and identity networks in the brain. This makes the experience more emotionally meaningful and strengthens dopamine release. Imaging studies demonstrate that when people listen to music they love, the dopamine system – the brain's core pleasure circuit – becomes far more active than when hearing unfamiliar or neutral music (Salimpoor et al., 2011).

In clinical practice, this means we shouldn't assume "calming classical" is best. A quick conversation about what a patient actually wants to hear can make the intervention far more effective. One patient asked for gospel songs that reminded her of childhood, another for heavy metal that made him feel strong, and another for a lullaby a parent once sang. These choices often surprised the staff, but each proved powerful because the music carried personal meaning as well as sound.

The key message is simple – classical music can help, but people benefit most when they listen to music they already love. Personal connection and emotional resonance matter more than genre labels when using music to manage pain.

> Think about the last time you were in pain – even something small like a headache or sore muscles after exercise. What music would you naturally reach for in that moment? Was it calming, distracting, or energizing? Take a few minutes just to recall and write down the tracks or artists you instinctively turn to. The goal here is to notice your natural preferences and the role they play in shaping your pain experience.

## Practical Applications and Guided Listening

A healing playlist works best when it reflects your own taste. Slow to moderate tempos (around 60–80 BPM) can help, but your favorite music will always matter more than technical rules. Choose tracks that feel familiar, comforting, and steady. If you ever need to choose between the "ideal" tempo and a song you love, always pick the one you love.

### *When to Use It*

You can use a healing playlist during flare-ups, before or after surgery, during rehab, or whenever pain feels intrusive. Gentle, immersive tracks can settle the nervous system, while slightly upbeat ones can bring energy for physiotherapy or moments of fatigue. Your favorite tracks will almost always work better than anything generic.

---

### Guided Listening

Play Ludovico Einaudi's "*Nuvole Bianche*" from Rob's Healing & Recovery Playlist. Notice how the repeating piano phrases create a steady, wave-like flow. Let your breathing follow the melody, releasing tension with each exhale. Simple, predictable patterns like this reduce cognitive load and help shift attention away from pain.

Alternatively try "Clara (the night is dark)" by Fred again... The driving beat and hopeful lyrics offer both distraction and emotional lift. Let the rhythm carry your attention outward. Even small movements – a nod, a tap – can release endorphins and shift the pain experience. This reflects the science. Rhythm boosts dopamine and movement; emotionally meaningful lyrics engage motivation and hope.

Finally, think of a lullaby, chant, hymn, or folk song from your own background. These often carry strong associations of safety and belonging. Neuroscience shows familiar, culturally meaningful music activates memory, identity, and emotional-safety networks (Janata, 2009), reducing the perceived intensity of pain.

Scan the QR code for Rob's Healing & Recovery Playlist.

Use the playlist for inspiration, not instruction. Calming piano, energetic pop, spiritual hymns, or traditional lullabies may all be useful – what matters most is personal resonance.

Choose soothing pieces for flare-ups or bedtime; use energizing ones during rehab or moments of fatigue. Headphones can increase immersion but keep the volume comfortable.

The guided examples above are starting points. Your own favorite tracks will nearly always work best.

---

Next time you feel discomfort – a headache, post-exercise ache, or chronic pain – press play on a playlist of your favorite tracks. Listen with full attention for 10 minutes and note whether it soothed you, distracted you, or lifted your energy. Over time, this will help you build a healing playlist that truly works for you.

## Perspectives

I still remember the moment it happened. I was at Birmingham University, playing serious basketball at the time, and I had agreed to help film a match for a BBC drama series about teachers. One wrong landing, one twist, and I tore the ligaments in my ankle. Within seconds the sharp, electric pain shot through me, followed by that heavy sinking feeling when you *know* something is badly wrong.

The days that followed were a blur of swelling, hobbling around campus on crutches, and waking up each morning to the same dull throb reminding me of what I'd lost. It wasn't just the physical pain – it was the frustration of being sidelined from the sport I loved, the loss of routine, the sudden absence of that outlet that anchored my well-being back then.

But something else showed up during that time too – music.

At that point in my life, I was deep into hip-hop, and one track in particular became my companion – "My Philosophy" by Boogie Down Productions. I listened to it endlessly. It didn't magically make the injury disappear, but it shifted my experience of it. The beat gave me something to hold on to. The flow distracted me from the discomfort. The energy helped me push through the physio exercises when motivation was low and progress was slow.

Music didn't just lessen the pain – it helped me reclaim a sense of momentum, even when my body felt stuck. It made the rehab sessions feel less like a chore and more like part of a journey I could shape. Looking back, that period was the first time I realized how deeply music can support physical healing, not in a clinical, abstract sense, but in a *human* one – by steadying your mindset, lifting your mood, and giving you strength when your body feels weak.

## Reflection Prompt

Think back to a moment when you were in pain or trying to recover. Was there a particular piece of music that helped you through it? Reflect on how it worked: Did it ease your body, change your emotions, or perhaps both at once?

Take a few minutes to write about what you listened to, why you chose it, and how it shaped your experience of that moment. How does it change your emotional state when you hear it today?

## Chapter Takeaway

Music may not eliminate pain, but it transforms how we carry it. By releasing natural painkillers known as endorphins – the body's own morphine-like chemicals that reduce pain and boost well-being – redirecting attention, and calming the nervous system, music becomes a powerful ally in healing. Just as importantly, the most effective music is often the music you love most – your personal favorites hold the greatest power to ease discomfort.

***Mantra:*** *Music may not cure pain, but it helps us carry it with more ease.*

# 9 Music, Sadness, and Emotional Healing

There are moments in life when silence feels unbearable. When loss or disappointment settles in and the world seems to quiet around us, words can start to fail. The sentences we reach for seem to fall short, and what we really feel remains buried – a weight in the chest, a knot in the throat. In those moments, music steps in. Not as a grand solution, but as a kind of translation. A melody can hold what we cannot express, a lyric can name what we cannot voice, and a familiar chord can feel like someone reaching out in the dark to say, "I'm here. I get it."

We often think of music as something that changes our mood, but sometimes its greatest power lies in meeting us exactly where we are. When sadness arrives – whether through heartbreak, illness, the slow drifting of friendships, or the unmistakable thud of life veering off course – music offers somewhere to rest inside the feeling. It gives shape to what hurts and makes it somehow bearable, even shared. Sometimes I think of it like leaning against a wall that won't move. It steadies you long enough to breathe. Listening becomes emotional breathing – a slow intake of memory, a release of pressure you didn't realize you were holding.

And yet, music also knows when to carry us forward. There are songs I've played on repeat during tough seasons – often late at night, sitting in the car outside the house for just a few extra minutes – that quietly nudged me back into motion. A rhythm can become a heartbeat we remember how to sync with and a harmony can crack a window where light begins to return. Healing rarely happens in a straight line; it moves like a dance between stillness and step, between sorrow and lift. As one friend once told me, "A sad song feels like a mirror; an uplifting one feels like a hand."

## What Is Sadness (and Emotional Healing)?

From a neuroscience perspective, sadness has a clear biological signature. Lower serotonin can accompany low mood, while hormones like prolactin help soothe us when we cry. Sadness isn't just emotional – it's a full-body response designed to slow us down, create space, and make connection more likely.

Sadness is one of our most human emotions – less a "quiet teacher" and more an unexpected companion who arrives when life knocks you sideways. It turns your attention inward, asks you to notice what matters, and gently nudges you toward support. But we often push it away. We apologize for tears in meetings, hide in emails, or scroll ourselves numb. In avoiding it, we miss what sadness is trying to reveal.

Often the first step is simply pausing – the moment you wait for the kettle to boil or sit on the edge of the bed before the day begins. In those small still moments, you might notice that sadness is already there, just beneath the surface. A little curiosity helps you meet it rather than outrun it.

Recognizing sadness starts with paying attention to what shifts. Sometimes it's obvious. A breakup, bad news, a conversation that lands wrong. Other times it's subtle. A heaviness in the body, canceling plans you'd normally enjoy, or realizing your favorite playlist suddenly feels flat. These signals are acts of self-communication. Naming them moves you from confusion to clarity – from being overwhelmed by the feeling to being in relationship with it.

Healing doesn't mean bypassing hard emotions; it means letting them move through safely. Think of listening to Adele's "Hello" – the slow tempo and raw vocal emotion give grief a place to land. I've had evenings where a song like that helped me release tension I'd been carrying all day. Music becomes a bridge. Not fixing what hurts, but helping you understand it and feel less alone. Healing isn't the disappearance of sadness; it's its integration – the way a sharp memory softens, or how sharing a tough moment turns isolation into connection.

Research backs this up. Studies in music and art therapy show that creative expression offers a safe container for emotion – a place to process without harm (Baker et al., 2018). A song can hold what feels too big to manage alone. Whether it's a melody that mirrors sorrow or a rhythm that lifts you slightly off the floor, music helps you feel fully – and in that fullness, helps you begin to heal.

## Why It's a Problem Today

In our fast-paced world – where phones buzz before we're even fully awake and messages stack up faster than we can clear them – we've grown uncomfortable with sadness. Modern life leaves little room for emotional depth. We jump between notifications, meetings, headlines, and noise, all while being fed highlight reels and quick-fix mantras that tell us to "keep going" even when we're exhausted. With social media serving curated snapshots of happiness and control, vulnerability can feel out of place. In a culture that rewards positivity and performance, sadness becomes something we try to patch over quickly – a glitch to fix rather than a signal worth hearing.

This avoidance creates a quiet but pervasive crisis. Unacknowledged sadness doesn't disappear; it reshapes itself. It shows up as fatigue, irritability, anxiety, cynicism, or burnout. I see it often in teams I work with – people powering through deadlines, fueling themselves with caffeine, squeezing in workouts not for joy but to outrun discomfort. We numb what we don't want to feel: the endless scroll, another coffee, another late night at the office. These habits offer momentary relief but steal real recovery. In the process, we suppress not only pain but also our capacity for empathy, creativity, and joy. Neuroscience shows that chronic emotional suppression heightens physiological stress responses and reduces resilience, keeping the brain in a low-level state of alert (Gross & Levenson, 1997; Butler et al., 2003).

Our discomfort with sadness has real consequences. Without safe spaces to feel and process emotion, people become disconnected – from themselves, from each other, and from meaning. I see it in workplaces when meetings become transactional rather than human, or in friendships where both people avoid naming what's actually happening. Teams lose empathy; relationships lose depth; mental health quietly deteriorates. We've mistaken emotional numbness for strength when, in reality, it's a form of disconnection. We need a reframe. Sadness isn't a malfunction but a message – a sign we've cared deeply, that something matters, and that something inside us needs tending.

This is where music becomes unexpectedly powerful. In a world obsessed with optimization and relentless positivity, music cuts through the noise. It slows us down, softens our edges, and gives us permission to feel. A quiet piano track, a melody from years ago, or a song you stumble across at exactly the right moment – it interrupts the rush. Sometimes it's the first thing that helps you breathe again. Music reminds us that feeling deeply isn't a weakness; it's a sign that we're still connected to ourselves, still human, still alive.

## How Music Helps (the Science)

Music engages the brain and body in ways that make emotional healing possible – and often surprisingly accessible. It can lower stress hormones, release dopamine and endorphins, and synchronize our internal rhythms (heart rate, breath, even brainwaves) back toward balance. This process is why a slow, steady track can calm anxious breathing or why a gentle rise in tempo can help us find energy again. Music doesn't just influence emotion; it shapes physiology.

From a neurological perspective, listening to music activates the amygdala (emotion), hippocampus (memory), nucleus accumbens (reward), and prefrontal cortex (reflection and meaning) (Koelsch, 2014). This is why music can make us cry one moment and feel relief the next – it helps the brain safely process complex feelings through sound.

Music tends to support emotional healing through two broad pathways: *presence and acceptance* and *shifting and lifting*. These are not rigid stages or a fixed sequence. Most people move fluidly between them, depending on the moment they are in and the depth of emotion they are carrying.

### *Presence and Acceptance (Sad or Reflective Music)*

Sometimes we reach for music that meets us exactly where we are. Slow, reflective, or melancholic tracks create emotional permission – a safe container to feel what's already inside us.

Songs like Adele's "Hello" or Max Richter's "On the Nature of Daylight" draw us inward. Their minor keys, slow tempos, and expressive dynamics mirror our emotional state, helping us name and release what we've been holding. Research shows that melancholic music activates the amygdala and hippocampus, helping us access and process emotional memories (Sachs et al., 2020). This emotional release is often accompanied by prolactin, a hormone linked to comfort and care, which explains why crying to music can feel strangely soothing.

Sad music doesn't keep us stuck – it helps us be honest. It gives emotion somewhere to go.

### *Shifting and Lifting (Upbeat or Rhythmic Music)*

Other times we turn to music to help us move. Upbeat, major-key, or rhythm-driven tracks activate the brain's reward system, releasing dopamine and endorphins (Ferreri et al., 2019). This explains why certain songs make us want to dance, nod our head, or simply smile.

Songs like Florence + The Machine's "Dog Days Are Over" combine rhythmic drive, energetic lifts, and lyrical optimism. That combination sparks motivation, engages the motor cortex, and reconnects us with vitality. It's not about forcing positivity – it's about giving the body a gentle nudge toward movement and possibility.

Together, these pathways help us move through sadness in a way that honors both truth and hope – *first inward, then upward.*

## Music and Coping Strategies

Most of us don't use music in just one way. We shift between coping styles based on what we need. Research identifies four broad types of coping that music can support (Lazarus & Folkman, 1984).

### *Problem-Focused Coping*

Using music to help think, plan, or take action. Instrumental or rhythmic tracks reduce mental fatigue and help maintain focus – a steady soundtrack when we need clarity. I often see people using ambient or electronic music in this way during deep work or when navigating difficult decisions.

### *Emotion-Focused Coping*

Here, music helps regulate feelings directly. A sad ballad can open the door to tears; a warm melody can steady the nervous system. By matching our mood first and shifting gently, music helps us soothe and reframe emotions safely.

### *Meaning-Focused Coping*

Reflective, spiritual, or lyrical music helps people make sense of difficult experiences. These tracks don't erase pain; they help us see it within a bigger story – turning hardship into insight and restoring a sense of continuity when life feels fractured.

### *Social Coping*

Shared listening builds connection. Singing in groups, attending concerts, or sending someone a playlist all release oxytocin – the hormone associated with trust and bonding. Music reminds us that our emotions aren't isolated; others feel them too.

### *Choosing Music Intentionally*

By tuning into what we need – comfort, release, momentum, clarity, or connection – we can choose music intentionally to support emotional regulation. These choices have measurable physiological effects – reducing cortisol, boosting dopamine and oxytocin, and bringing the body back toward balance.

In this way, music becomes both medicine and mirror. It reflects our emotional truth while helping us move through it with gentleness and agency.

## Practical Applications and Guided Listening

Understanding the science is only the beginning. The real shift happens when listening becomes intentional. Music can become a practical toolkit for emotional regulation, helping you move from heaviness to clarity.

Start by creating two playlists – one for Presence and Acceptance and one for Shifting and Lifting.

### *Presence and Acceptance (Reflective Tracks)*

Use this playlist when you need to sit with sadness rather than outrun it. Slower, minor-key tracks help you acknowledge and release emotion.

Take Adele's "Hello" as an example. Its slow tempo and emotional vocal delivery activate the brain regions involved in empathy, reflection, and emotional release. This style of music supports the parasympathetic nervous system – lowering heart rate and reducing stress hormones like cortisol – while hormones such as prolactin and oxytocin bring comfort and calm. This isn't wallowing; it's processing.

### *Shifting and Lifting (Energizing Tracks)*

When you feel ready to move forward, transition gently. This is where upbeat, rhythmic tracks help the body shift from stillness into renewed energy.

Fred again..'s "Turn on the Lights again.." is a great example. Its rising rhythm and sense of anticipation engage the brain's reward pathways, boosting dopamine and encouraging movement. It's not about "cheering up" – it's about reconnecting with momentum.

### *The Bridge Between Them*

Moving from a reflective track to an energizing one creates a subtle but powerful neurological handover – cortisol falls as dopamine rises. That shift mirrors the emotional journey from release to renewal, helping sadness soften into strength.

**Guided Listening**

You might begin by simply sitting with sadness. Choose a reflective track, close your eyes, and notice what arises – sensations in the body, memories, areas of tension or heaviness. If tears come, let them. This is about allowing the emotion to be present without rushing it away.

When you feel ready, you can shift and lift by playing a more energizing song. Let the rhythm gently guide your breathing or your movement, even if it's just a subtle sway or a deeper breath. Pay attention to how your body responds as the energy changes.

Finally, spend a few minutes reflecting. You might journal, jot down a few words, or record a short voice note about what shifted. This moment of reflection helps turn emotional release into insight, anchoring the experience rather than letting it pass unnoticed.

Scan the QR code for Rob's Sadness & Emotional Healing Playlist.

## *Making It a Habit*

Turn these playlists into simple rituals. Start or end your day with one track that matches your mood or use intentional listening before big moments – a meeting, a workout, or a difficult conversation. Over time, your brain learns that emotion is safe to feel and that you have tools to navigate it.

Music becomes not just a way to feel better but a way to feel *fully* – embracing sadness, strength, and everything in between.

For readers who want to explore this journey directly, the curated playlist mirrors the two pathways: reflective tracks first, then uplifting ones.

## Perspectives

During my experience with long COVID, the sadness of losing the joy of cycling hit hard in ways I didn't expect. Cycling had always been more than exercise – it was freedom, rhythm, therapy, escape. The steady pattern of pedaling, the rush of cool air on my face, the quiet satisfaction of powering up a hill – all of it formed a ritual that kept me mentally balanced for years. And then, almost overnight, it vanished. My body simply couldn't do it.

What surprised me most was the emotional weight of that loss. Without that outlet of movement, the days felt heavier, the world somehow smaller. My body was still trying to heal, but my mind needed somewhere to put the grief of suddenly being still.

That's when I turned, instinctively, to music. Not upbeat tracks designed to distract. Not motivational anthems trying to push me forward before I was ready. Instead, I gravitated toward songs that held a kind of emotional duality – melancholic enough to acknowledge what I'd lost, yet uplifting enough to remind me that the story wasn't finished.

One track became particularly important – "For You (Solomun Morning Version)" by Michael Mayer & Joe Goddard. It felt like the musical equivalent of recovery. It begins with a soft, introspective tenderness – a quiet emotional honesty that mirrored how fragile I felt. Then, gradually, layer by layer, it builds. Gentle at first. Curious. Then expanding into something brighter, more assured, as if reminding me that movement and energy would return in time.

Listening to it became a ritual. A small daily moment where I could sit with the grief of what had changed, while still holding onto hope for what might return. Over weeks and months, I started to notice how the rising rhythm of the track echoed my real-life progress. Tiny increases in energy, deeper breaths, more optimistic moments. It was as if the structure of the song was modeling recovery itself – starting in reflection, swelling with emotion, and resolving in a quiet, grounded optimism.

Music helped me process what I'd lost, soothe the ache of stillness, and reconnect to a sense of possibility. Even before my body could move freely again, the right track helped my mind remember how movement *felt*.

Music was a bridge back to myself.

## Reflection Prompt

When you're sad, do you tend to lean into the sadness with reflective music, or try to lift yourself with upbeat music? What happens when you try the other option?

Both pathways – Presence and Acceptance and Shifting and Lifting – are valid and valuable. There's no single right way to heal. What matters is awareness – choosing music consciously to meet yourself where you are and allowing sound to guide you toward where you need to be next. Sometimes that means slowing down to listen inward; sometimes it means turning up the volume and moving forward.

## Chapter Takeaway

Sadness is not something to fix, but something to feel. Music offers two healing choices – to sit with our sadness or to shift it – both are valid, and both help us heal. Let music meet you where you are and gently guide you toward where you need to be.

Music reminds us that healing is not a race but a rhythm. It teaches us to trust the cycles of feeling – to lean into what hurts, to rise when the moment calls, and to keep listening inward. Each song becomes a small act of courage, each note a reminder that even in sadness, we are still connected to something larger, something alive.

When we surrender to sound, we don't just recover; we remember. We remember that emotion is energy, that movement is medicine, and that to feel deeply is to be profoundly human. So, when the next wave comes – let the music meet it with you.

***Mantra:*** *Let the music hold you, then lift you.*

# 10 Music and Memory

Music can unlock time. The first time it happens, it almost feels like time travel.

A song you haven't heard in years drifts from a car radio, a café speaker, or a half-forgotten playlist – and before your brain has time to name it, your body already knows. Your heart quickens, your chest tightens, and you're back there again. The smell of warm air and spilled drinks. The faces. The feeling. It's not just memory – it's motion. Music doesn't simply remind you; it *re-members* you – stitching the past and present into a single, living moment.

Back in the day, I owned a London bar called barLocal with some mates. We decided to throw a spontaneous White Party, when the space was still a construction site – the walls freshly painted white, the bar half-built, wires coiled in corners. We cleared enough room for a sound system, poured some drinks, and filled the shell with people. When I dropped Pete Heller's "Big Love (The Dronez Dub)," the room erupted. The bass line rolled through the floorboards, vibrating up through our shoes, glasses rattling on the bar as flickering lights painted the white walls with color. The scent of paint mixed with sweat and euphoria. Builders, friends, strangers – all suddenly on their feet. Dancing on chairs. Shouting, laughing, surrendering to the rhythm.

The air was electric. The crowd pulsed as one – breathless, alive, connected. Every flash of light, every hit of the kick drum etched itself into my mind like a photograph made of sound. Even now, when I play that track, I'm transported straight back to that moment – the echo of laughter, the smell of paint, the feeling of pure release. It's a reminder that memory doesn't live only in the mind; it lives in the body, in the beat, in the breath between notes.

Memory isn't static – it moves through us. It's not an archive, it's an experience – and music is the bridge that brings it vividly back to life.

## What Is Memory?

To understand what was happening that night at barLocal, we need to step inside the mind's recording studio – where sound becomes memory and feeling becomes story. One chord from a summer track can take me straight back: the people, the light, the emotion. Memory is rarely neutral, right?

Think of memory as *emotion in motion*. Songs hit hard because they carry the emotional fingerprints of when we first heard them. When music triggers a memory, that emotional energy wakes up – helping us re-feel rather than simply recall.

Memory isn't a filing cabinet – it's a recording studio with rough takes beside polished ones. Faders shift, new tracks appear, and older versions get remixed as we grow. Our senses capture the raw audio of experience, while different brain regions act as producers, shaping what gets stored, edited, or replayed (Levitin, 2024). Like a producer layering sound, the brain blends sensory detail, emotion, and meaning into memory.

### *The Memory Studio*

*Sensory Memory* acts like a microphone, briefly capturing fleeting input before it fades away (Baddeley, 2003). From there, *Working Memory* functions more like a mixing desk, looping short clips, adjusting levels, and deciding what is important enough to keep in play (Zatorre & Salimpoor, 2013). What survives this process may then be stored in *Long-Term Memory*, which resembles an archive vault designed for future playback. Within that archive, different systems do different jobs: episodic memory stores lived moments and personal experiences in the hippocampus, procedural memory holds skills and habits in the cerebellum and basal ganglia, and emotional memory shapes the tone and feeling of experiences through the amygdala.

But structure isn't the whole story. Music taps directly into the emotional brain. Daniel Levitin notes that music strongly activates autobiographical memory because it blends pattern, prediction, and feeling (Levitin, 2024). Rhythm gives the brain a scaffold that strengthens recall. As Levitin says in *Music as Medicine*, "Prediction and anticipation are at the heart of the musical experience – and of how we remember."

When an experience pairs with melody or rhythm, we anchor it in predictability and pleasure. Dopamine flows when musical patterns resolve, reinforcing the pathways that hold memory in place (Zatorre & Salimpoor, 2013).

Music also becomes the mastering process of memory. Each replay subtly remixes the track – new layers, new meaning, small shifts based on who we are today. Music lets us join the process, helping us reframe the past and bring coherence to our story. It helps us not just remember – but feel remembered.

### *Music and Collective Memory*

Music also shapes the memories we share. That swell in your chest when a crowd sings the same line – it's powerful. Songs become cultural markers: soundtracks to eras, movements, crises, and celebrations. They help us remember not just our own past but our shared one.

Shared musical rituals – from community singing after tragedy to national ceremonies – help people process collective emotion and build resilience.

Examples of collective memory in action are all around us in music. "Imagine" by John Lennon has become a global anthem of hope, resurfacing again and again during moments of uncertainty or collective grief. "Three Lions" by Baddiel, Skinner & The Lightning Seeds acts as a kind of emotional shorthand for belief, disappointment, and hope, carrying decades of English football history in just a few familiar lines. For younger generations, "This Is Me" from *The Greatest Showman* has emerged as a powerful empowerment anthem, closely tied to identity, self-expression, and belonging.

Together, these songs show how music becomes a living archive. It doesn't just store individual memories, but holds shared emotional experiences that can be reactivated instantly, reconnecting people to moments, movements, and meanings that extend far beyond the music itself.

As we move from collective memory to the challenges of remembering in a distracted age, one thing is clear – music doesn't just connect us to the past – it cuts through the noise. Notifications, stress, and information overload distort how we record and retrieve moments. Even the best studio picks up interference. Today, attention is the rarest instrument in the orchestra of the mind.

In the next section, we'll explore how music helps us tune back into focus, presence, and feeling.

## Why Memory Is Challenged Today

Picture a typical weekday morning. Your phone lights up before you're fully awake, emails stack up, the news scroll tugs at your attention – and before coffee, your mind already feels crowded. Modern life overwhelms the brain. Notifications, multitasking, lack of sleep, and stress all compete for our limited attention, fragmenting focus and memory. Every alert hijacks the mind's recording studio, interrupting the process of laying down coherent tracks. The result? Mental noise. We remember information but lose the meaning behind it.

Daniel Levitin argues that in an age of information saturation, what we lack isn't storage – it's significance. I feel this myself on chaotic days where one song can pull everything back into perspective. We're drowning in data but starved of meaning. Music cuts through the noise and reminds us what matters. Its structure and emotion give shape to experience, transforming scattered moments into something memorable. As Levitin puts it, music reintroduces *context into chaos* – turning signals into stories and helping us reconnect with the bigger picture of our lives.

Biologically, stress and overload run deep. Chronic stress floods the brain with cortisol, damaging the very structures we rely on for memory. Prolonged exposure weakens neurons in the hippocampus – the brain's memory hub – making it harder to transfer short-term experiences into long-term storage. You can feel this on stressful days where conversations slip, names vanish, simple tasks feel strangely difficult. The prefrontal cortex, responsible for focus and decision-making, also takes a hit, making it harder to sort what's important. Meanwhile, the amygdala – our emotional alarm system – becomes overactive, nudging us toward threat and worry. Together, these changes shape a mind that remembers stress more easily than joy.

Sleep deprivation only adds to the problem. Without enough slow-wave and REM sleep, the brain struggles to consolidate memory or clear out waste through the glymphatic system. Even a single night of poor sleep can reduce hippocampal activity by up to 40%, impairing learning and recall. Then there's dopamine-loop scrolling – that reflexive refresh – reward cycle built into apps. Our attention skims across countless micro-moments, never settling long enough to capture emotional meaning.

We're also facing a new challenge – the digital memory shift. Streaming services and algorithmic playlists act as external hard drives for emotion. We no longer *need* to remember; technology does it for us. Convenient, yes – but when algorithms predict everything, they can also flatten surprise. I often wonder which songs have resurfaced only because a platform nudged them. . . and which favorites have quietly disappeared because the algorithm stopped showing them? Music in the digital age preserves the past, but it can also quietly edit it.

We live in an age of perfect recall but imperfect presence. Our memory systems are overloaded and out of tune. Yet music offers a way back – a way to restore rhythm to attention and reconnect emotion to experience. It slows us down, anchors awareness, and gives meaning back to moments. In a world full of noise, music helps the mind find harmony again.

## How Music Helps (the Science)

Let's return to the idea of the brain's orchestra discussed in Chapter 1, "Music and the Brain" – not as a neat metaphor, but as the living system behind how memory forms. Music doesn't just light up the brain; it recruits a full ensemble. It's one of the most widely activating human experiences (Levitin, 2006; Koelsch, 2014), engaging memory, movement, emotion, and reward all at once.

### *The Brain's Orchestra*

Each section of this inner symphony adds its own line to the score. The hippocampus encodes experience, particularly when it is tied to sounds that feel meaningful or familiar, helping moments become memories rather than passing impressions (Janata, 2009). The amygdala tags those memories with emotion, increasing the likelihood that they will stick and be recalled later (Juslin & Västfjäll, 2008). The prefrontal cortex plays a coordinating role, directing attention and pulling relevant memories forward when they are needed, while the auditory cortex interprets the raw musical ingredients of pitch, rhythm, and tone. Alongside this, the cerebellum and wider motor system help keep time, which is why tapping a foot or moving along to music can noticeably boost recall. When all of these elements align, the brain's reward circuits are activated, releasing dopamine as patterns and pleasure come together – reinforcing, not just the musical experience, but also the memory it carries (Zatorre & Salimpoor, 2013).

There are a number of mechanisms in practice:

### *Encoding Aid*

Pairing learning with melody helps turn abstract information into something memorable (Ludke et al., 2014). Singing gives ideas shape and rhythm the brain can replay. It's why children learn the alphabet through song and why adults remember sung phrases more easily.

In one study, adults learning Hungarian phrases recalled them far more accurately when sung – immediately and hours later. Melody provided structure, while singing linked auditory and motor systems, improving pronunciation and embedding the rhythm of the language. Recall accuracy can rise by up to 20% when information is sung.

### *Cueing and Retrieval*

Songs act as keys that unlock stored pathways (Janata, 2009). When a melody resurfaces, the brain reactivates the original network of sensory and emotional signals tied to it. One opening chord can return you to an entire scene – who you were with, how you felt, even the smell of the room.

### *Emotion Tagging*

Music's emotional charge strengthens memory (Koelsch, 2014). Emotion is the glue of recall, and music provides a direct route into the amygdala. A song linked to joy, heartbreak, or hope becomes a multisensory imprint – part sound, part feeling.

### *Neuroplasticity*

Regular engagement with music builds cognitive resilience, especially in aging and dementia (Altenmüller & Schlaug, 2015). Because music activates multiple regions at once, it reinforces existing connections and helps create new ones. This "cross-training" effect keeps cognitive flexibility alive.

### *Why Alzheimer's Patients Remember Lyrics When Other Memories Fade*

Research by Janata (2009) and Sacks (2007) shows that musical memory is unusually resilient – often surviving long after verbal or episodic memories disappear. That's because musical memories are stored across several systems including: auditory, motor, emotional, and reward.

Caregivers see this daily. For example, someone who no longer recognizes their daughter can still sing every word of a favorite song. Familiar rhythm and melody activate networks illness cannot fully erase, briefly restoring connection, language, and a sense of self. Identity often lives in sound long after it slips from words.

Music turns moments into melodies – and melodies back into moments. It transforms sound into story and emotion into connection. The brain doesn't just process music – it *remembers through it.*

Music is far more than entertainment; it's a biological symphony linking sound, movement, emotion, and memory. In the next section, we explore "Music as Memory Medicine" – how rhythm restores balance, melody repairs emotional pathways, and harmony helps the mind recover from illness, trauma, and time.

## Music as Memory Medicine

Lifelong musical engagement may help protect the brain as it ages. Studies of older adults who sing in choirs, learn instruments, or attend concerts show stronger cognitive reserve and lower dementia risk than non-musical peers – a pattern many clinicians observe too. MRI research from Helsinki and Harvard shows that active musical participation helps maintain grey matter and strengthens connections between auditory and memory regions (Wan & Schlaug, 2010; Särkämö et al., 2014).

A 2023 AARP and Global Council on Brain Health study also found that older adults who play or listen to music daily show better cognitive function and reduced dementia risk. The World Health Organization (2019) now recognizes music engagement as an accessible lifestyle factor that supports healthy aging.

Even simple, regular listening boosts neuroplasticity and emotional steadiness. Many people describe how a favorite album with morning coffee keeps them mentally sharper and more grounded. Music doesn't just restore – it protects. As Levitin (2024) notes, melody can both preserve and heal memory.

### *Example Healing Pathways*

Let's explore a few healing pathways in action:

**Dementia and Recognition** In dementia, familiar songs can reawaken recognition and calm (Sacks, 2007). Hearing a beloved track can spark emotional engagement and activate the hippocampus and limbic system, even when verbal memory has faded. Patients may smile, hum, or join in – briefly reconnecting with themselves and those around them. These moments show how music taps into a deeply preserved network of autobiographical memory.

**Rhythmic Entrainment and Recovery** Rhythmic entrainment helps rebuild speech and movement after stroke (Altenmüller & Schlaug, 2015). By synchronizing brain rhythms with external beats, damaged circuits can relearn timing. Rhythmic stimulation helps survivors walk more evenly, while melodic intonation therapy supports speech recovery by turning words into song.

**Personalized Playlists and Cognitive Reserve** Personalized playlists can strengthen cognitive reserve by activating multiple sensory and emotional systems at once. Meaningful music creates redundancy in memory circuits, helping maintain flexibility, attention, and emotional regulation even as decline progresses.

**Distributed Memory Networks** Because musical memories are stored across auditory, motor, emotional, and reward systems, they often endure longer than language or logic. Families often notice this resilience long before diagnosis. When other abilities fade, melody remains – a thread of identity and continuity.

**Real-World Music Programs in Dementia Care** NHS dementia wards are piloting MELODIC (Music therapy Embedded in the Life of Dementia Inpatient Care). Early results show fewer distress incidents on music-therapy days, with patients calmer and more communicative.

A UK study, *How and Why Music Therapy Reduces Distress and Improves Well-Being in Advanced Dementia Care* (Thompson et al., 2024), found that personalized music reduces agitation and strengthens emotional connection by activating preserved musical memory networks. Programs like Music for Dementia and the Alzheimer's Society's Singing for the Brain are bringing these insights into daily practice.

Globally, initiatives such as Music & Memory (US/Canada) and Playlist for Life (UK) use personalized playlists to help people recall key moments and reconnect with loved ones. The science of music and memory isn't confined to labs – it's unfolding in care homes, hospitals, and community centers every day.

Next, we'll explore practical ways to use music in daily life to strengthen memory, focus, and emotional well-being.

## Practical Applications and Guided Listening

Music's healing power isn't limited to clinical settings – it's something we can all use in everyday life. Even short, intentional listening can lower cortisol, elevate dopamine, and activate the neural pathways that support learning and memory. The key is being purposeful in choosing what we play, when we play it, and why. That simple shift turns music from background noise into an active tool for self-regulation and reflection.

When we listen with intention, we can guide our mental and emotional state as deliberately as we train our bodies through movement. We've learned that a calming playlist can slow breathing and ease tension; and an energizing set can lift motivation. In a similar way, a nostalgic track can reawaken memories that anchor identity. Music becomes a conversation with the nervous system – tuning mood, memory, and motivation in real time. By curating playlists that match specific emotional or cognitive needs, sound becomes a daily well-being ally rather than just a soundtrack.

---

**A Short Intentional Guided Listening Session**

Try this simple ritual – 10 minutes is enough.

1. **Set your intention.** What do you need most? Focus, calm, clarity? Ask yourself honestly, *where's my head right now?*
2. **Create the space.** Sit somewhere quiet, soften the lighting, silence notifications. Think of this as a mindful pause, not background music.
3. **Press play.** Close your eyes as the first track begins. Notice one element at a time – rhythm, tone, texture, the feeling behind it. Let memories surface if they do.
4. **Reflect.** When the track ends, jot a few lines in a journal or voice note. What shifted? What came up? Over time, this becomes a small map of the songs that steady or energize you.

This ritual can help you spot patterns – the tracks that sharpen focus, calm the mind, or reliably reconnect you with yourself.

Scan the QR code for Rob's Memory Playlist.

For this one, I've had a bit of fun and dropped a bunch of tracks that all have strong memories for me. They won't necessarily mean much to you, but it is an exercise that you can do to create a playlist to take you back.

### *Practical Memory-Based Playlists*

Use Table 10.1 as a starting point. Adjust tempo, genre, or mood until the music feels right in your body.

**Table 10.1 Memory-Based Playlists**

| Playlist Type | Purpose | Ideal Tempo | Example Tracks | Notes |
|---|---|---|---|---|
| **Study and Focus** | Enhance concentration and working memory | 60–80 BPM | Einaudi – "Experience," Tycho – "Awake" | Repetitive instrumental textures reduce distraction |
| **Calm and Grounding** | Support relaxation and emotional balance | <70 BPM | Nils Frahm – "Late," Ólafur Arnalds – "Near Light" | Slow tempo and gentle harmonics promote alpha brain waves |

(*continued*)

**Table 10.1** (*continued*)

| Playlist Type | Purpose | Ideal Tempo | Example Tracks | Notes |
|---|---|---|---|---|
| **Life Review** | Reflect on personal milestones | Variable | Fleetwood Mac – "Landslide," Bill Withers – "Lovely Day" | Ideal for journaling or life-review therapy |
| **Motivation and Energy** | Boost dopamine and recall through rhythm | 100–130 BPM | Fred again.. – "Danielle (Smile on My Face)," Macklemore – "Can't Hold Us" | Syncs motor rhythm with emotional arousal |
| **Sleep and Restoration** | Encourage slow-wave relaxation and memory consolidation | 40–60 BPM | Sigur Rós – "Samskeyti," Brian Eno – "An Ending (Ascent)" | Best used as part of a nightly ritual |

This visual helps translate theory into practice – curating playlists that support memory, focus, reflection, and recovery through intentional tempo and tone. Over time, adapt your playlists depending on the time of day, your emotional state, or the energy your body needs.

### *Music for Emotional Memory Journaling*

As you listen, jot down the emotions or memories that arise – images, scents, sensations, or sudden flashes of recognition. This turns passive listening into reflective storytelling, helping you understand how sound traces your life's timeline. People often discover patterns: tracks that reliably surface during transitions or melodies that mirror shifts in identity.

One music-therapy participant once told me that playlist journaling felt "like finding a map back to myself." Hearing that reminded me how reflection through sound can open emotional insight in ways words sometimes can't.

### *Life-Review Therapy Through Music*

Many therapists use *life-review playlists* to help people explore identity across time. Create one that spans key chapters of your life – childhood, adolescence, early adulthood, relationships, career, personal turning points. Sit with the playlist and ask, *Who was I then? Who am I now? What connects the two?*

Sharing your playlist with someone close can turn this into a powerful relational exercise. Swap stories. Explain why certain songs matter. This transforms solitary reflection into shared meaning – strengthening memory and deepening connection.

Music is one of the simplest daily ways to strengthen memory, emotional awareness, and connection. When we turn listening into a small ritual, we rediscover why sound is such a potent form of medicine. In Chapter 22, "Mark – The Power of Music to Connect, Heal, and Hold Us Together," we'll hear from people who've used music to reconnect with their pasts, rediscover lost memories, and rebuild their sense of self – showing that music doesn't just preserve memory; it awakens it.

## Perspectives

There are certain friends who become part of your emotional wiring – people who shaped you long before you realized you were being shaped. For me, one of those people is my old mate Paul "Griffo" Griffiths. We were inseparable growing up: school years, weekends, shooting hoops in long summers that felt like entire lifetimes, all stitched together by the soundtrack of whatever we had on repeat.

For us, that soundtrack was R&B – especially anything touched by Teddy Riley. New Jack Swing was our world. Wreckx-N-Effect, Guy, Blackstreet . . . and above all, "Rump Shaker." The moment that sax riff kicked in, we were gone – laughing, messing about, thinking we were far cooler than we actually were.

We eventually drifted apart after university, as people do. Different cities, different lives, different routines. But every time I play those tracks now – especially "Rump Shaker" – something in me snaps back into place. I'm instantly transported to those years: the pure fun with a basketball in hand, the ridiculous confidence, the feeling that the world was opening up and we were racing toward it.

Music does that. It brings people back – not just faces and places, but *feelings*. And sometimes, it reconnects you with parts of yourself you didn't realize you were missing.

## Reflection Prompt

Think about how your musical tastes have evolved over time. Which artists or songs defined different stages of your life – childhood, adolescence, early adulthood, and today? What do these shifts reveal about how you've grown, what you've valued, and how you've changed? Reflect on how music has shaped your identity through time, acting as both a mirror and a timeline of who you are.

Music can preserve parts of us that time tries to erase. Which memories deserve a soundtrack – and which songs help you remember who you are?

Build your own Memory Mixtape – five tracks marking life's key chapters. Note what each song represents, and how it connects to who you've become.

## Chapter Takeaway

Music is more than sound – it's storage. When words and facts fade, melodies remain, carrying our emotional and personal history. Across this chapter, we've seen how music shapes memory – from the neural symphony that encodes emotion to the melodies that reawaken recognition and restore identity. We've traced its impact from classrooms to clinics, from personal playlists to collective healing.

*Music doesn't just help us remember – it helps us remember ourselves.*

Returning once more to our discussion of the brain's orchestra, the melody of memory completes the symphony. Each recall, each song, each emotion plays like a reprise – reminding us that music, at its core, is how our inner orchestra keeps time with who we are.

> ***Mantra:*** *Press Play, and it comes back.*

# 11 Music and Neurodivergence

The world can feel too loud, too bright, too fast. For many neurodivergent people, sound doesn't just travel through the ears – it floods the body. A sudden noise can jolt the nervous system; overlapping voices can feel like static. But when the right song or piece begins – familiar, rhythmic, structured – the chaos softens. The rhythm becomes an anchor.

Before diving into the science, it's worth naming what many people feel instinctively. Music can act as both shield and translator for neurodivergent minds. It filters sensory overload and turns unpredictable sound into something safe. A steady rhythm can ground attention; a melody can bridge the gap back to calm.

Catherine Ritchie, Senior Wellbeing and Experience Leader at a global elite law firm, clarity coach, and proud autistic woman, described music as her emotional language – a way to regulate, process, and reconnect: "It was sometimes the only way I could process the world." The right rhythm slows her breathing, steadies her body, and restores clarity. Music, for her, is structure in a world that often feels unpredictable.

## What Is Neurodivergence?

Neurodivergence is not a mental illness. And here's a question worth pausing on. What if these differences aren't obstacles at all, but alternate ways of sensing the world? It describes the natural variations in human brain wiring that shape how we think, feel, and process the world. This includes autism, ADHD, dyslexia, dyspraxia, Tourette's, and other forms of cognitive difference. These conditions don't represent flaws but form part of the diversity of human cognition – a spectrum of perception, attention, and emotion that adds depth and creativity to our shared experience.

### *The Science of Difference*

Each neurotype processes information differently. Neurodivergent brains often show greater variability in connectivity between brain regions – meaning signals move along unique pathways that can amplify certain skills while challenging others. This explains why someone with ADHD may find it hard to focus on repetitive tasks but can hyperfocus for hours on something they love; or why an autistic person may find social cues confusing yet excel in recognizing patterns, systems, and details invisible to most. Dyslexic thinkers often have exceptional spatial reasoning and problem-solving abilities, while dyspraxic individuals may bring intuitive understanding of movement, timing, and rhythm.

These differences aren't random – they have evolutionary purpose. Diversity in brain wiring has helped humanity innovate, adapt, and survive. The same traits that make a classroom challenging for one person might make them a brilliant coder, designer, musician, or scientist in another context. Seen through this lens, neurodivergence isn't pathology – it's potential.

### *Sensory Worlds*

This brings us to one of the hallmarks of neurodivergence – sensory variation. If you've ever felt overwhelmed by a room that others barely notice, you'll recognize this instantly. Many autistic or ADHD individuals describe heightened sensitivity to sound, light, or texture. Everyday stimuli – humming lights, a ticking clock, overlapping voices – can be physically painful or emotionally overwhelming. Yet that same sensitivity can translate into profound artistic perception. Neurodivergent people often report deep, multi-sensory experiences of music: hearing texture, seeing rhythm, or feeling vibration as color or movement.

This is why music feels especially powerful for neurodivergent listeners. It mirrors how their brains naturally work – rhythmic, patterned, immersive. Music can help organize chaotic sensory input, offering both grounding and stimulation in a way that feels safe. It becomes a translation layer between inner experience and outer world.

### *Emotional Regulation and Time Perception*

Differences in emotional regulation and time perception also play a major role. You might know the feeling – when your emotions arrive like a wave, before you've had time to brace for it. Many neurodivergent people experience emotions with greater intensity and may struggle to modulate them in real time. Music helps bridge that gap – matching emotional intensity while guiding the listener toward balance. Rhythmic entrainment (the syncing of body rhythms to external rhythm) is a natural biological process that supports this regulation, helping restore coherence to breathing, heartbeat, and movement.

Similarly, for those who experience time differently – common in ADHD and autism – music provides an external structure that anchors the moment. The tempo of a song can act as a clock, marking passage and pacing tasks. A playlist can turn abstract time into something tangible and felt.

### *The Cultural Shift*

Stepping back from the science, culturally, we are living through a major shift in how neurodivergence is understood. You can feel this everywhere – in conversations at work, in classrooms, in families finally finding language for experiences long unnamed. Once pathologized and hidden, it is now increasingly recognized as part of human biodiversity. The neurodiversity movement reframes these differences as natural and valuable variations in cognition – a call to redesign systems that honor diverse ways of being. This means moving from accommodation to celebration, not asking how to make neurodivergent people fit the world, but how to make the world fit them.

Music sits beautifully at the heart of this reframe. It does not demand conformity or verbal explanation. It meets people exactly where they are – in rhythm, pattern, and emotion – offering connection without translation. Through rhythm, tone, and resonance, music becomes both a well-being tool and a form of social inclusion.

### *Creative Expression – Seeing Sound*

A striking example of neurodivergence expressed through music is Pharrell Williams, who experiences synesthesia – a blending of senses where sound and color interact. For Pharrell, melodies appear as hues and shapes, allowing him to compose in three dimensions of feeling and light. This sensory crossover isn't a disorder but a creative amplifier – showing how neurodivergent wiring can open new pathways for artistic expression. Like many synesthetes, Pharrell doesn't just hear music; he sees and feels it, turning sound into color and emotion into movement.

### *Why It Matters*

Understanding neurodivergence isn't about diagnosis – it's about empathy. When we understand how different brains experience the world, we can design more inclusive environments, practices, and well-being tools. Music offers one of the most universal bridges for doing this. It helps neurodivergent minds regulate, express, and thrive – translating the invisible language of feeling into rhythm, melody, and meaning.

## What Are the Challenges Facing Neurodivergent People Today?

All of this lands in a world that moves at a relentless pace – one not designed with neurodivergent minds in mind. Open-plan offices, constant digital pings, and overstimulating classrooms can turn daily life into a sensory assault. For those with heightened sensory awareness, this environment can lead to exhaustion and burnout long before the day ends. Our culture often rewards speed and multitasking – yet many neurodivergent people thrive in depth, focus, and pattern. The mismatch between how society works and how their brains work can create a chronic state of dysregulation.

The rise in neurodivergent diagnoses reflects both progress and pressure. Greater awareness means more people are finally understanding themselves and accessing support, but it also highlights how unprepared our systems remain.

### *Autism*

Diagnoses in the United Kingdom increased nearly eightfold between 1998 and 2018 (Russell et al., 2021). In England, around 1.22% of males and 0.35% of females now have a formal autism diagnosis. Research suggests up to 90% of older autistic adults remain undiagnosed (EurekAlert, 2024).

### *ADHD*

Diagnoses and prescriptions have risen dramatically, with a 20-fold increase among men aged 18–29 and a 50-fold rise in prescriptions since 2000 (UCL, 2023). Adult ADHD prevalence now sits at 3–4%, though only a fraction of people receive support (BDA, 2024). Referrals for ADHD assessment in England rose another 13.5% year-on-year in 2025 (NHS Digital, 2025).

This surge in awareness has not yet translated into environments that support neurodivergent regulation. Schools, workplaces, and communities continue to reward conformity and penalize difference. Many neurodivergent people are expected to mask their traits – hiding stimming behaviors, forcing eye contact, suppressing emotion – all of which take a toll on mental and physical health. The result is a silent epidemic of burnout.

### *The Education Gap*

Education remains one of the clearest examples of this gap. Traditional classrooms favor verbal instruction, linear thinking, and stillness. For many neurodivergent students, these conditions are the opposite of what helps them thrive. Without quiet zones, flexible pacing, or sensory-friendly design, classrooms can become environments of constant stress. Teachers may misread coping behaviors as misbehavior – labeling a dysregulated child as disruptive, when in truth they are overwhelmed.

Music-based approaches could transform this dynamic. Research in music therapy and education shows that rhythm and structured sound help regulate arousal levels, increase attention, and support memory formation. Integrating rhythmic transitions between activities or encouraging brief "sound resets" between lessons could help young people manage energy and emotion. Schools that embrace music as a learning tool not only support neurodivergent students – they improve focus, collaboration, and creativity for everyone.

### *The Workplace Challenge*

In the workplace, the same issues repeat. Open-plan offices, constant video calls, and noisy environments demand levels of sensory tolerance that many neurodivergent people simply don't have. Few organizations provide soundproofed quiet zones or allow flexibility in communication methods. Even fewer use music intentionally – as a focus aid, a relaxation tool, or a bridge for inclusion. Yet music can be a leveler, providing rhythm and flow where verbal or social interaction may be difficult.

Employers who incorporate musical well-being practices – such as optional focus playlists, calm zones with ambient sound, or rhythm-based breaks – can create environments that support neurodivergent employees rather than overstimulate them. The evidence is clear: when we design for difference, performance and well-being rise for everyone.

### *Regulation – The Core Challenge*

At its root, this is a regulation issue. Many neurodivergent people live in constant adaptation mode – trying to manage sensory input, emotional energy, and social expectations in systems not built for them. This chronic effort leads to fatigue, anxiety, and loss of self-trust. The problem isn't the brain's difference; it's the world's rigidity.

Music offers a rare antidote – direct, portable, and intuitive. It communicates directly with the nervous system through rhythm and frequency. A steady beat can ground racing thoughts; a familiar melody can restore safety. The predictability of musical structure provides something the external world often doesn't – coherence. Whether through headphones, playlists, or spontaneous dance, music gives neurodivergent minds a way to re-establish balance on their own terms.

In a world that rarely adapts to difference, music becomes an adaptive companion – portable, non-judgmental, and profoundly regulating. It helps people manage emotion, energy, and focus in real time, and offers both grounding and expression when words fall short.

*More people are identifying as neurodivergent – but our systems haven't yet learned to listen.*

## How Music Helps (the Science)

To understand why music works so powerfully here, it helps to look at what's happening in the brain. Music activates a network of brain regions involved in attention, emotion, memory, and sensory regulation – making it one of the most accessible and effective tools for supporting neurodivergent well-being. You've probably felt this yourself when a single track shifted your entire state within seconds. The following sections explore how music influences the brain and body, turning sound into structure, rhythm into regulation, and emotion into clarity.

### *Sensory Regulation*

Predictable rhythm and steady frequency patterns calm hyperactive neural networks and ease amygdala overactivity – the same surge you feel when a sudden noise sends your system into alert (Thaut & Hoemberg, 2014). For autistic listeners who often experience sensory overload, music's repetitive and structured nature offers a reliable sense of safety. Unlike environmental noise, which is random and uncontrollable, music is intentional and patterned. This predictability gives the nervous system a clear signal – *you're safe now.*

Slow tempos and low frequencies lower physiological arousal, steadying heart rate and breath. Many neurodivergent individuals use playlists intentionally – switching between calming and energizing tracks to stabilize sensory input throughout the day. In this way, music becomes a self-directed sensory tool, providing order in a world that often feels chaotic.

### *Dopamine and ADHD*

Anticipating a beat boosts dopamine in the brain's reward centers, lifting motivation and improving focus (Salimpoor et al., 2011). For people with ADHD, who tend to have lower baseline dopamine levels, this can be transformative. Rhythm provides an external pacing mechanism, stimulating reward and attention pathways without the need for external pressure.

Mid-tempo, rhythmic music – particularly electronic, instrumental, or lo-fi genres – can help maintain focus over long periods, while upbeat music can counteract low-energy dips. Some individuals use "rhythmic entrainment" playlists to match tempo with task difficulty: slower tracks for deep work, faster ones for activation. In essence, music acts as a dopamine regulator, turning distraction into direction.

### *Autism and Entrainment*

Musical rhythm creates synchrony between brain regions involved in communication, emotion, and motor control – strengthening connection and expression (Grahn & Brett, 2007). This synchronization – known as *entrainment* – allows the brain and body to align with rhythmic patterns, creating coherence across movement and emotion.

For autistic individuals, group drumming, singing, or rhythmic play can enhance joint attention and empathy, offering shared experiences that don't rely on spoken language. Music provides a structured form of social interaction, helping individuals connect through timing and shared feeling. This isn't just about therapy – it's about belonging. Within rhythm, everyone can participate at their own pace.

### *Frequency Sensitivity*

Many neurodivergent people experience hyperacusis – an increased sensitivity to sound. Low-intensity soundscapes or binaural beats soften intrusive noise, supporting calm and concentration (Koelsch, 2014). Ambient or nature-inspired tracks are particularly effective, acting as "acoustic blankets" that smooth harsh frequencies and mask unpredictable sounds.

In neurodivergent-friendly environments, curated soundscapes can replace silence with safety – not through stimulation, but through consistency. Companies and classrooms experimenting with adaptive music technology report improvements in focus, mood, and inclusivity. These soundscapes create a gentle sense of containment, allowing overstimulated minds to rest.

### *Flow and Predictability*

Repetition and structure create predictable sensory patterns that invite immersion and self-regulation. It's why some songs feel like coming home – they arrive exactly the same way every time (Levitin, 2006). For many neurodivergent individuals, especially those with ADHD or autism, time can feel abstract or disjointed – a concept known as *time-blindness*. Music restores temporal order. The steady progression of beats and melody provides a tangible sense of movement and continuity, anchoring thought and emotion.

This predictable flow also supports transitions. A playlist can serve as a signal between work and rest, stimulation and recovery, or isolation and engagement. By offering a framework for pacing and change, music becomes both a regulator and a companion – an external rhythm that helps internal rhythms find harmony again.

### *Emotional Regulation and Neuroplasticity*

Music doesn't only stabilize the moment – it changes the brain. Through repeated engagement, musical experiences strengthen neural pathways that support attention, coordination, and emotional balance. This process, known as *neuroplasticity*, shows how the brain adapts and rewires through rhythm and repetition.

Neurodivergent individuals often describe feeling emotions intensely but struggling to label or release them. Music bridges that gap. It validates emotion through sound and offers a safe route for expression. Over time, musical engagement can increase emotional literacy, helping individuals identify and regulate their feelings more effectively. Whether through listening, playing, or moving, music becomes both expression and integration – an evolving rehearsal for resilience.

Together, these mechanisms reveal why music is such an effective ally for neurodivergent well-being. It doesn't demand language or conformity. Instead, it creates a structured, empathetic space where people can regulate, recover, and reconnect – not by changing who they are, but by finding rhythm in how they feel.

## Practical Applications and Guided Listening

With the science in place, the next question is: How do we use it day to day? Music's power lies in its adaptability – it can be tuned to the needs of each individual. For neurodivergent people, intentional listening can transform sound from background noise into a tool for focus, calm, and connection. The following practices translate the science of rhythm and regulation into everyday action.

### *ADHD Focus Mix*

People with ADHD often describe difficulty sustaining attention on routine or low-stimulation tasks. Mid-tempo music (100–120 BPM) with minimal lyrics helps regulate dopamine release, sustaining motivation without distraction. Artists like Tycho, Bonobo, and Jon Hopkins offer immersive yet unobtrusive soundscapes that support deep concentration. These tracks act as a pacing mechanism – rhythmic enough to engage the brain, steady enough to keep it from wandering.

Create a "Focus Flow" playlist. Start with slower tracks for grounding, build to moderate tempos for active work, and close with gentle downtempo sounds to signal completion. Over time, your brain begins to associate this musical pattern with productive attention.

### *Sensory Soother*

For autistic or highly sensitive individuals, overstimulation can lead to emotional or physical fatigue. Ambient and binaural soundscapes – such as Brian Eno's *Music for Airports*, Ólafur Arnalds' piano textures, or Marconi Union's "Weightless" – help regulate the nervous system by reducing unpredictable sensory input. Low-frequency drones and slow harmonic transitions calm the amygdala and promote alpha-wave brain states linked to relaxation.

When feeling overwhelmed, pause for three minutes and listen to a track with gradual, sustained tones. Focus on your breath aligning with the music's rhythm. This practice can reset your nervous system and restore balance.

**Guided Listening**

Many neurodivergent people find comfort in repetition and rhythm – a pattern that feels safe and grounding. Minimalist composers like Philip Glass and Max Richter use looping motifs that mirror the structure of predictable thought. These compositions create a sense of temporal order, helping the listener find focus or emotional stability through sonic symmetry.

Choose one minimalist piece and listen to it daily for a week. Notice how the repetition shifts from monotony to meditation. For some, this becomes a form of mindfulness – a musical anchor for attention and calm.

Scan the QR code for Catherine Ritchie's Neurodivergent Focus & Calm Playlist.

### *Expression and Connection*

Movement-based musical practices can transform emotion into expression. Drumming, humming, or singing releases energy, stimulates endorphins, and fosters oxytocin-driven connection. Group drumming sessions or spontaneous "dance breaks" can act as rhythmic resets for both body and mind.

When you feel tension building, play a track with a strong beat and move intuitively. Allow your body to respond freely. This isn't performance – it's self-regulation in motion. As Catherine Ritchie described in her story, "Dancing is a form of stimming – my body's way of finding balance again."

### *Building Musical Rituals*

The key to using music therapeutically is consistency. Just as mindfulness works through repetition, musical rituals train the nervous system to respond predictably. Morning playlists can lift mood and activate focus; evening ones can slow tempo and support rest. Over time, these cues help the body anticipate and regulate transitions.

Design a "Daily Sound Cycle." Identify three key transitions – waking, working, resting – and assign each a playlist that matches the energy you want to feel. These become your musical non-negotiables – reliable rituals that tune your day to your rhythm.

## Perspectives

These ideas come alive in real stories. Music becomes deeply personal when filtered through lived experience. Each of these stories illustrates how sound helps neurodivergent people regulate, connect, and thrive – not as therapy, but as expression and empowerment.

### *Finding Focus Through Rhythm – Gabby's Story*

For my daughter, Gabby, maintaining focus during schoolwork can feel like trying to hold water in her hands – it slips away the moment she tries to grasp it. But she's discovered that the right music can change everything. When she works on long creative assignments or art projects, she puts on "Emotion" by Purple Disco Machine – a repetitive, steady electronic track with just enough rhythm to keep her attention anchored.

"The beat feels like something my brain can lean on," she explained. The pattern gives her structure, and the predictability of the rhythm keeps her energy steady. It's neither too stimulating nor too quiet – a balance that helps her ADHD brain find its rhythm.

With the music playing, she feels time stretch and soften. Tasks that once felt overwhelming become more manageable. The beat gives her momentum, while the melody keeps her grounded. It's not just background sound – it's scaffolding for focus, turning chaos into flow.

Gabby's story illustrates a wider truth. For many neurodivergent minds, repetition and rhythm provide an external framework that the world rarely offers. Music becomes a cognitive anchor – a rhythm for attention, a tempo for thought, and a bridge to sustained concentration.

### *Catherine – Joy as Regulation*

Catherine's story brings all of these threads together. As a proud autistic woman, she uses music to regulate emotion, navigate energy, and reconnect to joy. Dancing, for her, is both expression and stimming – a physical form of emotional release that restores equilibrium. "When I move to music," she explained, "my body understands what my brain can't say." Her story shows that joy itself can be a form of regulation – that pleasure, rhythm, and belonging are not luxuries, but essential forms of balance.

Each of these experiences reminds us that music isn't just art – it's architecture for emotional balance, a rhythm the nervous system understands when words or logic cannot.

## Reflection Prompt

How does music help you find focus, calm, or comfort when the world feels too loud or too fast? What sounds feel like home to your mind?

Now, take this further by reflecting on the soundscape of your day – from the moment you wake up to the time you wind down. Where are the moments that feel harmonious, and where do the dissonant notes arise? How might you use music to restore balance between the two?

Try tracking your energy patterns alongside the music you play. Notice how different tempos affect your focus or mood, and when silence feels supportive vs. overstimulating. Over time, you may start to see a rhythm emerging – your own symphony – a blend of sound, energy, and feeling that reflects how your brain finds balance.

Music is not a single cure, but a mirror. Each track can reveal something about how your body responds to the world. When you listen intentionally, you learn not only to manage your environment but to understand yourself.

## Chapter Takeaway

Stepping back one last time, music acts as translation for neurodivergent minds – transforming the sensory world into something manageable, structured, and meaningful. It offers rhythm where there is chaos, pattern where there is noise, and expression where words may not reach.

Neurodivergent minds don't need fixing – they benefit from tuning.

***Mantra:*** *Different brains, same music.*

# 12 Music and Anxiety

It came out of nowhere. One moment I was sitting in a bright Melbourne office, making small talk before a meeting; the next, my heart was hammering in my chest as if it were trying to escape. Jet-lagged and thousands of miles from home, a sudden rush of heat swept up my neck. My vision narrowed. My breath slipped into those quick, shallow sips that feel like breathing without receiving any air. A familiar world abruptly felt foreign – unsettling in a way that catches you off-guard.

At first, I didn't recognize what was happening. Anxiety wasn't something I typically battled, and panic attacks were things other people talked about. Yet here I was – dizzy, unsteady, trapped inside a body that had mistaken a quiet Tuesday morning for an emergency. It's a strangely lonely feeling when your mind and body stop agreeing on what's real.

I muttered something about grabbing a coffee – which, in Melbourne, is always a believable excuse. But stepping out wasn't about caffeine. It was about escape. Space. The hope that a few breaths of fresh air might let me catch up with myself.

Outside, the sunlight felt sharper, the sounds louder, my thoughts noisier. My senses were dialed up just a bit too high. But muscle memory – or something deeper – nudged me toward my headphones. I opened my phone with shaking hands and tapped the one track I knew instinctively might help – "Silence" by Delerium and Sarah McLachlan.

The first chords landed softly, like a steadying hand. Then came the grounded chant. I focused on a single inhale. Then an exhale. Inhale. Exhale. Slowly, the rhythm began to weave its way through the panic – not erasing it, but meeting it. Matching it. Softening its edges.

With each breath, the static loosened. My heartbeat, once frantic, began syncing subtly with the song's pulse. My mind – spiraling moments earlier – found something to hold onto. Something steady.

Standing on a street corner halfway around the world, I felt myself return. Not because I thought my way out of panic, but because the music offered a rhythm my body could lean into. Anxiety rarely responds to logic – but rhythm can reach places logic can't.

It was frightening to feel so untethered, especially for someone who doesn't typically experience anxiety. But that moment taught me something essential. When our mind spins out of control, music can guide us home. It offers a center of gravity when our own feels gone.

## What Is Anxiety?

Anxiety is one of the most human experiences there is. At its core, it's another one of the body's built-in alarm systems – a protective mechanism designed to keep us safe. In short bursts, it works beautifully. It sharpens our senses, heightens awareness, and prepares us to respond to potential danger. But when that alarm system starts going off too often, too loudly, or without a clear reason, things begin to unravel.

Think of anxiety as *anticipatory fear* – the mind rehearsing danger that hasn't happened yet. It's an overactive imagination wired to an overly sensitive threat system – an internal weather forecast predicting storms even beneath a clear sky. And that kind of constant prediction is exhausting.

Inside the brain, anxiety is closely tied to the amygdala – the emotional center – and the wider limbic system, which handles threat, memory, and survival. When these systems sense danger (real or imagined), they flood the body with cortisol and adrenaline. Your heart picks up pace, your breath shortens, your muscles tighten, and your thoughts race ahead as if trying to outrun something.

Because the body reacts first, often long before we've had a chance to think, anxiety shows up physically before it feels psychological. Your chest may tighten, your stomach may churn, your muscles may ache with tension. You might feel restless, struggle to sleep, or find yourself strangely wired but completely exhausted. It's the body working overtime – even when you desperately wish it wouldn't.

### *Anxiety vs. Stress – Why They Feel Similar but Aren't the Same*

Stress and anxiety often get grouped together because their symptoms overlap – a racing heart, tight chest, or mental overload. But they come from different places. Stress is situational – your body reacting to a real-time challenge like a deadline or a difficult conversation. When the moment passes, the body usually settles. Anxiety, on the other hand, is anticipatory. It's the mind leaping ahead, imagining what could go wrong, and preparing the body for danger that hasn't arrived.

If stress is a spike – sharp and temporary – anxiety is more like a lingering hum. The timing difference matters as stress lives in the present, while anxiety lives in the future. Stress gears the body up for action; anxiety keeps it geared up long after the moment has passed. No wonder it's draining.

Of course, the two can fuel each other. Long stretches of stress can tip into anxiety, and intense anxiety can trigger the physical stress response. They're distinct but intertwined – partners in an uneasy dance of overactivation.

### *A Crucial Truth – Anxiety Isn't a Personal Failure*

Before going further, it's important to name something clearly. *Anxiety is not a weakness.* It's not a character flaw nor a sign you're broken or failing. It's biology doing what biology does – just doing it a little too well.

The goal isn't to eliminate anxiety altogether; that wouldn't be human. The aim is to regulate it, to help the body relearn safety, and to find ways to interrupt the loop before it spirals.

That's where music becomes a powerful ally.

## Why Anxiety Is a Problem Today

If anxiety is the body's alarm system, then modern life can feel like living beside a smoke detector that won't stop chirping – not because there's a fire, but because the batteries are fading or someone burnt the toast. Our environment is constantly nudging us into a state of low-grade vigilance, priming us to anticipate threat even when there is none.

We wake to alerts and notifications before we've taken a breath. Our days fill with deadlines, performance pressure, and an endless stream of comparisons we never asked for – scrolling past highlight reels while wondering, quietly and constantly, whether we're keeping up. No wonder our nervous systems rarely get the chance to settle.

Anxiety has become one of the defining mental health challenges of our time. The World Health Organization estimates that more than *1 billion people* experience anxiety symptoms or disorders regularly (World Health Organization, 2023). In the United Kingdom, around *one in six adults* report anxiety in any given week (National Health Service Digital, 2023). Among younger people, the rise is even steeper – a sign that our cultural environment is fundamentally misaligned with what human biology was built to manage.

Technology amplifies this mismatch. Our phones – essential, helpful, but relentlessly interruptive – act like portable micro-stressors. Each ping or vibration pulls at our attention, subtly training the brain to stay watchful and braced for whatever might happen next. It's anticipation on a loop.

The media adds more fuel. Negativity drives engagement, and engagement drives revenue. Research shows we are *three times more likely* to click a negative headline than a positive one (Soroka et al., 2019), so we are fed a steady flow of fear and outrage. This drip-feed of threat cues keeps the nervous system scanning, guessing, and tensing – even when our logical mind knows there's no immediate danger.

Add to that the pressures of the cost-of-living crisis, global instability, environmental worry, the accelerating pace of work, and the quiet expectation to be "on" at all times, and you have more than a stressful moment – you have a system pushed past its natural limits. In this context, feeling anxious rarely means something is wrong with you; it means your nervous system is responding exactly as it was designed to, but in conditions it was never designed for.

Culturally, anxiety has become the low-level hum behind daily life. We talk about being *busy*, *stretched*, or *burnt out*, but beneath those words is a deeper truth. Many of us are carrying a steady sense of unease that never quite lifts. We're restless and wired, tired and tense. Stress overwhelms; anxiety traps – keeping us rehearsing what-ifs and scanning the future for danger.

And it isn't just emotional. Chronic anxiety reshapes how we breathe, digest, sleep, recover, and connect. It scatters attention, drains energy, and narrows our sense of what's possible.

This is why music can feel like a lifeline. Not because it erases pressure, but because it offers something the anxious mind seldom finds on its own – steadiness. A rhythm instead of a worry. A pattern where there was chaos. A place to land when the world feels uncertain.

## How Music Helps (the Science)

Music interacts with anxiety on multiple levels – neurological, physiological, emotional and relational. And while it shares some mechanisms with how music supports stress recovery, the intention is different. With stress, we unwind from what *has* happened; with anxiety, we're trying to steady the body before imagined threat takes over. Music becomes a cue of safety – a predictable structure in a moment that feels uncertain.

Stress recovery happens *after* the storm; anxiety regulation happens *before* it breaks. In that sense, music works like a lighthouse – a steady point of reference when everything inside feels unsettled. It offers direction when your internal world feels scattered – a rhythm the nervous system can lean into.

### *Amygdala Regulation – Quieting the Alarm System*

Calming or emotionally familiar music can dial down activity in the amygdala, the brain's alarm center. When it senses threat, it primes the body for action. Soothing music, nostalgic tracks, or songs linked with comfort send a competing message – *you're safe*. Research shows that emotionally positive or gentle music lowers amygdala activation (Levitin, 2006), helping the brain shift from threat to reassurance.

This is why a familiar song often steadies you before your thoughts can catch up. Logic is slow. Music works instantly.

### *Autonomic Balance – Syncing Breath, Pulse, and Rhythm*

The autonomic nervous system has two branches: the sympathetic (fight or flight) and the parasympathetic (rest and restore). Anxiety traps us in the sympathetic state – fast breath, racing heart, tight muscles. Slow, rhythmic music helps guide the body back toward balance.

When we hear music with a steady tempo, our breath and heartbeat often align with it – a process called entrainment. This activates the parasympathetic system, reducing physiological arousal (Chanda & Levitin, 2013). It's the body's way of saying; *you can settle now.*

If you've felt your breathing deepen a minute or two into the right track, that's entrainment doing its work.

### *Neurochemistry – Softening the Internal Weather*

Anxiety is not only emotional, it's biochemical. Elevated cortisol tightens both body and mind. Music shifts that internal chemistry.

Listening to pleasurable music increases dopamine (motivation and reward) and endorphins (natural pain and stress relievers). Together, they loosen cortisol's grip and create more internal space (Chanda & Levitin, 2013). It's not about sudden joy – it's about easing intensity.

One track really can change the tone of a moment.

### *Predictability and Control – Giving the Mind Something Steady*

Anxiety thrives on uncertainty. Music offers the opposite – structure. A clear rhythm, a reliable pattern, a beginning and an end.

Repetitive or familiar music provides a sense of reliability. Your mind knows what comes next, and that predictability is regulating. Even a chorus looping back around can act like an auditory mantra (Levitin, 2006). It restores order when everything feels disorganized.

This is why many people return to the same tracks when anxious – predictability feels like safety.

### *Co-Regulation – Feeling Accompanied, Even When You're Alone*

Humans regulate each other emotionally through voice, breath, presence, and rhythm. This is co-regulation – and music can mimic it.

A steady beat can feel like a companion. When anxiety isolates, music offers a sense of being accompanied – something external helping stabilize your internal world.

This isn't poetic; it's neurological. Your nervous system entrains to the music, softening the intensity of your own state. Music becomes a relational cue of safety.

Music doesn't just relax us. It helps the nervous system remember what safety feels like.

## Practical Applications and Guided Listening

This is where the theory becomes something you can actually use – not in an abstract way, but in the moments when anxiety is real, physical, immediate. And the good news is that you don't need musical training, perfect playlists, or any special equipment. You just need sound, intention, and a little consistency.

Before getting practical, it helps to keep this distinction in mind: *stress playlists help you slow down after intensity; anxiety playlists help you feel safe before the spiral begins.* Both benefit from slower tempos, warm tones, and minimal surprises, but anxiety responds especially well to music that feels predictable, steady, familiar, and emotionally grounding – a kind of sonic environment that tells your nervous system, *Nothing unexpected is coming. You can settle now.*

### *Habit Stacking – Making Music Part of a Safety Ritual*

One of the most powerful ways to use music for anxiety is to pair it with another grounding practice. This is habit stacking – linking two actions so the brain begins to treat them as one. When you consistently pair music with breathwork, journaling, grounding exercises, or gentle movement, your body learns to associate the music with calm. Over time, the first few seconds of a familiar track can act like a cue, a small psychological exhale that signals your system to soften.

You might play the same track each time you practice box breathing or choose a soft instrumental to accompany your evening journaling. Slow ambient music can sit beneath a few minutes of stretching before bed, helping you unwind at a pace your body can follow. You may even select one specific song as a personal "reset button" – a track that reliably meets you where you are and brings you home.

Used this way, music stops being passive background noise and becomes an active stability practice: intentional, repeatable, and soothing.

### *Playlist Design – Building the Right Soundscape*

Different moments call for different forms of support, and designing a playlist with intention can make a meaningful difference. A grounding playlist tends to sit in the 50–70 BPM range, with warm tones and slow, steady rhythms. These tracks – gentle piano, soft guitar, ambient textures – feel like emotional weight, in the best way, helping you settle into yourself.

A breath-syncing playlist works slightly differently. These tracks mirror a slow breathing pattern, roughly six breaths per minute, guiding your breath without effort and helping your body shift out of its anxious pace. And then there's the familiar or nostalgic playlist: songs linked with positive memories or calmer times. Emotional familiarity reduces threat perception, making these tracks especially powerful when anxiety arrives unexpectedly.

### *Micro-Scenarios – Real Moments, Real Tools*

Think about the moments in daily life when anxiety is most likely to spark. Before a presentation, you might press play on a steady instrumental track and combine it with slow, deliberate breathing as you prepare to step into the room. On a commute, low-tempo music can give your mind something steady to hold onto instead of looping through worry. In the evening, a gentle playlist that gradually slows in tempo can help you transition into rest – a musical dimmer switch signaling to your body that the day is closing.

### *Integrating Music into Daily Practice*

Music becomes most effective when woven naturally into the rhythms of your day. It can accompany a simple breathing exercise, giving your inhale and exhale a rhythm to follow. It can sit beneath a short stretching routine, helping release tension and reconnect you to your body. Grounding techniques – like noticing a few things you can see, feel, or hear – become more embodied when paired with soft, stable sound. Journaling feels safer and more reflective when the same track opens the space each time. And a short evening check-in becomes easier to slip into when music gently signals that your system can slow down.

These aren't dramatic interventions. They're small anchors – each one offering a quiet reminder: *You're safe. You're here. You can settle.*

## Guided Listening

To help you begin, here are a few tracks that often work beautifully for anxiety. "On the Nature of Daylight" by Max Richter offers slow, emotional coherence and deep grounding. "Memories of Wandering" by Robert Rich provides gentle entrainment and is ideal for syncing your breath. And "Still Water" by Trevor Hall brings warmth, reassurance, and a quiet sense of presence. These aren't prescriptions – simply starting points. You'll know the tracks that speak safety to your system.

Scan the QR code for Rob's Grounding Playlist.

## Perspectives

In my conversation with Sarah Restall, a well-being professional with lived experience of anxiety, for Chapter 25, "Sarah – Music, Anxiety, and the Art of Being Human," she talked about music as an Immediate Regulator: "When anxiety tightens around me, the first thing I do is get outside. Headphones in. Music on. Step into sky. The more compressed I feel internally, the more I need a place that expands. Sometimes I cry while walking – not in despair, but in release. The music meets me where I am and gives me permission to feel everything fully."

### *Harmonizing the Mind Demonstration – What Anxiety Sounds Like*

In my Harmonizing the Mind show, I often demonstrate what anxiety can feel like sonically by playing two versions of "Clocks" by Coldplay at different tempos. When the tracks overlap, the clashing cascade of dissonance creates a chaotic, swirling soundscape that mirrors the mental experience of anxiety – the waterfall of intrusive thoughts, the racing internal tempo, the feeling of being pulled in multiple directions at once. It's a powerful auditory metaphor for the cognitive overload many people describe during anxious moments.

## Reflection Prompt

Take a moment for some soft journaling or quiet reflection. A moment that invites you back into your breath, your body, and the safety that music can restore.

Think about a time when music helped you steady your breath. Maybe it was a song you turned to without thinking, or a track that found you at exactly the right moment. What was playing? Where were you? And what did it teach your body about safety, grounding, or coming back to yourself? Write about the moment as you remember it – the sounds, the sensations, the shift inside you.

As you reflect, notice what patterns emerge. Was the music familiar? Slow? Warm? Did it meet you where you were or move you somewhere softer? Sometimes the story of the song tells us something about the story our body is holding.

## Chapter Takeaway

Anxiety is rhythm out of sync – the body anticipating danger before it arrives. Music offers a pulse that says, you are safe, you are here, you can breathe again.

Just as music can serve as a lighthouse before the storm, guiding us through uncertainty, it can also light our way home after it. The same rhythmic beam that steadies us in moments of anxiety can remind us of where safety lives – in the body, in the breath, in the beat.

You can't always think your way out of anxiety, but you can feel your way back into rhythm.

> ***Mantra:*** *When the mind races, let the music set the pace.*

# PART II

# How Music Shapes Our Lives

Music has the power to connect us with ourselves and others.

# 13 Music and Identity

I grew up in a decent neighborhood in Birmingham, but as a teenager playing for the Birmingham Bullets youth teams, I wanted more than anything to belong. Basketball gave me a place to stand, but music hinted at who I might become. The soundtrack around the team was split between rap and dancehall – or Ragga, as everyone called it – and if I wanted to fit in, I had to understand it. Not just nod along, but really *get* it.

As a white kid trying to find my place, Jamaican patois felt like both a barrier and a key. I'd sit on buses or in changing rooms, listening intently, trying to translate enough of the lyrics to feel part of the conversation. Then one day it happened – a lyric clicked. Tiny moment, but it felt like a door unlocking. A click of belonging, an invitation into a world I'd admired from the outside.

From there, the whole universe widened. Tracks like "Rumours" by Gregory Isaacs, "Twice My Age" by Shabba Ranks, "Here I Come" by Barrington Levy and Gregory Peck, and "Murder She Wrote" by Chaka Demus and Pliers became the soundtrack of that period. I became obsessed with *riddims* – the way one instrumental could be used by many different artists, each track with its own personality. The Bam Bam *riddim* especially fascinated me. Produced by Sly & Robbie and used by more than 140 artists, it felt alive, constantly renewing itself.

One night stands out vividly. I was about 17 when some teammates took me to what they called a proper "Dance." It was in someone's house, but stepping inside felt like entering another world. Floor-to-ceiling speakers towered over us, and the bass hit so hard it made my chest and throat vibrate. I was nervous, but having several enormous basketball players vouch for me gave me enough courage to stay. Then the music swallowed the room.

It was the first time music felt like more than sound – part of the room itself, messy and overwhelming, something you stumbled into rather than a perfect cinematic moment. That physical hit of bass stayed with me for years. I didn't know it then, but it was planting the early seeds of my love for DJing – the idea that one day I might be the person behind the decks, shaping that same charged atmosphere for others.

Maybe that's why those early experiences mattered so much. Hearing the same rhythm carry so many different voices made me wonder if there might be space for mine somewhere in the mix.

## Why Music and Identity Are Intertwined

Music has a habit of tagging along with us, often quietly, and then suddenly throwing something back that feels strangely familiar. It reminds us of who we think we are and sometimes nudges at parts we haven't quite figured out. We usually define identity through the big things – where we grew up, what we believe, who we love – but our soundtrack is just as revealing.

These days, a big part of my identity is wrapped up in DJing. Shaping atmospheres, reading a room, knowing instinctively what sound will carry a moment forward. It means I listen to a lot of House Music. At the time of writing, "Shadow of Love – Echonomist Remix" is a defining track for me – one I often open sets with because it captures the mood I want to create – deep, emotional, slightly dark, hopeful.

But long before I touched a set of decks, music was shaping me in quieter ways. It was the backdrop to bus rides, changing rooms, friendships forming and fading. It helped me understand worlds bigger than mine. It helped me communicate when I didn't yet have the language or confidence. It gave me a sense of belonging at a time when I was desperate to figure out who I was.

But there's another side to this too. When I'm experiencing depression, I can lose interest in music completely. It's as if the illness strips it out of my identity for a while – like a dimmer switch being turned down inside me. That absence is an early warning sign. And just as powerfully, the moment music starts to matter again is usually a sign I'm rejoining the light.

Music often sits in the background – something we only appreciate in hindsight – the soundtrack that's been quietly running underneath everything else. The songs we grow up with weave themselves into our emotional architecture. They become shortcuts to remembering who we were with, what we were learning and who we were trying to become.

And sometimes music does the talking for us, especially when we can't find the words ourselves. It shapes feelings we can't articulate and gives voice to the parts of our identity that are still forming. It lets us try on different selves safely – a way of rehearsing who we might be.

Music doesn't just sit alongside our identity – it quietly helps shape it, piece by piece.

## The Soundtrack of Your Life: Autobiographical Memory

Music has an uncanny ability to pin moments of our lives into place. A single track can pull you straight back to a version of yourself you'd forgotten. The person you were on a first date, the kid staring out of a rainy bus window, the friend laughing in a kitchen at 2 a.m. These connections aren't accidental – they're the result of how tightly emotion and memory are wired together. When a moment matters, the music around it gets stored too.

Most of us have songs that act like emotional time machines. The ones that transport us instantly – sometimes joyfully, sometimes painfully. For Sarah Restall, opera will always smell faintly of cleaning products because her dad used to blast it while scrubbing the house. For me, "Dancing Queen" by ABBA will forever be paired with the sound of a vacuum, my mum doing housework on a Sunday morning. These memories don't just remind us of a time – they remind us of who we were in that time.

And that's the quiet power of autobiographical memory. It lets us revisit former selves with compassion, curiosity, or even gratitude. It gives us a sense of continuity in a life that's always changing.

## Nostalgia: Returning to Ourselves

Nostalgia has a way of sneaking up on us – often in the space of a single chord, a familiar intro, or a fragment of melody. It's not just remembering the past; it's momentarily *being* the person we were in that moment. That's why nostalgic songs can feel like emotional anchors. They remind us of our own continuity, especially during times when life feels uncertain or fast-moving.

There's real comfort in hearing "home" in a song. Sometimes it's literal – a track your parents played, a song tied to childhood routines, or something that lived in the background of your early life. Other times it's emotional. The feeling of being young, hopeful, connected, or even heartbroken in a way that shaped you. These songs pull threads through our story, giving us a sense of who we've been and the parts of us that haven't changed.

Nostalgia also stabilizes us. When we're overwhelmed, stressed, or unsure of ourselves, hearing a track tied to a safe or meaningful memory can pull us back into our center. It's a reminder that we've lived through things before, that we carry history inside us, and that our identity isn't as fragile as it sometimes feels.

And for all its gentleness, nostalgia can be surprisingly powerful. Dr. Hazel spoke about this in her interview with me for Chapter 27, "Dr. Hazel and Phillipa – How Music Holds Us in Grief" – how revisiting meaningful songs can restore emotional strength, reconnect us to belonging, and even help with mood regulation. It isn't about living in the past; it's about borrowing emotional resources from it and, often, looking to the future.

Nostalgic music helps us return to ourselves – not the version we wish we were, but the version we've always been.

## Belonging: The Music That Helps Find Our People

We often talk about belonging as if it's built from big moments – joining a team, finding a group of friends, stepping into a new community. But music creates belonging in quieter, faster ways. Sometimes it happens in seconds. The moment a bass line drops, a chorus hits, or someone across the room mouths the same lyric you love. It's one of the fastest pathways humans have to connection.

Musical subcultures shape this deeply. Metalheads, ravers, punks, indie kids, club-goers, choir singers – each group has its own rituals, aesthetics, shared language, and emotional codes. When you find the music that resonates with you, you often find the people who do too. For teens especially, this can be life-changing. Music becomes both shield and signal – a way of saying "this is who I am" long before you have the confidence to explain it.

And belonging through music isn't limited to youth culture. In workplaces, families, and communities, shared taste bridges generations and backgrounds. A single song can connect a parent to a child, a manager to a team, a stranger to a stranger. Choirs are a powerful example of this. As musician and speaker Dr. Mark Deeks often says, the magic isn't just in the sound – it's in the sense of unity that forms the moment people breathe together, sing together, and feel part of something bigger than themselves.

Music helps us find our people. Sometimes quickly, sometimes slowly – but always in ways that feel deeper than words.

## Musical Taste as Self-Definition

Our taste in music is often one of the first ways we express who we are – sometimes deliberately, sometimes without even noticing. Before we can articulate our values or describe our personalities, we're already signaling them through bands on a hoodie, posters on a bedroom wall, the playlists we build, or the artists we defend a little too fiercely.

Musical taste can feel like quiet self-branding. The genres we cling to, the artists we rave about, the eras we feel pulled toward – they all reveal pieces of how we see ourselves. Sometimes we use music to project who we want to be – confident, alternative, emotional, rebellious, refined, joyful, introspective. Other times, a song just feels like us, even if we can't explain why.

And we do get defensive. Ask someone to justify their favorite artist and you'll usually hear more about *them* than the musician. Taste is tied to memory, belonging, self-image – which makes preference feel personal rather than purely aesthetic.

Taste evolves too. The songs we loved as teenagers often stay with us for life, but new genres and artists slip in as we change careers, become parents, navigate relationships, move cities, or recover from hard seasons. Sometimes a shift in what we listen to is the first clue that our identity is shifting as well.

There's some light personality science behind all this – loose links between traits and genres – but the reality is far messier. No chart or quiz can pin us down. We're too contradictory, too fluid, too human to be summarized by a playlist.

And because honesty matters here, the first record I bought was "Some Girls" by Racey. I was seven. It's absolutely awful – and probably always was – but it still tells a true story about who I was then.

## When Identity Shifts: Letting Music Help Us Become Someone New

There are moments in life when who we are begins to change – sometimes gently, sometimes all at once. These transitions can feel disorienting, such as the end of a relationship, becoming a parent, changing careers, recovering from illness, moving cities, or simply realizing that the version of ourselves we've been carrying no longer fits.

In these in-between spaces, music can act as both guide and companion. We often find ourselves drawn to new genres or artists without fully understanding why. A sound that never meant much before suddenly feels right. A lyric lands differently. A track you've never heard before seems to describe exactly what you're going through. These shifts in taste aren't random – they're clues. They're the soundtrack of a self that's still forming.

During my own periods of change, I've noticed how certain songs become footing when everything else feels uncertain. They help me hold onto hope, or grit, or a sense of possibility when I can't articulate any of it yet. Sometimes building a playlist is the first step in understanding the person I'm becoming.

Music doesn't just reflect identity – it can help shape the next version of it. When life rearranges us, the right song often arrives to help us find our new center.

## Practical Applications and Guided Listening

These small practices don't take long, but they can gently reconnect you to the parts of yourself that music has shaped – and the parts still taking shape.

- **Life Chapters Playlist:** Choose one song for each meaningful moment of your life – childhood, adolescence, early adulthood, challenges, wins, turning points. Don't overthink it. Let instinct choose.
- **Return to 14:** Revisit the music you loved at 14. Notice what still resonates and what no longer does. Ask yourself what that younger version of you was trying to feel or express.
- **A Playlist for Who You're Becoming:** Pick three to five songs that match the energy, values, or emotional tone of the person you want to grow into. Let it be aspirational but honest.
- **Nostalgia as a Tool:** When you're feeling unsettled, play a track tied to a safe or grounding memory. Notice what emotion or memory surfaces – and what it offers you now.
- **Emotional Home Tracks:** Identify the songs that feel like home – the ones that settle you, lift you, or remind you who you are. Keep them close for when you need them.

---

### Guided Listening

Scan the QR code for Rob's Music & Identity Playlist.

Which song feels like a part of who you are – and what does it reveal about the version of you it represents?

---

## Chapter Takeaway

Your identity has a soundtrack – one that doesn't just remind you who you were, but helps you remember who you still are.

# 14 Rituals and Habit-Building with Music

There's a particular kind of stillness on the start line of a cycling time trial. You can hear the hum of turbo trainers and the clicks of cleats, but inside, everything narrows. A time trial is you against the clock – no teammates to hide behind, no tactics beyond managing your mind and your effort. Push too early and you blow up; hold back and you waste the ride.

My warm-up ritual became the way I bridged that gap between nerves and readiness. Twenty minutes, always the same structure. Harder than people expected – sharp efforts, rising intensity, the kind of work that shocks the system awake. And every phase was built around one playlist.

As a regular racing cyclist, my legs often felt rubbish in the warm-up – a side effect of the constant training load and back-to-back racing. That heavy-legged sluggishness could play tricks on the mind, but the music helped me push through it, lifting me out of doubt and into intention.

"What I've Done" by Linkin Park lit the fuse – a jolt that shifted me from fog to focus. Then "Eye of the Tiger," predictable but perfect, tightening my cadence and settling my mindset. When "Move Your Body

(The House Music Anthem)" by Marshall Jefferson kicked in, everything clicked. House music dissolved any hesitation – it helped me stop overthinking and simply move. Those three tracks were for the legs – activation, rhythm, honesty.

Then everything softened. I'd lower the power and let "*La Ritournelle*" by Sébastien Tellier wash over me. Spacious, calm, almost cinematic. It slowed my breathing and pulled my attention inward. It wasn't for the muscles anymore – it was for the mind.

Only later did I realize what I'd created – a ritual of state change. A psychological ramp from activation to focus to flow to calm. Music as the cue, the warm-up as the behavior, and that quiet, centered readiness as the reward. By the time I rolled to the line, the playlist had already built the version of me I needed to become.

## Why Rituals Matter

Rituals are the small actions that steady us – the things we return to not because we have to but because they make the day feel more anchored, more deliberate, more ours. They don't need ceremony. Sometimes a ritual is nothing more than that moment when you hit play on the same track as the kettle boils or choose the same playlist every time you open your laptop. These tiny repetitions create edges in the day – soft boundaries that offer a sense of control when everything else feels scattered.

Part of their power comes from the way they slot neatly into how the brain prefers to operate. There's always a cue – the smell of coffee, the start of the commute, the familiar click of a door closing behind you. Then the behavior – selecting a track, stepping into a rhythm, letting a beat guide you into the next moment. And finally, the reward – the small lift in mood, the shift in focus, the quiet drop in tension. Music strengthens this loop. The reward arrives almost instantly. One bar, one chorus, one rising melody – and something inside you starts to shift.

Most habits work on a single level. Music works on several at once. A chosen track can steady your breathing, sharpen your attention, or release the emotional clutter you've been carrying without realizing it. This is why a short musical ritual – even 90 seconds long – can sometimes make more difference than a long list of well-being techniques you keep meaning to try.

Think of the parent who hums the same lullaby every night or the runner who knows the first beat of a certain track means "time to go." Tiny acts, but they change the internal weather.

These rituals settle into your day in ways you often only recognize afterwards. An energizing track can wake something up in you; a calming piece can soften the edges; a shared playlist can create a moment of closeness; a nostalgic song can pull an old memory gently to the surface. There's no need to analyze any of it – the music simply does its work quietly in the background.

In a noisy world, rituals give you something predictable to hold on to. And when music becomes part of that pattern, the ritual doesn't just shape what you do – it shapes how you feel. It helps you shift gears, change emotional lane, and step into the moment ahead with a little more steadiness. That's why rituals matter. And it's why music so often becomes the thread that ties them together.

## The Psychology of Rituals in Daily Life

Rituals don't happen by accident. They form because they speak to something deep in how humans make sense of the world. And when music becomes part of that pattern, the ritual gains texture, emotional memory, and a sense of identity that's hard to replicate with anything else.

### *Rituals as Identity Cues*

We often think of identity as something fixed – who we are, rather than what we do. But in reality, identity is shaped in tiny, repeated choices. The tracks we reach for at certain moments reveal who we believe ourselves to be, and sometimes who we're trying to become.

A runner who begins every long Sunday run with the same track isn't just warming up – they're stepping into their "athlete self." A parent playing the same bedtime lullaby becomes the version of themselves who soothes and protects. A DJ cueing up a familiar track during setup steps into their craft, their focus, their history. Personally, when sound checking, I always use "Your Love Will Set You Free (C2 Remix)" by Caribou – ever since I heard an engineer in Ibiza do the same and was completely transfixed by it.

Music helps us remember the version of ourselves we want to inhabit. The right ritual doesn't just change your day – it quietly shifts your self-perception.

### *Rituals as State-Shifters*

Rituals also help us move from one internal state to another. A lot of life's friction happens in the transitions – work to home, busy to calm, tired to focused, restless to steady. Without something to bridge the gap, you carry the residue of one state into the next.

Music is one of the fastest ways to smooth that transition. An uplifting track can help you move out of a stress response. A calming instrumental can down-regulate a racing nervous system. A familiar groove can lift your energy when the day has flattened you.

Research tells us that music can accelerate recovery from stress by helping the autonomic nervous system return to balance more quickly. But you don't need the science to recognize the feeling – that moment when one song changes the pace of your breathing or loosens something in your chest.

### *Rituals as Emotional Regulators*

Music has always been a tool for managing emotion, especially the difficult ones. A good ritual gives you a predictable way to meet yourself. When you know which track brings calm, which one brings lightness, which one helps you release tension, your emotional landscape becomes more manageable.

And intention matters. Studies show that pairing a deliberate intention with positive music enhances the mood-lifting effect – you're not just listening, you're aligning. It's the difference between *hearing* a song and *using* it.

Emotional regulation sounds clinical, but in practice it's deeply human. It's the song you play before a tough conversation, the track that helps you reset after bad news, the playlist you rely on when you need courage rather than calm. A ritual turns these moments into something predictable and grounding. You don't have to decide what to do – you already know.

## Types of Musical Rituals

Musical rituals show up in all kinds of moments – small, repeated pockets of the day where music helps you shift gear, find focus, or settle your internal world. They don't need to be formal or planned. Most of the time, they begin almost accidentally, then become the patterns we rely on.

### *Morning Reset Rituals*

For many people, the day doesn't really begin until a certain track plays. It might be an energizing song as the kettle boils, or a gentle piano piece that helps you arrive in yourself before the noise of the day begins. Morning rituals set tone, mood, and pace.

### *Focus Rituals*

A lot of us have a go-to track or playlist that signals, "Right – time to get into it." Music can thin out distraction, narrow attention, and create just enough structure for focus to take hold. Even a single track can define the moment when work truly starts.

### *Movement Rituals*

Whether you're heading out for a run, stepping into the gym, or beginning a training session, movement rituals help the body and mind sync. The first beat becomes a cue – lift your energy, find your rhythm, get going. These rituals are some of the easiest to maintain because the physicality reinforces the music.

### *Calming Rituals*

Not all rituals are about activation. Some are about release. A calming track during a commute home, or an evening playlist that tells the body it's safe to slow down, can act as a bridge between the demands of the day and the softness of rest. These moments link directly to the ideas explored in Chapter 5, "Music, Sleep, and Restoration," – where we look at how a consistent pre-bedtime music ritual can help the nervous system shift into a state that supports deeper, more restorative sleep.

For me, certain tracks have become part of that wind-down pattern. "Milky Sleep" by Brian Eno and Beatie Wolfe, and "LA3" by Moby both have a softness and spaciousness that signal to my body that it's time to settle. When these tracks play, something inside loosens – breath deepens, thoughts slow, and the day begins to let go. Over time, they've become cues in their own right – small signals that guide me toward rest.

### *Connection Rituals*

Shared rituals – couple playlists, family songs, the tracks that always play during dinner or on long drives – create a sense of belonging. They become part of a shared language, moments that connect people without needing words. For me and my daughter Gabby, two tracks have become part of our own soundtrack: "Pink Matter" by Frank Ocean and "Eventually" by Tame Impala. They're songs we return to often.

### *Memory Rituals*

These are the rituals that transport you. A nostalgic track that takes you back to childhood, a song linked to a friend, or music tied to a particular life chapter. These rituals help you hold your history and revisit the emotions that shaped you. Some rituals form in a single moment yet echo for decades – like a wedding first-dance song. You may only dance it once, but every time it plays afterwards, the emotional meaning reactivates. That's still a ritual, just a ceremonial one that lives in the background of a relationship.

And then there are the tracks that bring back very specific – and sometimes cringeworthy – memories. "Jump Around" by House of Pain will always transport me straight back to the choreographed dance my groomsmen and I performed at our wedding. A single beat of that song and I'm right there again, equal parts joy and embarrassment.

### *Creative Rituals*

Artists, writers, and creators often rely on musical rituals to enter a creative state – the track that signals "we're starting now," the playlist that keeps them in flow, the soundscape that holds the mind open. For me, writing this book often began with listening to the tracks from the playlist that accompanied the chapter I was working on. It didn't always improve my focus, but it reliably dropped me into the headspace of the chapter – a kind of emotional tuning that helped me feel my way into the ideas rather than think my way in. These rituals help creativity feel less like a leap and more like a doorway.

Across all of these examples, the common thread is repetition and meaning. You return to the same tracks not out of habit alone, but because something in them reliably changes how you feel. They become small, steadying moments – oases you carry with you.

## Behavioral Science: How to Build a Ritual That Lasts

Rituals don't last because we force them. They last because they fit. They slide into the rhythm of daily life in a way that feels natural, rewarding, and easy enough to repeat even on the messy days. Behavioral science gives us some simple truths about why certain rituals stick while others fade – but the real magic happens when these principles meet music.

The first truth is that rituals grow best when they begin small. Not grand commitments, but barely noticeable shifts. A single track you press play on while making your morning coffee. A two-minute reset song before opening your inbox. A calming piece that signals the moment you put your phone away at night. When a ritual is tiny, it doesn't provoke resistance. It simply becomes part of the background of your day.

Rituals also last when they attach themselves to cues that already exist. The brain loves predictability. If you always step into your run just as the first beat lands and your shoes strike the pavement, or if the start of your working session is marked by the same song rising gently beneath the hum of your desk, the cue and the behavior begin to merge. Before long, the track itself becomes a doorway into the state you're aiming for – focus, calm, movement, or reflection.

Pleasure matters too. We repeat what feels good. A ritual built around music has a built-in reward such as the emotional lift, the grounding feeling, the moment of clarity or release. This isn't about discipline – it's about creating experiences that your mind and body want to return to.

Intention amplifies the effect. Research shows that when you pair a clear intention with positive music, the mood-boosting impact increases. It doesn't have to be dramatic – a simple, quiet inner statement like "I'm settling," "I'm arriving," or "I'm letting the day go" can turn a moment of listening into a moment of alignment.

And rituals work best when they're flexible rather than rigid. They should bend with the day, not break under it. Some mornings you may want an energizing track; other days you may need something softer. The ritual is not the song – it's the act of choosing music with purpose.

What keeps a ritual alive isn't perfection. It's meaning. It's knowing that each time you return to the track, you're also returning to yourself – the breath, the beat, that small internal shift – even if only for a moment.

## The Meaning Layer – Rituals as Personal Culture

Rituals aren't just habits. They're a form of personal culture – the small, repeated gestures that shape how we move through the world and how we relate to ourselves. When a ritual lasts, it's rarely because it's efficient or productive. It lasts because it feels like *you*. It carries memory, intention, identity. And music amplifies that meaning in a way almost nothing else can.

Every musical ritual – whether it's a morning reset track, a focus playlist, or a calming song before bed – becomes a kind of daily declaration. A quiet reminder that your inner world matters. These aren't grand statements, but soft ones: "I'm here." "I need grounding." "I want to arrive in this moment with care." Over time, these small choices weave themselves into the fabric of your life.

Rituals also create a thread that connects your days. They bring a sense of continuity; a feeling that even in a busy, unpredictable life, there is something you can return to that steadies you. The playlist you use to begin writing, the track that brings your nervous system down at night, the song you share with someone you love – these aren't just behaviors. They're part of your emotional architecture.

When repeated with intention, rituals become acts of self-respect. Not because they're impressive or productive, but because they honor your needs. They acknowledge your desire for steadiness, connection, clarity, or rest. In a world that often pulls us toward noise and haste, these moments of musical ritual are small acts of reclamation. You choose them. You shape them. They belong to you.

For me, this became especially clear coming out of a period of depression, when I'd lost my connection to music for a while. The simple act of playing a track again felt like both a signal and a symptom of recovery – proof that something inside me was reawakening. I even built a playlist called Out of the Woods for those moments. One track in particular, "Forms of Love" by Adam Port and Alan Dixon, still feels like a marker of that turning point – a reminder that music can guide you back to yourself when you've drifted far away.

This is why rituals sit so naturally alongside larger well-being practices without ever feeling like "another thing to do." They're not tasks – they're expressions of who you are and who you're becoming. And when they're supported by music, they take on an emotional resonance that's hard to articulate but easy to feel. They turn well-being into something lived rather than prescribed.

Everything in this chapter points to a simple truth. Rituals endure not because they are perfect, but because they are meaningful. They become part of your personal culture – the soundtrack you build, consciously or not, to help you move through life with a little more presence and a little more heart.

## Closing Reflection – Your Life Already Has a Soundtrack

Rituals rarely announce themselves. They emerge quietly – in the way you reach for a track that helps you settle, or the song that steadies your nerves before a challenging conversation, or the playlist that signals the beginning or end of your day. They're already part of your life, even if you haven't named them yet.

Music gives these small moments emotional shape. It helps you shift state, connect to meaning, and come back to yourself when the world pulls you in every direction. You don't need to overhaul anything. Change starts with one track, one moment, one decision to listen with intention.

**Guided Listening**

Scan the QR code for Rob's Music Rituals Playlist.

What is one piece of music that reliably shifts something in you – your mood, your energy, your sense of calm – and how might you turn it into a small ritual in your day?

# 15 Music and Grief

It happened on a dancefloor in Ibiza, long after the lights should have come up.

Rachel had spent the week celebrating her wedding – a whirl of sunshine, family, and the strange, tender joy that comes when life allows you to love again after unthinkable loss. Six years earlier, she had lost her husband, Ant, to suicide while pregnant with their son. Grief had wrapped itself around every part of her life. Their first dance – "Everywhere" by Fleetwood Mac – was a song she couldn't bear to hear for years. It held too much. The joy of the life they had built and the devastation of the life suddenly gone.

She hadn't looked for signs of him during the wedding. Grief had taught her they come when they want to, not when you call for them. And yet, on their final night – at the Melon Bomb closing party at Pikes – the universe shifted.

The DJ played the last tune. The lights brightened. Guests drifted away. Rachel and her new husband started to leave the floor, ready to close the chapter on a beautiful week.

And then it happened.

The unmistakable opening bars of "Everywhere" filled the room.

A song of hope. A song of beginnings. A song she had danced to with Ant on their wedding day and then listened to again 18 months later while staring at his coffin, unable to comprehend the world she was now living in.

Rachel and her new husband froze – not in shock, but in recognition. Something had arrived. Or someone.

They turned to each other with the same realization, the same quiet gratitude. She felt him. She felt both of them – the love she had lost and the love she had found. For a moment, the boundaries between past, present, grief, and joy dissolved.

They stepped back onto the dancefloor. Wrapped in music, held by the glow of the disco ball, they danced with tears in their eyes – the three of them – suspended in a moment that was beautiful, magical, joyful and heartbreaking all at once.

This is what music can do. It can collapse time. It can return someone to you. It can hold your grief and your hope in the same breath. It can remind you that love doesn't end; it finds new shapes.

*With thanks to the Music to Die For team for permission to share this story. More details can be found in Part III, "The Stories We Carry," and at* www.musictodiefor.co.uk.

## What Grief Really Feels Like – And Why Music Finds Its Way In

Grief rarely arrives in a straight line. It moves in waves – abrupt and unpredictable. One moment you feel numb, the next overwhelmed. Some days you can talk about what happened; on others, even a passing lyric can undo you. This non-linearity isn't a flaw in the grieving process; it *is* the grieving process.

And this is precisely why music finds its way in so naturally. Music can meet you where you are emotionally, even when you're not entirely sure where that is yourself.

Music doesn't require you to be in any particular state. It doesn't ask you to explain. It doesn't judge whether you're coping well or falling apart. It simply offers a space – a rhythm, a structure, a sonic landscape – where your feelings can exist without needing to be packaged neatly for the outside world.

For many people, grief feels like an internal chaos of tangled memories, sudden jolts of longing, anger at the unfairness of it all. Music can help bring shape to that chaos. A melody can mirror what feels jagged.

A lyric can articulate something you haven't yet had the strength to say. And sometimes, even a single sustained note can hold a feeling you're not ready to speak.

The connection runs deeper than emotion alone. Music engages the emotional centers of the brain, which is why it can unlock feelings that have been held tight or frozen. It activates autobiographical memory networks, bringing certain moments or people vividly back to life. And even in sadness, music can stimulate dopamine and endorphins – the brain's own stabilizing and soothing chemicals. This is why a sad song can feel strangely comforting and why a familiar track can provide relief rather than collapse.

In grief, people often talk about feeling disconnected from themselves, from others, or from the world. Music can restore a sense of connection – not by removing the pain, but by acknowledging it. Music doesn't take the pain away; it sits beside you. And sometimes that companionship is the beginning of healing.

And because grief shifts so often, the music we need shifts too – from the quiet that holds us to the songs that let us break open.

Before we go further, it's worth looking more closely at some of the emotional states grief can pull us through – not as rigid stages, but as common experiences many people recognize. And alongside each, we'll explore how music can help us navigate, express, or simply survive them.

## State One: Shock – When the World Goes Quiet

Shock is rarely loud. It's the quiet that follows the moment your world changes – a kind of muted stillness where everything feels far away, including yourself. People often describe this early state of grief as moving through fog. You can see shapes, you can hear sounds, but none of it lands. The body protects you by turning the volume down on your emotional world.

In this phase, music often becomes less about expression and more about containment. You might find you can only tolerate sound that asks nothing of you – slow, predictable, almost neutral in tone. Ambient textures, gentle piano, soft classical pieces. Music that seems to sit at the edges rather than the center, offering reassurance without intrusion.

There's a physiological reason for this. In moments of shock, the nervous system shifts into protective mode. Music with a steady, uncomplicated structure can help regulate this response, supporting the body's stress recovery systems and allowing the mind to begin making sense of what has happened – at its own pace.

What matters here is not feeling deeply but feeling *safely*. Even the quietest music can serve as a grounding anchor. A reminder that the world is still moving, that breath is still possible, that you are still here.

A track such as "Opening" by Philip Glass might fulfill this purpose.

## State Two: Pain and Longing – When Emotion Finally Breaks Through

If shock is the silence, this is the moment when the sound returns – raw, sharp, and somehow both too much and not enough. Pain in grief is rarely tidy. It can feel like being pulled under by an emotional riptide – the memory, the realization, the truth of what has been lost all surging up at once. Many people describe this as a kind of emotional thawing with the numbness loosening, the ache stepping forward.

In this state, music becomes a companion to the breaking open. Sad songs carry a quiet kind of bravery. They don't rush you toward the light or pretend things are fine. They simply sit beside you and make room for the emotion to rise. A lyric can voice what you cannot yet say. A melody can soften the edges of pain just enough for you to keep breathing through it.

There's a strange comfort in listening to sorrow when you're already submerged in it. Music activates emotional memory networks, helping feelings come in waves rather than in overwhelming floods.

And sorrow in music has shape – a beginning, a swell, a release. That shape can make your own grief feel less like an endless blur.

For many people, this is the phase where certain songs become lifelong companions. Tracks once shared with the person you lost. Songs that hold a room, a day, a version of your life that now only exists in memory. Sometimes you avoid them for years, knowing how sharp they are. And then one day you let them play again – not because the pain has gone, but because you've grown strong enough to hold it.

I was reminded of the power of music in this state during the memorial service for my friend and extraordinary public servant for mental health, Gregor Henderson. I had known Gregor for years – admired him, learned from him, laughed with him – and yet, somehow, I never knew how deeply music lived in him. His service revealed parts of him I had never seen.

A choir opened the ceremony. Then came beatboxers – unexpected, joyful, defiantly alive. And the music choices were astonishing: "Into My Arms" by Nick Cave, "All I Do" by Stevie Wonder, "Something About Us" by Daft Punk, "Running Up That Hill" by Kate Bush. Each track felt like a small doorway into Gregor's inner world – his tenderness, humor, and quiet depth.

As each song played, I found myself not only grieving a friend but discovering him anew. Music helped me say goodbye – and, at the same time, introduced me to the parts of him I never had the chance to know. That is one of the quiet powers of music in grief – it doesn't just hold your emotions; it reveals the person you're mourning, sometimes more clearly than memory alone.

## State Three: Anger – The Chaotic Phase

If pain is the collapse inward, anger is the flare outward. It's the part of grief we don't talk about enough – the sharp edges, the restlessness, the sudden eruptions of feeling that seem to come from nowhere. Anger can feel confusing or even shameful, but it's a natural response to loss. Something precious was taken. Something that mattered ended. Anger is the mind trying to make sense of the senseless.

This state often arrives with a kind of frantic energy – a buzzing under the skin, an inability to sit still, a desire to shout, move, break, release. And this is where music, especially intense or high-energy music, can become a safe container rather than an accelerant.

Heavy beats, distorted guitars, rapid rhythms – these sounds can give form to what feels formless. They offer a place to discharge emotion without directing it at yourself or anyone else. For many people, the physicality of loud or fast music becomes a kind of emotional pressure valve.

I've spoken to people who say that in their deepest grief, metal was the only thing that understood them. Mark Deeks, who has spent decades in the heavy music world, explained that metal isn't about darkness – it's about *honesty*. It lets big feelings exist without apology. In grief, that can be a lifeline.

There's also a physiological side to this. Up-tempo, high-intensity music can help the body move through the stress response, releasing some of the pent-up tension that grief often lodges in the muscles, chest, and jaw. It's not about "fixing" anger – it's about letting it move so it doesn't consume you from the inside.

This phase can feel chaotic, disorienting, even frightening. But anger isn't the enemy. It's part of love. Part of loss. And when music gives it a shape, it becomes something you can work with rather than something that overwhelms you.

For me, tracks that resonate this way are "Nothing Else Matters" by Metallica or "Hurt" from the Nine Inch Nails.

## State Four: Searching – Trying to Reconnect

After the sharpness of anger, many people find themselves reaching – not forward, but back. This is the phase where the longing takes on a quieter shape. It isn't only about missing someone; it's about trying to feel close to them again, to remember them clearly, to hold onto something that feels like connection.

This is often when music becomes a bridge. A single song can act like a portal, pulling a memory into the present with astonishing clarity. You replay tracks you shared with the person you lost. You follow the thread of a melody back to a kitchen, a car journey, a dancefloor, a moment that once felt ordinary and now feels sacred.

There's a reason for this. Music is deeply tied to autobiographical memory. The brain doesn't just store the song – it stores who you were with, where you were, what the room smelled like, what you felt in your body. Hearing it again can feel like stepping back into a life that no longer exists.

In this state, people often create small rituals without even realizing it. Playing "their song" on anniversaries. Listening to certain tracks when they need guidance or reassurance. Returning to playlists that once filled a home with laughter or softness. These rituals aren't attempts to hold on to the past; they're ways of maintaining connection with someone who mattered.

Sometimes, this searching can also reveal gaps – things you didn't know about the person you lost, memories you wish you had asked about, parts of them you missed. Music can soften this ache by offering something to reach toward, even if only for a moment.

And occasionally, in the middle of this searching, a song will arrive unexpectedly – through a radio, a shop speaker, a shuffled playlist – and it will feel like a message. Whether it's coincidence or something more, the effect is the same. A brief, powerful reminder that love does not disappear; it just changes form.

Tracks that can evoke that sense of reaching back for me include "Holocene" from Bon Iver and "Your Hand in Mine" by Explosions in the Sky.

### State Five: Acceptance – Moving with Grief

Acceptance in grief is often misunderstood. It isn't about being "over it," nor is it about closing the door on what happened. It's quieter than that – a gentle widening of life again, even while the loss remains part of your inner landscape. In this phase, grief doesn't vanish; it simply stops taking up the whole horizon.

This state can feel fragile at first. You may notice moments of lightness appearing unexpectedly – a laugh you didn't see coming, a day that doesn't feel heavy from the moment you wake. You might catch yourself planning something, or looking forward to something, and feel a rush of guilt before remembering that healing doesn't betray the person you've lost. If anything, it honors them.

Music in this phase can support a sense of gentle forward motion. Not the euphoric tracks that feel too sharp against tender skin, but songs that hold a quiet uplift – melodies that rise slowly, beats that move at a walking pace, lyrics that speak of carrying on rather than moving on.

These are the songs that help you take the next step, and then the one after that. Music that reminds your body how to move again, how to breathe into the day, how to feel connected to a future that once felt unthinkable.

For some, these songs become part of rebuilding identity. Not the life before, not the life after – but the life that's forming now. A life that carries the loss with tenderness rather than collapse.

"Dancing in the Moonlight" from Toploader is an example of a reminder that moments of lightness can return, gently, alongside the grief.

## State Six: Integration – When Grief Finds Its Place

Integration is the long view of grief – the point at which the loss is no longer an open wound but a part of your emotional landscape. Not healed, not forgotten, but woven in. You carry it without having to hold it tightly. It lives with you rather than against you.

This phase isn't marked by big moments. It arrives quietly, almost unnoticed. When you can tell a story about the person you lost without bracing yourself; when an old song makes you smile before it makes you cry; when grief feels like a companion rather than a collapse.

Music often becomes part of this long-term relationship with loss. Songs turn into markers of remembrance – the track you play each year on their birthday, the one you put on during a quiet evening when you want to feel close, the playlist that holds the chapters of a life that shaped you. Choirs, community singing, shared rituals – all of these become ways of keeping connection alive, together rather than alone.

Here, music doesn't reopen the pain; it honors the love. It gives you permission to remember without losing your footing, to feel without falling. Over time, these musical rituals become part of how you continue the relationship – differently, but genuinely.

"*Hoppípolla*" by Sigur Rós; "Guiding Light" from Foy Vance are examples of songs that might fit in this stage. But, here more than elsewhere, such tracks will be intensely personal to you.

## Practical Applications and Reflection

Grief is personal, and the music that holds it is too. These prompts are an invitation – not to fix anything, but to notice what moves in you when you listen.

**Music and Grief Prompts**

A song that represents your connection to what you've lost might bring that person, place, or chapter of your life back into the room for a moment. Notice what shifts in your body when it plays. There may also be a track that helps you stay with pain – not to deepen it, but to hold it without tipping into overwhelm. Perhaps there is a song that represents gentle movement, one that helps you breathe a little deeper or imagine taking a small step forward.

Use these reflections whenever the grief feels distant one moment and sharp the next. Let your answers change as you do.

In this chapter, more than any other, your songs will be highlighted personal to you. However, for comparison, please scan the QR code for Rob's Music and Grief Playlist.

Grief doesn't disappear; life simply grows around it. The music that holds you in the early days may not be the music that carries you later – and that's the point. As your relationship with loss evolves, so does the soundtrack that supports it.

Some songs will stay with you forever. Some will arrive only once, at exactly the right moment. Some will break you open; others will help you rise. Together, they form a kind of map – not of where you've been, but of how you've felt, loved, endured, and begun again.

Music can't take grief away. But it can sit beside you. It can remind you of connection, of memory, of meaning. And in time, it can help you remember that even in loss, you are still capable of joy.

In the end, music doesn't heal grief. It accompanies it – and it accompanies you.

# 16 Music in Community: Culture, Connection, and Collective Healing

On a cool March evening in Milan, when the world felt unusually quiet, a single violin note drifted out over a courtyard of shuttered windows and closed-in lives. People had spent days behind their doors – listening to news about COVID that made their bodies tighten, trying not to think too far ahead. The kind of silence that lives inside a pandemic lockdown isn't just the absence of sound; it's the absence of each other.

Then the music arrived.

Aldo stepped onto his small balcony with his violin and no plan beyond offering something – anything – that might lift the heaviness of the evening. The apartments around him were dark, anonymous, indistinguishable. But as the melody rose, something subtle shifted. Lights flicked on. Windows cracked open. Curtains lifted just a little.

And suddenly the courtyard wasn't empty anymore.

Someone gasped softly at the first familiar phrase. Another leaned out with a hand to their chest. A child appeared at the corner of a window, eyes wide, listening. Nobody spoke, and yet the entire building seemed to breathe more deeply.

By the end of the piece, applause erupted – not the polite kind, but the relieved kind. The grateful kind. The "we're still here" kind.

It lasted longer than the music itself.

In that moment, people who had been strangers the week before were connected – not through words, or shared history, or even proximity, but through a sound that seemed to travel straight into the space where fear had been sitting. A courtyard that had felt like a collection of sealed lives was suddenly a single, shared room.

They didn't know the musician. They didn't know each other. But they knew what it felt like to be held, briefly, inside the same emotional shelter.

Music has a way of doing that – of reaching places conversation can't quite get to. It helps us remember each other – and connect with people we've never actually met.

Even when the world asks us to stay apart.

*For Aldo's full story and personal journey, see Chapter 21, "Aldo – Music as a Language, a Lifeline, and a Lighthouse."*

## Why Shared Music Connects Us

There's something unmistakable about the way music reshapes the atmosphere when we experience it together. You can feel it in a stadium crowd when a single drumbeat turns thousands of strangers into one voice or in a small festival tent when the first chord drops and everyone instinctively leans in. Shared music doesn't just entertain us – it reorganizes us.

I've felt this myself many times over the years. Back when I worked in executive search, I occasionally took clients to concerts – Foo Fighters, Muse, Linkin Park – the kind of shows where sound becomes a physical force. What always struck me was how quickly the usual corporate armor fell away. People who were guarded over lunch or polite over drinks suddenly opened up in the surge of a guitar line or the rise of a chorus. Standing shoulder to shoulder in a sea of noise created a kind of shortcut to trust. We weren't "networking"; we were just two humans having the same experience at the same moment – and strangely, that felt far more honest than any meeting room ever could. And that, it turned out, went far deeper than any formal meeting ever would.

What I felt in those arenas is something workplace choir leader Mark Deeks sees every week – the same shift, just on a far more intimate scale. The first few minutes often carry that familiar awkwardness – people clearing their throats, glancing sideways, trying to work out where they fit. But the moment voices blend, something shifts. Breath aligns. Bodies soften. The group becomes more than the sum of its parts. No one intends it; it just happens. And that effortless synchrony is part of what makes communal music so powerful. *(See Chapter 22, "Mark – The Power of Music to Connect, Heal, and Hold Us Together," for Mark's full story.)*

You don't need to know the people standing next to you – or even exchange a single word – to feel connected to them. Music does the work for you – quietly aligning heart rates, softening social edges, and giving everyone permission to feel something together.

Shared rhythm is shared humanity. It's why these moments stay with us long after the final note.

## The Human Voice – Our Most Ancient Instrument of Connection

There's something deeply human about the sound of a voice meeting another voice. Long before instruments, before notation, before stages and sound systems, we had breath and tone – and the instinct to use them together. You can feel this instinct come alive in a choir rehearsal, even in those first uncertain moments when people shuffle into a semi-circle and try to decide where to stand. There's a kind of collective hesitation – a few nervous laughs, a clearing of throats, the soft rustle of people adjusting their posture as if preparing to be seen.

Just as concerts connect us through scale, choirs connect us through closeness. But then someone sings a note, and another joins, and another. The sound doesn't just fill the space – it reshapes it. When voices blend, something settles. The room feels less like a room and more like a shared pulse. Breath synchronizes without instruction. People who walked in as individuals begin, almost imperceptibly, to lean into one another's sound.

Mark talks about this moment – the point in a choir rehearsal where the group moves from *trying* to sing together to *trusting* that they already can. The hierarchy of the day dissolves. Job titles evaporate. Age, background, confidence, experience – none of it matters when everyone is holding the same vowel. The voice is the great leveler. No equipment, no training, no prerequisites. Just bodies, breath, and the willingness to create something in unison.

This is the smallest scale of communal music, and in some ways the most intimate. Concerts connect thousands, but choirs connect dozens – sometimes fewer. And because your instrument is your body, the connection feels immediate, unfiltered. You're not just listening to music; you're *part of it*. You feel the vibration in your ribs, the faint scent of the wooden floor rising as people shift their weight. You hear how your sound changes when someone next to you releases a little more confidently. You notice your breath matching the person beside you.

There's something ancient about this – as if singing together taps into a memory older than language. A reminder that we once used our voices not only to communicate, but to belong.

## The Hidden Mechanics of Musical Togetherness

For all the emotion and instinct we feel in shared musical moments, there's also a quieter story unfolding beneath the surface – one written in breath, heartbeat, hormones, and the subtle choreography of human bodies responding to one another. We don't consciously control it; it simply happens when we make or experience music together.

Take a choir, for example. Long before the harmonies lock in, something physiological is already shifting. Studies show that when people sing together, their heart rates begin to synchronize – rising and falling in gentle unison as phrases lengthen and resolve. It's the body's way of saying: *I'm here with you. I'm moving with you.* The breath patterns that shape each note become shared patterns, and without ever discussing it, the group slips into a common rhythm.

Part of that shift is chemical too. Singing in a group has been shown to increase oxytocin – the hormone associated with trust, bonding, and social connection. It's why people often describe choirs as feeling like family, or why standing in a stadium with thousands of strangers can create a sense of belonging that surprises even the most introverted among us. Our biology is wired to respond to shared sound.

And it isn't only singers. Drummers synchronize movement; dancers match tempo; audiences mirror the micro-expressions and breathing of performers on stage. Neuroscientists call this *co-regulation* – the process by which our bodies calibrate to one another in shared emotional experiences. When Aldo stepped onto that balcony and began to play during lockdown, the crowd didn't just hear the music – their nervous systems adjusted to it. Fear softened. Shoulders dropped. People breathed together again.

Then there's emotional contagion – the way a melody, a beat, or even a single held note can ripple through a group and change how everyone feels. It's why a room can tilt collectively toward joy, or grief, or quiet reverence. No one decides it. No one directs it. It emerges from the simple act of feeling something at the same time.

This is the hidden mechanics of musical togetherness. A biological choreography that unfolds every time humans gather around sound. We often talk about music as a cultural force, but at its core, it is also a physiological one – a way our bodies find alignment, trust, and connection without needing a single word.

## Cultural Echoes – Humans Have Always Made Music Together

If you look across cultures, across history, across every place humans have ever gathered, you will find music. Not as decoration, and not as entertainment, but as a way of holding communities together.

The balcony concerts that swept across cities during lockdown were a modern expression of something ancient. People stepped outside not just to sing, but to signal: *we are still here; we are still connected.* The instinct behind those moments echoes traditions that stretch back thousands of years.

Across Ireland and Scotland, folk sessions in small pubs have long acted as social glue – musicians taking turns, listeners joining in on choruses, strangers becoming briefly bound by melody. In gospel churches, entire congregations rise and fall together on a tide of harmony. In Indigenous communities, drumming circles align breath, heartbeat, and identity. And in stadiums around the world, crowds chant in unison, finding belonging in a melody sung by tens of thousands.

Music is one of the oldest ways we've had of saying: *This is who we are. This is where we belong.* National songs, regional tunes, family lullabies – these shared sounds become emotional shorthand for home. I was reminded of this years later when my daughter was born. Without thinking – just as I described in Chapter 5, "Music, Sleep, and Restoration" – I found myself singing a single line from "Ring Ring Ring" by De La Soul. Not a traditional cradle song, but something instinctive, familiar, and soothing. Lullabies aren't always passed down; sometimes they emerge spontaneously from the soundtrack of our own lives.

Some evolutionary theorists believe this goes even deeper. Scholars such as Mithen (2005) and Cross (2003) argue that singing may have emerged before language – that early humans used melodic vocalizations to soothe infants, coordinate movement, signal safety, and strengthen bonds long before structured speech existed. In that view, music was our first emotional technology, a tool for survival that helped us regulate fear, build trust, and recognize one another as part of the same group.

If that's true, then singing together isn't just cultural – it's biological. When we join our voices, or our footsteps, or even our listening, we're participating in something woven into us long before history began. Community music is not a modern invention. It's why even now, a simple chorus can make strangers feel like kin. It's one of the ways we first learned to be human.

Community music is ancient, universal, and foundational to human connection.

## Shared Healing – What Happens When We Feel Together

There are moments in life when words falter, when a community faces something too heavy or too beautiful or too bewildering to express directly. And yet, in those moments, music often arrives effortlessly, as if it already knows what to say.

You can see it at vigils, where a single voice begins a familiar song and others join, quietly at first, then with strength. The melody becomes a container – a place where grief can sit without overwhelming, where people who do not know one another can stand side by side and feel less alone. No one sings to fix anything. They sing to *hold* something together.

At weddings, it works differently but with the same emotional architecture. A song rises, and the room lifts with it – not just celebrating a couple, but acknowledging the layers of family, history, and love that brought everyone there. In those moments, you can feel the room itself responding – a soft rustle of clothing, a shared intake of breath, the subtle hush that falls when everyone leans into the same emotion. The music helps people belong to the moment, and to one another.

You see it in protests, too. And the same quiet alchemy happens in smaller, more ordinary spaces as well. Chants and call-and-response rhythms create a kind of shared spine, uniting people in urgency and purpose. Even in fear, voices find coherence. Music gives shape to what collective courage feels like.

And in smaller, quieter ways, this happens in choirs every week. People come in carrying the weight of their own lives – loneliness, worry, the ache of feeling unseen – and something begins to loosen as the harmonies form. Breath aligns. Shoulders drop. Hearts steady. Singing together doesn't erase difficulty, but it offers a space where difficulty can be carried *with* others rather than alone. It's why so many describe choir rehearsals as therapeutic, even if the word feels too clinical for what is, at its core, a human experience of being witnessed.

Aldo's balcony audience felt that, too. In those brief nightly gatherings, fear eased not because circumstances changed, but because people remembered how to feel together. The music created a soft landing place for everything they didn't have language for.

Shared music doesn't solve grief or fear or uncertainty. But it does something subtler and just as important: it transforms isolation into companionship. We heal most easily when we don't have to heal alone. It happens in the spaces where our emotions meet and settle into rhythm with someone else's.

## Practical Invitations – Small Ways to Bring More Community into Your Life

The beautiful thing about communal music is that it doesn't ask for talent or confidence or training. It asks only for willingness – the willingness to show up, to participate, to let yourself be carried for a moment by something larger than your own thoughts.

For some people, this begins with joining a choir. Not because they believe they can sing, but because they're curious about what it might feel like to let their voice mingle with others. The first rehearsal is often a tangle of nerves, but that feeling usually dissolves within minutes. Before long, the music becomes a weekly anchor – a place to breathe, to belong, to exhale the day.

For others, it's attending a live performance with intention. Stepping into a gig or concert and choosing not just to listen, but to pay attention to the shared experience unfolding around you – the subtle sway of bodies, the collective exhale when the lights drop, the way strangers mirror each other's energy without even realizing it.

And for some people, belonging arrives through making music rather than simply listening to it. Joining a band, picking up an instrument with a friend, or taking part in a local jam night invites a different kind of connection – one built through shared creativity, attentive collaboration, and a willingness to play. You don't need to be accomplished. The act of creating something together is often the connection itself.

Sometimes it's simpler still. Sharing a song with a friend because it reminds you of them. Starting a family ritual where everyone picks a song for Sunday breakfast. Playing something uplifting in the office on a Friday afternoon. These tiny gestures carry more connection than we realize. Music creates a soft bridge between people, even when the conversation doesn't come easily.

Leaders feel this intuitively too. A well-chosen piece of music can shape the mood of a room, soften tension, or signal that a space is safe to speak. When used with care, music becomes a subtle tool for creating belonging.

You don't need to be musical to bring more community into your life. You just need to start noticing the musical moments that are already happening around you – and step toward them.

## Closing Reflection – A Soft Landing

Community music doesn't require grand gestures. It doesn't ask us to perform, or perfect, or impress. It simply invites us to be present – with ourselves, and with one another – in a way that words often can't reach.

As you finish this chapter, take a moment to think back. When did music last make you feel part of something bigger than yourself?

Maybe it was a chorus at a gig, a chant on a football terrace, a hymn you haven't heard in years, or the quiet joining of voices at a difficult moment. Whatever it was, notice how the memory feels in your body. Notice what it stirred, softened, or steadied.

These moments stay with us because they remind us of something essential. We are not meant to navigate life alone. We are shaped – and sometimes healed – not in isolation, but in the quiet company of others.

# 17 Music and Digital Solutions for Well-Being

You've had one of those days at work where everything seems to land at once. By the time you're leaving the office, your jaw aches from clenching and you're half-walking, half-jogging to catch the train. You slip through the doors just as they're closing and, to your relief, spot an empty seat by the window. You drop into it, your bag still digging into your side, and take a moment before fishing out your headphones.

A well-being app loads on your phone. You pick a guided stress-relief track almost without thinking – something gentle, something that doesn't ask too much of you. A calm voice settles into your ears, carried by a slow wash of sound. As you breathe with the guidance, you notice how tightly you'd been holding yourself. Your shoulders begin to fall back into place. Your breath evens out. The day's noise, which felt so loud a few minutes ago, starts to lose its grip.

When the session ends, you open your eyes more slowly than you expected. The countryside is slipping past in a soft blur – fields, hedgerows, a lone dog walker on a path you only glimpse for a second.

The carriage smells faintly of damp coats and takeaway chips from someone's bag. Across the aisle, a passenger opens a can of gin and tonic, the crack-hiss briefly punctuating the quiet. You catch it, note it, and feel a small, private gratitude for choosing something different tonight – not better, just better for you.

As the train rolls into your station, you feel more like yourself again. Not perfect, not transformed – just steadier. You step onto the platform with a little more room inside your chest and begin your evening in a different headspace (pun intended).

This is the new frontier of music for well-being – from passive listening to personalized emotional support.

## Why Digital Platforms Matter

Digital platforms have transformed how we access music – but more importantly, they've begun transforming how we *use* it. What was once a passive soundtrack is now becoming an active tool for mood regulation, stress relief, sleep support, and emotional clarity. Music is no longer just something that fills the silence; it is an entry point into self-awareness and a bridge to better mental health.

For many people, these tools offer structure where there was once overwhelm, and permission to care for themselves in moments when life feels too fast or slightly out of reach. Maybe it's the end of a long day when your shoulders are still tense from a meeting that ran over, or the moment you collapse onto the sofa after the school run and realize you haven't taken a proper breath in hours. These are the small, private thresholds where digital music tools can provide grounding – not by fixing anything, but by helping you notice yourself again.

In this chapter, we explore how apps blend music, psychology, and technology to support real-world well-being, tracing the shift from generic playlists to emotionally responsive systems that adapt to who we are and what we need. We look at how these tools help people navigate mood, anxiety, sleep, identity, and the everyday pressures of modern life, as well as the promise – and the limitations – of algorithmic support.

At its heart, this chapter is about reconnection. Digital tools can guide us back to something we often forget in the rush of daily life, that music is a powerful, accessible, deeply human way to feel better – not perfect, not fixed, just better enough to start again.

## The Problem

We now live in a world with more music at our fingertips than at any point in history – yet somehow this abundance often makes it harder, not easier, to know what to play when we truly need support. Faced with endless choice, many of us drift into passive listening, letting music blur quietly into the background instead of using it to steady ourselves or shift our mood. In those moments when we're anxious, low, overstimulated, or simply struggling to focus, the sheer volume of options can leave us hesitating on a single question. *Where do I even start?*

Digital well-being tools are stepping in to soften that friction. They cut through the overwhelm of choice at the very moment you feel least able to decide. Instead of scrolling through playlists and hoping to land on something that helps, these tools bring music back into the foreground as something intentional rather than accidental. They strengthen emotional awareness by nudging you to notice how you feel and to choose sound that meets you there. For those who rely on screens late at night, they offer calming audio that works with the body instead of against it; for those battling distraction, they create soundscapes that feel protective rather than intrusive.

In essence, these tools don't replace your musical instincts – they give them shape. They offer a gentle starting point when your mind is scattered, a framework when silence feels too sharp, and a way of tuning back into yourself when the day has pulled you in too many directions. They turn what used to be guesswork into something more grounded, more intentional, and far more supportive.

## The Science

Digital solutions are built on well-established music science – much of which we explored in Part I, "The Power of Music." We now know that music can soften the stress response, steady the nervous system, and help the body recover more quickly after periods of pressure. We've seen that intentional listening, not just passive consumption, has a measurable effect on mood and emotional regulation. We know that tempo and rhythm can influence our ability to focus, energize, or sustain effort, and that calming, predictable sound can support better sleep by easing the body into a slower physiological state. Music also boosts memory, emotional processing, and learning – which is why guided practices work so well when paired with sound.

What digital well-being tools do is take this foundation and weave it into everyday behavior. They don't just offer music; they offer *structure* around music, using principles from behavioral science to help us build habits that stick. Nudges, prompts, streaks, and mood-check-ins encourage us to notice how we feel and choose music with intention. Suggestions are shaped around what we're likely to do in real life, not what we wish we'd do in theory. Over time, these small behavioral cues help turn music from something we reach for occasionally into a reliable, science-backed component of our well-being routines.

In this way, the apps act as a bridge – translating scientific insights into everyday practice, helping us turn knowledge into behavior, and behavior into support we can actually feel.

## The Landscape: Three Waves of Digital Musical Well-Being

Before we break these waves down, it's helpful to understand why this framework matters. Digital tools are not replacing the ways we've always used music – they're expanding them. Each wave represents a different kind of relationship with sound, from the playlists many of us rely on every day to the responsive systems that are beginning to shape personalized emotional support. Think of these waves as overlapping rather than sequential. Most of us move between them depending on our energy, our mood, and what life is asking of us in that moment.

With the scientific foundations from Part I in mind, this framework helps show how those principles come alive in the real world – through the ways we choose, use, and respond to music in daily life.

### *Curated Playlists (Spotify/Apple Era)*

Most of us still access music for our well-being in the simplest and most familiar way, through curated playlists from platforms like Spotify and Apple Music. These playlists – for focus, chill, sleep, energy, or "deep work" – remain the primary route into intentional listening for millions of people. In fact, for many, they are not a stepping stone but the *main* way they use music to support their mood, their work, or their evenings winding down.

And there is a lot to celebrate here. Curated playlists offer instant, low-effort support. They are convenient, reliable, and available the moment you need to shift gears – whether you're trying to concentrate after a busy morning, settling into a late-night writing session, or finding a steady rhythm for the school run. They create atmosphere without requiring decisions, which is often exactly what we need when we're tired or overwhelmed. In Part I, we also explored the power of building your *own* playlists – a personal musical toolkit shaped by memory, emotion, and meaning. These self-curated playlists can be even more effective because they draw on your lived experience, strengthening the emotional connection to the music you choose.

But curated playlists, particularly algorithmic ones, do have natural limitations. They aren't typically built around your emotional state in real time, which means they can miss the subtle shifts that determine whether a piece of music soothes, overstimulates, or simply drifts past without impact. They support intention, but they don't always respond to need.

In this sense, curated playlists remain a powerful entry point into intentional listening – and for many, they are more than enough. But they do not yet personalize the journey moment-to-moment, nor do they help us reflect on how our listening habits interact with our well-being. Those are the gaps newer digital tools are beginning to explore, offering layers of guidance that playlists alone cannot provide.

And this is where guided audio steps in.

### *Guided Audio Experiences (Headspace, Calm, Spoke)*

Guided audio experiences represent the moment when music stops being something we *put on* and becomes something that actively *guides* us. Unlike curated playlists, which set a mood, guided audio uses a blend of voice, sound design, and intentional structure to help shift our emotional state. These experiences sit at the intersection of music, psychology, and storytelling: part meditation, part coaching, part sonic environment. They support listeners by offering direction when the mind feels scattered, companionship when emotions feel heavy, and gentle structure when focus is hard to find.

What defines this wave is not the specific style of music, but the presence of a guiding voice or narrative arc – something that meets the listener where they are and leads them somewhere steadier. The guidance is what transforms the experience from passive listening to active regulation. For some people, this kind of narration is grounding and supportive; for others, it can feel intrusive, especially on days when the mind wants quiet more than instruction. But when it works, guided audio can feel like a companion – one that knows how to steady your breath and help your thoughts settle.

With that in mind, the following examples illustrate how different apps interpret and deliver this approach, each offering its own tone, texture, and emotional flavor.

Headspace is built around simplicity and calm. Its music and sound design are engineered to support focus, relaxation, and sleep, often using minimalistic rhythms and predictable sonic patterns to help the mind settle. Their Sleepcasts and guided meditations use music as a soft bed for emotional grounding, helping listeners ease into rest or manage daily stress.

Calm leans more into storytelling, atmosphere, and rich soundscapes. The app features original music created specifically for relaxation and sleep, celebrity-led sleep stories, and cinematic ambient tracks designed to support deep rest. Calm approaches musical well-being through immersion – creating audio environments that soothe the nervous system and quieten mental chatter.

Spoke takes a different path, blending trauma-informed spoken word with music and lyrical guidance. Its content is expressive, culturally diverse, and emotionally direct, offering practices that support self-reflection, emotional regulation, and healing. Spoke shows how music and voice can work together in a way that feels therapeutic without being clinical.

### *Emotionally Responsive Systems*

Guided audio is powerful, but it remains largely one-directional – the listener receives support, but the experience itself doesn't adapt in real time. Wave 3 begins where that limitation becomes most visible – at the point where our emotional state shifts and we need something that shifts with us.

Wave 3 represents a shift from guided experiences to systems that respond to the listener in real time. Rather than offering a fixed library of practices or pre-curated journeys, these tools adapt to your emotional state, your habits, and the patterns emerging in your daily life. They are less about instruction and more about reflection – helping you build emotional awareness by noticing how your listening connects to how you feel.

ISO-1 sits at the forefront of this space. Unlike traditional well-being apps, ISO-1 begins with the listener's *mood*, not the music itself. Users journal how they feel, pairing emotional states with the tracks they naturally gravitate toward. Over time, ISO-1's AI learns these connections and begins offering personalized recommendations – not based on genre or popularity, but on the emotional tone embedded in the music. The process is gentle, reflective, and intentionally human. The goal is not to prescribe solutions, but to help people understand their own emotional landscape through the music they already love.

What makes ISO-1 distinctive is its blend of psychological insight and musical intuition. By turning mood journaling into a musical practice, it encourages self-awareness without pressure or perfectionism. The app becomes a mirror, helping users recognize patterns – the songs that soothe them when anxious, the tracks that help them reset after difficult moments, or the rhythms that lift their mood when energy is low. In this way, ISO-1 isn't just a tool for well-being – it's an invitation to understand yourself more deeply through sound.

*It's important to note that we have no affiliation with any of these apps. They are included purely as illustrations of how digital platforms are using music and sound to support well-being. (The only personal connection in this book is the interview with Russ Newell, the founder of Isofi featured in Chapter 26, "Russ – Tuning Technology to the Human Heart.")*

## What Digital Music Tools Get Right – and Where They Fall Short

Digital music tools have opened up new ways for people to care for themselves, and much of their power lies in their simplicity. They meet us where we already are – on our phones, in moments of stress, or when we're searching for a shift in mood – and offer support that feels immediate and approachable. A supportive track is only seconds away, and because people interact with these apps far more frequently than they access formal care, the consistency of that contact can be quietly transformative. Many tools also adapt to our listening habits, learning what helps us focus, what calms us, and what lifts our mood, turning music into a personalized well-being companion. Their prompts and gentle nudges borrow from behavioral science, helping us build small, repeatable routines that anchor us through the week. And crucially, music itself feels safe. It doesn't demand vulnerability or expertise – it simply meets the listener with familiarity and warmth.

But even the most thoughtful tools have limits, and recognizing those limitations helps us use them more intentionally. Algorithms, no matter how advanced, do not understand context. They cannot tell the difference between a low mood caused by grief and one caused by tiredness, or between needing soothing and needing silence. The increasing use of mood tracking also raises natural questions about data privacy – especially when emotional information is involved. Recommendations can misfire, landing as too upbeat, too slow, or too intense for the moment you're in. And while these tools can support emotional awareness, they can also create a subtle dependence if we begin outsourcing our internal listening to technology rather than developing practices of our own. Cultural bias can shape how emotions are categorized and understood, meaning the tools may not always reflect the nuance or diversity of human feeling.

Used well, digital tools can be powerful allies – not perfect, not complete, but supportive. Understanding both their strengths and their limitations helps us choose them with clarity and rely on them in ways that genuinely deepen our well-being rather than dull our instincts.

## Practical Guidance

Digital tools can be powerful, but they work best when used with intention. A simple rule of thumb is to let them guide you without handing over the steering wheel. Start by noticing how you feel in the moment, then choose the kind of support that matches your state – whether that's a grounding track, a guided reset, or a calming soundscape for sleep. Small rituals can make these tools even more helpful – a playlist that marks the transition from work to evening; a short, guided practice before bed; or a focus soundtrack you return to when concentration wavers. And remember the work you did in Part I, "The Power of Music." Your own personally curated playlists remain one of the most powerful tools you have. Digital platforms can complement them, but they don't replace the emotional wisdom you've already built.

Use technology as a companion, not a director – something that helps you tune in rather than tune out.

---

What digital tools – if any – are already part of your musical life? How intentionally do you use them? What small shift could improve the way they support your well-being?

---

# 18 Music Therapy and Clinical Insight

Most of us already use music instinctively – to calm ourselves, lift our mood, focus our attention, or get through difficult moments. We reach for it without instruction, often without conscious deliberation. In everyday life, music is familiar, flexible, and typically experienced as low risk.

That position shifts when music is used deliberately in care.

When music is introduced with therapeutic intent – to reduce pain, support emotional regulation, aid recovery, or reach someone who is struggling – it moves beyond background comfort and begins to carry clinical responsibility. In healthcare and therapeutic settings, music is not neutral. While it can soothe and stabilize, it may also evoke memories, emotions, or physiological responses that require appropriate containment and professional judgment.

This chapter examines that boundary – where intuitive, self-directed listening meets formal clinical practice. It explores what distinguishes music therapy from everyday use, why those distinctions matter, and what can be learned from clinical contexts without reframing listening as treatment.

The pages that follow stay with this shift in responsibility – not to medicalize listening, but to understand what becomes possible, and what must be handled with care, when music is used intentionally in clinical contexts.

## What Is Music Therapy? (and What It Isn't)

Music therapy is a regulated clinical practice delivered by trained and accredited professionals. It involves the intentional use of music – and musical interaction – to support physical, emotional, cognitive, and social needs within a therapeutic relationship. Crucially, the music itself is not the treatment in isolation; it is the way music is used, adapted, and held within a clinical context that gives it therapeutic value.

Unlike everyday listening, music therapy is guided by assessment, professional judgment, and ethical responsibility. Sessions are shaped by the needs, capacity, and readiness of the individual and are adjusted in real time based on their responses. This is why music therapy sits alongside, rather than outside of, healthcare and psychological practice.

It is equally important to be clear about what music therapy is *not*. It is not simply listening to calming playlists, however beneficial those may be. It is not generic sound healing, nor is it a substitute for medical or psychological treatment. Instead, music therapy complements existing forms of care, often working in partnership with multidisciplinary teams.

Within clinical practice, music therapy can take different forms. In active music therapy, individuals may sing, play instruments, improvise, or use rhythm and movement as a way to express, regulate, or rehabilitate. In receptive music therapy, listening is used more deliberately – for emotional processing, relaxation, imagery, or pain management – with the therapist guiding the experience and supporting what emerges.

Music therapy may be delivered one-to-one or in group settings, depending on context and need. What remains consistent is the presence of a trained therapist who attends not just to the music, but to the person experiencing it. This relational dimension – the ability to notice, respond, and contain – is what distinguishes music therapy from even the most intentional forms of self-directed listening.

## Why Music Works When Words Don't

One of the most distinctive features of music, psychologically and in therapeutic contexts, is the way it reaches us without requiring words. Long before we can articulate how we feel, we can often feel *something* shift in response to rhythm, harmony, or melody. This is not accidental. As we have previously discussed, research in affective neuroscience shows that music engages brain systems involved in emotion, memory, movement, and reward – many of which sit outside, or upstream of, conscious verbal processing (Koelsch, 2014).

Unlike spoken language, which asks us to name, explain, or justify our inner experience, music offers structure without demand. It can hold emotional states without requiring them to be translated into narrative. For people who are overwhelmed, cognitively impaired, traumatized, or simply unable to find the right words, this matters. Music creates a shared space where experience can be expressed, regulated, or contained without explanation.

Rhythm plays a particularly important role in this process. Regular pulse and timing provide external structure that the nervous system can synchronize with, supporting attention, coordination, and regulation. In clinical settings, this is why rhythm is often used to support movement, gait, or focus when internal control has been disrupted. The body can follow a beat even when conscious instruction fails.

Melody and harmony, meanwhile, act as emotional containers. They shape expectation, tension, and release, allowing feelings to emerge and resolve safely over time. This makes music especially useful in contexts where emotions are complex, mixed, or difficult to tolerate. Rather than forcing clarity, music allows ambiguity – and in doing so, often makes experience more bearable.

Taken together, these qualities help explain why music can be effective when conversation reaches its limits. It does not replace verbal therapy or medical intervention, but it extends the range of how care can be offered. In clinical practice, this capacity – to meet people where language falls short – is one of music therapy's most distinctive strengths.

## Clinical Areas Where Music Therapy Shows Strongest Evidence

This chapter does not attempt to catalogue every context in which music therapy has been applied. Instead, it focuses on areas where the evidence base is relatively well established and where clinical consensus is strongest. The aim is not to overstate impact, but to illustrate the kinds of challenges music therapy is particularly well suited to support.

### *Pain and Physical Recovery*

Pain is one of the contexts in which music has been most consistently studied in clinical settings. Across post-operative care and chronic pain conditions, music therapy and structured music interventions have been shown to reduce reported pain, anxiety, and distress, often alongside standard medical treatment. Importantly, these effects do not rely on music as a substitute for analgesia, but as a complementary, non-invasive form of support.

In recovery contexts, music is often used to provide predictability and a sense of safety at times when the body feels unfamiliar or out of control. This can be particularly valuable after surgery, where anxiety, uncertainty, and heightened sensitivity can amplify the experience of pain. Music does not remove pain, but it can alter how pain is perceived, tolerated, and emotionally processed.

An important clarification here is that music therapy is not presented as a cure for pain, nor as an alternative to medical care. Its value lies in supporting recovery and reducing distress in ways that are low risk and adaptable to individual needs. Large-scale reviews have highlighted these benefits while also emphasizing the importance of appropriate timing, delivery, and patient preference (Hole et al., 2015).

### *Neurological Rehabilitation*

Neurological rehabilitation is another area where music therapy has a well-established role, particularly in conditions such as stroke and Parkinson's disease. Here, the clinical value of music is closely tied to rhythm and timing. When neurological injury disrupts internal motor control, external rhythmic cues can provide a scaffold for movement, coordination, and gait.

In these contexts, music is not used for emotional expression alone, but as a practical tool to support relearning and re-patterning. Regular pulse can help organize movement when conscious instruction is insufficient, allowing the body to regain a sense of flow and predictability. This is why rhythmic auditory stimulation has been widely studied in motor rehabilitation.

It is important to state this limitation clearly. Music therapy does not reverse neurological damage, nor does it replace physiotherapy or medical intervention. Its role is supportive and integrative, contributing to rehabilitation by engaging systems that remain responsive even when others are compromised (Thaut et al., 1996).

### *Mental Health Support*

Music therapy is used across a range of mental health settings, including work with anxiety, depression, and trauma-related difficulties. In these contexts, its value often lies less in symptom reduction alone and more in emotional regulation, expression, and relational safety.

For individuals who find verbal therapy overwhelming or inaccessible, music can offer an alternative entry point. It allows feelings to be expressed and contained without requiring immediate insight or explanation. This can be particularly helpful in early stages of therapy, or during periods of heightened distress.

At the same time, the evidence base here is appropriately cautious. Reviews of music therapy for depression, for example, suggest modest but meaningful benefits when delivered by trained professionals, often as an adjunct to other treatments. Music therapy is not positioned as a standalone solution, but as part of a broader therapeutic landscape (Aalbers et al., 2017).

### *Dementia and Memory Care*

One of the most striking areas of music therapy practice is dementia and memory care. Even as other forms of memory and communication decline, musical memory and responsiveness are often preserved for longer. Familiar music can support recognition, emotional regulation, and a sense of identity when other cues fail.

In care settings, music therapy is used not to restore memory, but to maintain connection and dignity. Music can help people feel oriented to themselves and others, reducing agitation and supporting moments of shared presence. These effects are not uniform and depend heavily on personal history, cultural context, and delivery.

A further limitation is essential to acknowledge here. Music therapy does not halt cognitive decline, nor does it work universally. Its value lies in quality of life, emotional well-being, and relational connection – outcomes that matter deeply, even when cure is not possible (Baird and Samson, 2015).

## Music Therapy vs. Self-Directed Listening

This distinction matters not to elevate professional practice above everyday listening, but to protect both. Confusing the two risks medicalizing something that is often deeply personal, while also underestimating the skill and responsibility involved in clinical work.

Self-directed listening is something most of us already do. We choose music to suit our mood, energy, or situation. We skip tracks that don't feel right, return to ones that comfort us, and use music as a companion through daily life. This kind of listening is driven by agency and choice. Its strength lies in flexibility, intuition, and the freedom to engage – or disengage – as we need.

Music therapy operates in a different context. Here, music is used intentionally within a therapeutic relationship, guided by assessment, professional judgment, and ethical responsibility. The therapist's role is not to select the "right" music, but to create a safe container in which music can be explored, responded to, and integrated. This is particularly important when individuals are vulnerable, overwhelmed, or unable to regulate their emotional or physiological responses on their own.

The difference is not simply one of expertise, but of containment. In music therapy, someone else is holding the space – noticing shifts, responding to distress, and helping to make sense of what emerges. In self-directed listening, the listener holds that responsibility themselves. Both can be valuable. Both can be appropriate. But they are not interchangeable.

Understanding this distinction allows readers to engage with music more thoughtfully, without turning listening into treatment or assuming that more structure is always better. Music therapy offers guidance and support when it is needed. Everyday listening offers autonomy and self-connection when that is possible. Recognizing when each is appropriate is part of using music with care.

## The Role of the Therapist: Holding the Space

At the heart of music therapy is not the music itself, but the relationship within which it is used. While music provides the medium, it is the therapist who holds the space – attending to the person, the moment, and the meaning that emerges between them.

The therapeutic alliance is central. Trust, attunement, and emotional safety allow music to be explored without overwhelm. A trained music therapist listens not only to what is played or heard, but to how it lands. Changes in breath, posture, affect, or energy are signals that help guide pacing, choice, and intervention, particularly when individuals are unable to articulate their experience verbally.

This relational attention is especially important when working with vulnerability. Music can open emotional territory quickly – sometimes more quickly than words. The therapist's role is to notice when something shifts, to slow or redirect when needed, and to help contain what arises. In this way, music therapy is less about eliciting response and more about supporting regulation.

Music itself can function in multiple relational roles. At times it acts as a bridge, enabling connection where direct conversation feels too exposed. At other moments it becomes a mirror, reflecting emotional states that may be difficult to recognize or name. It can also serve as a regulator, offering rhythm and structure that support the nervous system in finding steadiness.

By foregrounding relationship over technique, music therapy reinforces a wider truth echoed throughout this book – healing does not happen through optimization or perfect solutions, but through being met, understood, and supported in context.

## Clinical Moments from the Evidence

Rather than relying on individual stories or illustrative vignettes, clinical insight in music therapy is often drawn from patterns that appear consistently across the research literature. These moments are not dramatic turning points, but quiet observations about how people respond when music is introduced with care and intention.

In neurological rehabilitation, for example, rhythmic cueing is repeatedly used to support timing and coordination rather than strength. Studies describe how patients are sometimes able to initiate or sustain movement more fluidly when guided by an external pulse, even when conscious control is impaired. What appears to matter here is not motivation alone, but the way rhythm provides an organizing framework the body can synchronize with when internal regulation has been disrupted.

In dementia and memory care, a different pattern emerges. Familiar music is frequently associated with improved emotional regulation, recognition, and social engagement, even when other forms of memory are compromised. These moments are not about recovering lost information, but about preserving a sense of identity and connection. Music offers continuity when cognitive systems fragment, allowing people to remain present with themselves and others for brief but meaningful periods.

Pain and anxiety research points to another recurring observation. Music is often described as reducing distress not through distraction alone, but by creating predictability and emotional containment. In situations marked by uncertainty or loss of control, music can provide a stable reference point – something known, structured, and temporally bounded – that helps make discomfort more tolerable.

Taken together, these clinically observed moments illustrate how music tends to function in therapeutic contexts, not as a solution, but as a support. Across different conditions and settings, its value lies less in changing outcomes outright and more in shaping experience – offering structure, safety, and connection at times when these are most needed.

## Boundaries, Ethics, and Caution

The clinical use of music comes with responsibilities as well as possibilities. While music is often associated with comfort and pleasure, it is not inherently soothing, nor is it universally safe. In therapeutic contexts, this complexity must be acknowledged rather than overlooked.

Music can surface difficult emotions, memories, or bodily responses, sometimes quickly and unexpectedly. For individuals with a history of trauma, loss, or heightened sensitivity, certain sounds or pieces of music may be activating rather than calming. What supports one person may overwhelm another. This is why timing, readiness, and personal history matter as much as musical choice.

Ethical music therapy practice involves careful pacing and consent. Therapists attend closely to signs of distress or dysregulation and are trained to slow, adapt, or stop when necessary. The goal is not to push emotional material into awareness, but to create conditions in which people feel safe enough to encounter their experience gradually and with support.

These boundaries also matter outside formal therapy. When music is used informally to cope with stress, grief, or low mood, it can still stir powerful feelings. Noticing when music intensifies distress rather than easing it – and being willing to pause or seek support – is an important form of self-care.

Above all, it's important to recognize the value of trained professionals and the difference between individuals. Music therapy works best when it respects the uniqueness of each person's nervous system, history, and capacity in the moment. Used with care, music can support healing. Used without awareness, it can inadvertently do harm. Holding this distinction is part of using music responsibly.

## What This Means for You (Without Making You a Therapist)

Listening does not need to become therapeutic in order to be meaningful, nor does music need to be used to manage every difficulty. What matters instead is orientation – approaching music with a little more awareness of why it can feel supportive, and of when greater care is needed.

Clinical practice offers useful cues here. Music tends to be most supportive when it is engaged with intentionally, at a pace that feels manageable, and in ways that respect capacity in the moment. This does not require specialized knowledge or techniques. It simply involves paying attention to how music affects the body, mood, and sense of safety.

Choice plays an important role. In everyday listening, being able to skip a track, change the volume, or turn the music off altogether is not a failure of engagement, but a form of self-regulation. Listening *with* yourself means noticing when music supports you – and when it does not – and responding accordingly.

A final shift in expectation is worth holding. Music does not need to fix, optimize, or transform in order to matter. Sometimes its role is simply to accompany a moment, offering structure, familiarity, or emotional holding when things feel uncertain. Used this way, music remains a companion – not a treatment – and that distinction is worth protecting.

## Reflection Prompt

*When has music helped you feel held, rather than fixed?*

That distinction matters. Across clinical practice, music shows its value not by solving problems outright, but by shaping experience – offering structure, safety, and connection when words, certainty, or control are limited.

Everyday listening does not need to imitate therapy to benefit from this insight. It can simply take from it a quieter understanding – that music works best when it respects capacity, allows choice, and meets us where we are. Music does not need to cure, optimize, or explain in order to matter.

At its most powerful, music is not an answer in the conventional sense. It is a presence. Something that stays with us – through discomfort, recovery, and change – reminding us that being accompanied can be as meaningful as being solved.

# 19 Breaking Barriers to Musical Well-Being

One of the most common barriers people describe is time. Or more accurately, the belief that music for well-being requires extra time – something else to fit into already full days.

"I'd love to use music more intentionally, but I just don't have the time."

What sits underneath this is rarely a shortage of minutes. It's a shortage of permission. Music is often framed as an addition – a ritual, a practice, a separate activity that needs to be done properly to count. When life is busy, anything that feels optional is the first thing to fall away.

And yet, music is already threaded through daily life. It's there on the commute, in the background while cooking, during workouts, on walks, and in the quiet moments before sleep. The shift isn't about adding more music. It's about noticing what's already there, and how it's affecting you.

Musical well-being doesn't require carving out new time. It asks for a different relationship with the time you already have. Let's take a look at some common barriers.

## "I Don't Know What I Need"

For many people, the biggest barrier isn't just time or access at all. It's something quieter and harder to name.

You don't know what you need.

This isn't a failure of musical knowledge. It's a gap in self-awareness.

Most of us aren't taught how to check in with our internal state in any meaningful way. We learn to push through tiredness, ignore low-level stress, and normalize emotional flatness. We become skilled at coping, but less skilled at noticing. When someone asks, "What would help you right now?" the honest answer is often, "I'm not sure."

Music brings this gap into focus very quickly.

When people try to use music intentionally, they often reach for what they like rather than what they need: familiar favorites, old habits, algorithm-generated playlists designed to do the thinking for them. Sometimes this works; often it doesn't. And when it doesn't, it is easy to draw the conclusion that this doesn't work for me.

But usually, the issue isn't the music. It's the missing step before the music.

Using music for well-being asks a deceptively simple question – how am I actually feeling right now? And a second, more challenging one – what would support me, not fix me or distract me, but support me in this state?

These questions can feel unfamiliar. We're far more comfortable using music to boost, energize, or escape than we are using it to meet ourselves where we are. We know how to reach for motivation. We're less practiced at recognizing when we need grounding, containment, or permission to feel low.

This is why people often say, "I don't know what works for me." What they really mean is, "I haven't been taught to listen inwardly before I listen outwardly."

The good news is that self-awareness isn't a fixed trait. It's a skill. And music can help develop it.

For me, that awareness didn't arrive through theory or intention. It arrived through disruption. When long COVID took away my usual outlet of exercise – the thing I relied on to regulate stress, mood, and energy – I was forced to pay attention to what remained. Music was still there. And slowly, almost accidentally, I began to notice that it was helping me stay well.

Not in a dramatic way, but in small, cumulative ways – stabilizing my mood, giving shape to days that otherwise felt flat, offering movement when my body couldn't.

It was that loss that sparked my curiosity. Why was music helping when so many other strategies weren't available to me? That question sits at the heart of this book.

My hope for you, as a reader, is that it doesn't take a crisis to prompt that same awareness. That you don't have to lose something – health, time, capacity – before you start noticing what music is already doing for you.

Over time, intentional listening becomes a feedback loop. You notice how your body responds. Your breathing changes – or doesn't. Your thoughts soften – or sharpen. You feel steadier, more agitated, more present, or more distant. None of these responses are right or wrong. They're information.

Gradually, patterns emerge. You begin to recognize the difference between music that supports you and music that suppresses something – between music that helps you stay with an emotion and music that helps you step away from it. Trust builds, not because you've found the perfect playlist, but because you've rebuilt a relationship with your own signals.

## "I'm Not Musical"

Another powerful barrier is the belief that musical well-being is only for people who are "musical."

For many adults, this belief was formed early. A comment at school. A failed audition. Being told to mime rather than sing. Over time, music becomes something other people do, better than us.

This misunderstanding rests on a narrow definition of music – one that prioritizes performance, talent, and comparison. Musical well-being has nothing to do with any of these.

As Mark Deeks put it when we spoke, part of the challenge is how we frame our goals. If learning the piano is approached as a route to proficiency or performance, it's easy to feel intimidated or discouraged before you even begin.

But learning to play an instrument for the sake of the experience itself – for focus, absorption, expression, or simple enjoyment – is already a meaningful well-being outcome. It doesn't need to lead anywhere else to be worthwhile.

You don't need technical ability to respond to rhythm, repetition, melody, or harmony. You don't need to sing, play, or perform. You simply need to be human. Our nervous systems respond to sound long before we learn to judge it.

Musical well-being isn't about doing music properly. It's about allowing music to meet you where you are.

## When Pleasure Feels Indulgent

For some people, especially caregivers, high performers, and those shaped by strong productivity cultures, music carries a quiet sense of guilt.

Listening with intention can feel self-indulgent. Unproductive. Hard to justify.

In these contexts, music is often framed as escapism rather than regulation – something you earn after work is done, rather than something that helps you stay resourced enough to do the work at all.

But ignoring emotional and physiological states doesn't make them disappear. It delays them. Music, used intentionally, observable and responsive, functions more like maintenance than indulgence.

Pleasure isn't a reward. It's information – a signal about state, need, and regulation.

## "I Don't Trust My Response"

A quieter but deeply influential barrier is a lack of trust in our own responses to music.

People second-guess themselves. They worry their taste is unsophisticated. They feel their reactions are inconsistent. They defer to genres, experts, or trends, assuming there's a correct way to respond.

There isn't.

Your response to music is not something to correct or refine. It's the data. The body often registers safety, tension, familiarity, or discomfort before the mind has language for it. Learning to trust those signals again is part of the work.

## Barriers Don't Appear by Accident

These obstacles are not individual failures. They're shaped by culture.

Music education narrows rather than widens. Music slips into the background, heard constantly but rarely attended to. Wellness culture prioritizes optimization over connection. Feeling is outsourced to tools and techniques rather than cultivated from within.

Seen in this light, it's not surprising that many people feel disconnected from music as a source of well-being. What matters is recognizing that these barriers can be unlearned.

## Gently Clearing the Path

Breaking barriers to musical well-being doesn't require discipline or expertise. It requires small shifts.

From playlists to patterns.

From mood-changing to mood-meeting.

From judgment to curiosity.

From perfection to presence.

This might mean pausing before pressing play and asking, "What do I need right now?" It could mean noticing when a track helps you breathe more easily – or when it doesn't. It might mean allowing your relationship with music to change.

There's no need to get it right. Only to stay responsive.

## Music as Companion, Not Cure

Music doesn't fix us. It doesn't remove difficulty or erase discomfort. What it offers is something quieter and more enduring: *companionship*.

In moments of grief, transition, identity shift, or exhaustion, music doesn't rush us forward. It stays with us. And sometimes, that's enough.

Musical well-being isn't about doing more. It's about removing the reasons you stopped listening to yourself.

If there's one question worth carrying forward, it's not "What should I listen to?" It's "What do I need right now – and how might music help me meet it?"

# PART III The Stories We Carry

If you're lost, take a breath and let the music find you.

# 20 Catherine – The Autistic Raver: Joy as Regulation

Music doesn't just soothe or stimulate – it finds its own way of settling in the gaps of a busy day. Some mornings it steadies you; other times it surprises you. It's rarely neat, and that's what makes it real. For Catherine Ritchie, Senior Wellbeing and Experience Leader at a global elite law firm, Clarity Coach, and proud autistic woman, music is more than background; it's how she regulates emotion, navigates energy, and reconnects to joy. Her story reveals a truth that runs throughout this book. When we listen intentionally, music becomes not just something we hear, but something that helps us *feel* again.

## Finding Language Through Sound

Catherine grew up in a home where music and quiet were both sacred. There was always a record playing somewhere – a parent testing a new album, a sibling with headphones on, each of them finding calm in sound. Only later did she realize that much of her family was neurodivergent, instinctively using music to self-regulate before they had the language for why it worked.

"Music has always been like a vehicle or a conduit to expressing feelings or finding words for things," she told me. "Sometimes, especially as an undiagnosed autistic person, it was the only way I could process the world."

Music became her translation layer – not in a tidy, poetic way, but in the practical sense of helping her sort through feelings that didn't always line up with what was expected. Like many neurodivergent people, Catherine experiences heightened sensory input – light, sound, conversation, movement. Music doesn't drown it out; it organizes it. A song can transform overwhelming noise into order, giving shape to what might otherwise feel chaotic. This is what music does for all of us at times of overload – it holds emotion within structure, giving us something predictable to lean into.

Where words fall short, melody sometimes mumbles, sometimes shouts – and Catherine has learned to listen to both. For Catherine, this is not metaphorical – it's physiological. The right chord progression can relax her breathing. The repetition of rhythm can restore her focus. The moment of harmony can reconnect her to the world around her. Music doesn't just express how she feels; it *explains* it to her.

## The Art of Intentional Listening

Catherine's musical awareness evolved from habit into practice. She learned to notice what different sounds did to her mood and began using that knowledge deliberately. Predictable, rhythmic tracks help her focus. More complex, improvisational pieces – like jazz – help her break out of hyperfocus and transition into rest. Ambient textures help her wind down before sleep. Each playlist is designed to serve a function.

This is intentional listening at its most human – not a perfect system, but a gentle habit of asking, "What do I actually need right now?" and letting sound answer back. Catherine speaks about it as a form of dialogue with herself: "I love and accept that this is exciting to me, but I'm going to take control here to gently wind myself into a different headspace."

Music becomes her self-coaching language – a way to support rather than suppress emotion. She treats sound like a navigation system, adjusting tempo, texture, and tone according to what her body and mind need. It's a lesson we can all take into our own lives. Music can help us *move between states*, not just dwell in them.

Her approach reflects a core idea explored throughout this book – when we use sound intentionally, we can influence our brain chemistry. Music becomes an accessible form of biofeedback – a sonic mirror for mood, energy, and presence.

## The Playlist of Life

Catherine describes her relationship with sound as "the curation of life's playlist." Each song in her library holds emotional data – memories, feelings, milestones. The concept echoes the science explored in Chapter 10, "Music and Memory" – how melody and rhythm activate the hippocampus, embedding life experiences into musical form.

Her playlists trace emotional evolution. There are songs for confidence, grief, hope, and transition – a living archive of growth. She balances digital discovery with lived connection. Algorithms introduce her to new sounds, but real-world encounters – gigs, family recommendations, unexpected pub bands – make them meaningful.

Music connects her to people as much as to self. "He listens consciously," she says of her father. "We've always talked about music. I bought him a Bonobo CD years ago and said, 'I think you'll like this now.' It became part of our connection."

Music, for her, is a family language. It's also how she makes sense of belonging – a key theme throughout this book. Whether it's a live concert or a shared playlist, music reminds us that we're not alone in what we feel.

## The Autistic Raver

When Catherine calls herself "the autistic raver," she laughs – partly because it's true, partly because it still surprises people, and partly because she likes reclaiming a stereotype and turning it on its head. The image of an autistic person finding joy in a crowded dance space might challenge stereotypes, but for her, it's the ultimate expression of connection.

"There's such a shared energy," she said. "When everyone's feeling the same emotion – that collective swell – it's like empathy in sound. I feel people's joy as if it's my own."

In that moment, music transforms sensitivity into superpower. Her empathy amplifies, connecting her to the emotional current of the crowd. It's not overwhelm – it's resonance. As we've explored in relation to music and social connectivity, oxytocin and endorphins released through synchronized rhythm create shared euphoria. For Catherine, this isn't just theory; it's embodied truth. Joy is her form of regulation.

These moments of euphoric connection reframe what it means to be neurodivergent. They remind us that sensitivity is not fragility – it's depth. Music becomes a bridge between inner intensity and collective joy.

## Sensory Balance and Boundaries

With heightened perception comes the need for precision – or, as Catherine puts it, "the need to know when I'm about to get peopled-out." Catherine knows exactly where her sensory thresholds lie – when stimulation shifts from energizing to overwhelming. She builds boundaries, accordingly, using noise-canceling headphones, quiet recovery days, and open communication at work. Her sunflower lanyard signals her needs without words. Her playlists become tools for self-management.

"I'll put them on and pick a mix I know by heart," she said. "It blocks the world without pulling me into it."

In her corporate environment, she advocates for sound-conscious design – creating spaces that respect sensory diversity. She envisions "health hubs" where calming soundscapes replace silence and private zones where individuals can modulate volume and focus. "Sound is part of well-being," she told me. "Just like light or temperature."

This approach aligns with the broader idea of *environmental well-being*. We thrive when our surroundings support, not assault, our senses. For neurodivergent individuals, this isn't luxury – it's necessity.

## The Mindful Act of Curation

For Catherine, playlist-building isn't some serene ritual – it usually starts with her scrolling through her liked songs thinking, "What do I want for today?" or hitting shuffle and skipping until finding a track that feels right and then go down a rabbit hole of discovery. "It's a gift to yourself," she said.

"You can listen to one song and ask, *How does this make me feel? What do I need next*?"

Creating playlists is more than organization – it's emotional reflection. In a world of pre-made mixes and algorithmic curation, taking time to choose your own songs becomes an act of self-care. It transforms listening from passive to participatory.

This mindful approach reflects how intention is what transforms sound into healing. Curating music consciously strengthens emotional literacy. It helps us learn the subtle language of our own responses – to recognize when we need calm, energy, or catharsis.

Catherine's playlists aren't just lists; they're living documents of self-understanding. "You've put effort into it," she said. "It's yours. And it reminds you who you are."

## Designing a Neurodivergent Soundscape

When asked what she'd include in a neurodivergent playlist, Catherine imagined a sound journey that mirrors human energy itself:

- Euphoric builds for joy and motivation – high-tempo electronic music that lifts mood and ignites movement.
- Lo-fi and ambient tracks for focus – sounds that create safety and concentration without distraction.
- Acoustic and lyrical songs for grounding – musical honesty that validates emotion.

"It would move from euphoria to rest," she said, "a balance between stimulation and calm – or at least a decent attempt at it."

---

In designing your own playlist, try to mirror the biological rhythm of your day – the natural oscillation between activation and recovery. Music can guide that rhythm, offering stimulation when we need to rise, and soothing resonance when we need to settle. Her imagined soundscape becomes a metaphor for balance – not perfection, but *permission* to flow.

Scan the QR code for Catherine's Neurodivergent Focus & Calm Playlist.

---

## Joy as Regulation

Catherine's story is ultimately about awareness – the messy, ongoing kind. Knowing when to move, when to rest, when to disappear into headphones, and when to let joy recalibrate the whole system. Her playlists, her movement, her empathy – they're all expressions of the same wisdom – using music to come back to herself.

For her, joy isn't escapism. It's agency. It's how she takes back control from chaos, how she reclaims meaning in a noisy world. "Music meets me where I am," she said. "And it helps me get back to where I want to be."

It's a truth that sits at the heart of this book. Whether we are neurodivergent or not, music offers us a bridge between emotion and action, chaos and coherence, noise and meaning. Catherine's story reminds us that to regulate is not to flatten experience – it's to dance with it.

## Reflection Prompt

Take a moment for a reflective pause. Think of a song that helps you regulate – something you return to when you're overwhelmed, overstimulated, or in need of grounding. What about it restores balance? Is it the tempo, the texture, the lyrics, or the memories it evokes? How could you build small musical rituals into your own day – to move, reset, or simply breathe?

## Chapter Takeaway

Catherine's story shows that intentional listening can become a well-being practice in itself. Through rhythm, movement, and sound, music can help us navigate the sensory world with more grace and awareness. For some, it may mean using dance to release energy; for others, curating playlists that mirror emotional need. For neurodivergent and neurotypical minds alike, music offers agency – a way to guide, not just feel, our inner rhythm.

When we listen with awareness, we don't just hear music – we remember ourselves through it.

> ***Mantra:*** *Let joy be your rhythm. Let music meet you where you are.*

# 21 Aldo – Music as a Language, a Lifeline, and a Lighthouse

On a cold evening during the COVID lockdown, Aldo Cicchini stepped onto his small Milan balcony with a cheap speaker, his violin, and little more than a feeling. The courtyard below him was silent – two facing buildings, 180 families, each household sealed into its own private uncertainty. His hands were freezing. Nobody knew he was a professional musician. Nobody expected anything from him.

He lifted the violin to his shoulder anyway.

Three minutes later, when he finished the first piece, the night burst into applause – unexpected, generous, and almost disbelieving. He couldn't see a single person, but he could feel them. Balcony after balcony, neighbors leaning out into the early-evening air, responding to something that felt like normality. Like humanity.

The next night, he played again. Then again. Thirty-six evenings in a row, a ritual born from fear, generosity, and instinct. By the third night a neighbor had filmed him and posted it online. By morning it had been viewed ten million times in China alone. Within days, nearly 300,000 people were watching every evening – a global audience held together by the most fragile thread of hope.

"It wasn't about perfection," he told me. "It was about connection."

That line stayed with me. Because in many ways, Aldo's whole life has been a story of connection – found, lost, rediscovered – through music.

---

Scan the QR code for Aldo's YouTube video clip from the first balcony concert.

---

### The Three-Year-Old Who Shushed the Room

Aldo didn't grow up in a musical family. His father was an electrical engineer, his mother a pharmacist. Uruguay in the early nineties wasn't exactly overflowing with violin teachers for toddlers either.

But his grandfather – a builder by trade and an artist by heart – loved poetry, opera, and classical music. Every Sunday, symphonies drifted through the house during family lunches. Mozart, Puccini, Beethoven.

One day, a three-year-old Aldo heard the storm movement from Vivaldi's *Four Seasons – Summer*. He remembers the moment even now.

"I shouted, 'Stop, stop!'" he said. "I wanted everyone to be quiet. That music was giving me something I didn't understand, and I needed to focus on it."

His grandfather saw the reaction and, later, pressed the CD into his small hands and sent him home with it. From that day, Aldo had a ritual. Every afternoon, he'd return from kindergarten, go straight to his room, and listen to the entire CD from start to finish. Then he'd go outside to play.

It was early, instinctive, intentional listening – before he even knew what the word intentional meant.

When he was five, his parents finally found him a violin teacher. Within two weeks, the teacher realized Aldo had perfect pitch. For a painfully shy child who rarely spoke, it became his first fluent language.

"With music, I felt like a superhero," he said. "I could communicate without words."

He would invite neighborhood children over, ask them to play something on the radio, and then – every time – he played it back by ear.

Music wasn't just a talent. It was belonging. It was identity. It was safety.

---

Scan the QR code for Aldo's references and other pieces.

---

## Thursdays – The Quiet Before the Music

Decades later, Aldo now plays first violin in the National Symphony Orchestra of Italy. He performs live on European radio every Thursday and often on television. You'd imagine that performance days would be frantic or full of adrenaline.

For Aldo, they're the opposite.

He lives in Milan. The orchestra is in Turin. So, each Thursday starts with a long journey, a morning rehearsal, and then, hours of nothing. A rare, precious nothing.

"It's like a meditation day," he said. "It forces me to stop. To think. To breathe."

He sits in a small practice room until evening – playing, writing, reflecting, reading, sometimes watching a film. He lets his mind slow down. It's the one day he can't rush around or try to cram too much in. Life quietens itself a little, almost by force.

Thursdays became the first clue to something Aldo didn't fully see until the pandemic: stopping is not optional for musicians. It is part of the art. Part of the health. Part of the connection.

## When the World Paused, He Found His Why Again

During lockdown, Aldo was at home with his wife and two small daughters – almost one and almost four. Like so many of us, he felt helpless. Health systems were overwhelmed. Fear was everywhere. And Aldo, whose entire purpose was built on connection, suddenly had no way to reach people.

"I couldn't save lives," he said. "But maybe I could help protect their mental health."

At 5:55 pm on the first day of Italy's balcony flash-mob concerts, he looked at his wife and said, "I'm going to try this." He stepped outside with his violin and a speaker. Ten degrees Celsius, humidity wrecking the tuning, and not a soul in sight.

And yet, connection found him.

What began as a single 20-minute gesture became a nightly ritual that helped an entire courtyard feel human again. When the videos went viral and strangers across the world began sending messages of gratitude, Aldo realized something he had forgotten in the busyness of professional life.

"I am more me than ever," he said. "Because now I know my purpose. And if you know why you are doing something, the rest is just details."

He also says the experience changed him as a musician.

"I became less of a perfectionist. I stopped waiting for the perfect moment to start projects. During the worst situation, from my home in pyjamas, I had the biggest audience of my life. It taught me to do uncomfortable things – to say yes before I feel ready."

It's hard not to see yourself somewhere in that.

Sometimes the most human work we do emerges from imperfection.

Sometimes the healing shows up in unexpected moments – the ones we never plan and don't feel ready for.

## The Epiphany of the Mahler Moment

Ask Aldo to describe how music creates emotion and he doesn't talk about theory or technique. He talks about lived moments – about memories coded directly into melody.

He remembers playing Mahler's *Resurrection Symphony* for the first time with a full orchestra – 200 musicians, a monumental wall of sound.

"I was living that moment as a gift," he said. "And every time I play that symphony now, I go back to that exact feeling. I have chills for one hour and a half."

He talks about the "*Adagietto*" from Mahler's Fifth Symphony as his recovery music.

"It has the emotions of a lifetime inside eight or ten minutes," he told me. "It starts calm, rises like a volcano, then settles again like sunset."

And Strauss's *Four Last Songs*, which played in his mind as his children were born.

"If there is a heaven," he said, "I'm sure that's the music playing all day."

For Aldo, these pieces aren't just compositions – they're places he returns to. Portals. Time machines. Little emotional fingerprints you only notice when they press back.

You and I might have a favorite song from a teenage summer or a track we played on repeat after heartbreak. For Aldo, the depth is simply amplified through a lifetime spent inside the notes.

## The Conversation Without Words

Performing, Aldo says, is a dialogue. Not metaphorically – literally.

Even in classical music, where applause is saved for the end and etiquette is rigid, he feels the energy of the room. He listens for the unspoken feedback.

"It's like a conversation with the audience," he said. "I give something, and I feel something back."

He dislikes the strictness of traditional concert culture – the "don't clap between movements" rule that intimidates newcomers.

"People are not in jail," he laughed. "Gratitude is always good."

His mission with his string trio is to break some of those boundaries – to make music feel like a shared experience again, not a ceremony.

Because the magic for Aldo is not only in technical accuracy. It's in emotional reciprocity.

## Music as an Antidote to Anxiety

Later in our conversation, Aldo admitted something that many performers hide.

"I'm a very anxious person," he said. "I tend to live in the future."

Music forces him to come back.

"During concerts, if you don't live in the present, you screw up everything," he added. "You must be here, now. You must listen to yourself. You must trust your preparation."

So, he closes his eyes. Feels the bow. Breathes with the melody. Tunes into his colleagues. Tunes out the world.

The effect is oddly grounding – not quite meditation, more like remembering you have a body again.

And although the mechanisms differ – musicians perform while the rest of us listen – the outcome is surprisingly similar.

Music, when given our full attention, becomes a powerful anchor to the present. Anxiety lives in the future. Music tugs us back into the moment – sometimes gently, sometimes like a friend taking you by the shoulders.

And that's why being deliberate with music isn't just some neat idea – it genuinely changes how the moment feels.

## Listen to Yourself First

When I asked Aldo how people can build an intentional listening habit, he paused, then answered with something beautifully simple.

"First you must listen to yourself," he said. "Because you listen to music. Every day I need something different. So, ask yourself, *what do I need today?*"

If he feels sad, he deliberately chooses the saddest music he can find, to go deeper, to release it. A musical catharsis.

If he feels low and wants to lift himself, he finds brightness – Mozart, an Allegro, something playful.

"It's like choosing a movie after a bad day," he said. "Maybe you need comedy. Maybe you need to cry. But first you must listen to yourself."

This is the same principle I use in well-being work – the gift of self-reflection. A few minutes each day to ask: *How am I today? What's driving that? What do I need?*

Music simply becomes the tool that meets the moment.

And Aldo believes deeply that to feel the full effect of music, you must stop multitasking.

"To listen to music," he told me, "you have to force yourself to stop thinking about what you're thinking. To be present. And when you live the present, you start healing from the first moment."

> ***Mantra:*** *Stop. Listen. Be here. And let the music bring you home.*

# 22

# Mark – The Power of Music to Connect, Heal, and Hold Us Together

There are some people whose lives seem stitched together by music. Not as a hobby or a soundtrack running quietly in the background, but as a force that shapes identity, carries memory, creates community, and gives us a way to survive what words alone can't hold. Dr. Mark Deeks is one of those people.

A pianist, choir leader, speaker, with a PhD in heavy metal, Mark has spent his life moving between musical worlds that shouldn't, on paper, belong together – heavy metal, workplace choirs, Northumbrian folk traditions, piano coaching, and well-being retreats. Yet for him, they are all expressions of the same truth – music is the ultimate connector.

And perhaps more than anything, Mark is someone who understands the power of music not just to entertain us, but to heal us.

## The Thread of Identity

Mark's PhD explored how musicians express national identity through heavy metal – a study that takes him deep into the fascinating psychology of how we understand ourselves. He talks about ideas like *imagined communities* such as how fifty thousand people in a stadium might believe they are somehow the same because they love the same band, despite being wildly different in almost every other way.

Identity through music is rarely factual. It's a feeling, a story, something we build inside our own minds. A Nordic band playing a song about fjords taps into mythology for some listeners, history for others, or simply a sense of belonging for those standing shoulder to shoulder in the crowd.

It's why we describe an "Irish sound" or a "Finnish sound," even though the musical ingredients themselves might be almost identical. Music becomes a mirror we hold up to where we think we belong.

And perhaps that's why Mark, who lives in Northumberland, also smiles when he admits something many people wouldn't expect – that he finds Iron Maiden relaxing.

Not because the music is soft – but because it feels like home.

It's a reminder that the relationship between music and well-being is deeply personal. What calms one person may overwhelm another. What uplifts someone might unsettle someone else. The only thing that matters is whether it works for you.

## When Music Becomes Memory

Mark's relationship with music is not abstract – it is deeply lived. One of the most emotional parts of our conversation was when he spoke about losing his daughter, Laurie. At the 20-week scan, he and his wife received news no parent is prepared for – their unborn baby had two terminal conditions.

The song playing at that exact moment was "Nothing's Gonna Stop Us Now" by Starship – their wedding first-dance song, their happiest memory.

In seconds, it became tied to their worst.

For months, neither of them could listen to it. The song that once lifted them instantly became unbearable. They had to fight to reclaim it – listening to a verse at a time, leaving it for weeks, trying again, slowly extending what they could bear. Eventually, they managed to hear the whole song.

"It means a lot to us now," Mark says, "but in a very different way." It is no longer just the soundtrack to joy – it is a testament to their resilience.

Still, that moment wasn't the end of what music would mean in their grieving.

Mark's brother-in-law bought a star in the Andromeda system and named it after Laurie. The star's number coordinates were printed on a chart delivered to their home. Mark looked at the numbers, and something shifted. At three o'clock one morning, he woke with a thought that felt like it had been handed to him. *What if those numbers weren't coordinates? What if they were musical notes?*

He padded downstairs, still half-asleep, and pressed the piano keys softly – just enough to hear what those numbers might sound like.

A melody appeared.

It was instant, simple, and profoundly moving.

It was *hers*.

"If she hadn't existed," he says quietly, "the melody wouldn't exist either. Now she was real because the music was real."

The melody became the closing track on an album he was writing at the time. Most listeners will never know its meaning. To them, it is simply the end of a beautifully atmospheric record. But to Mark and his wife, it is Laurie's theme – a way of holding her in sound.

Performing that piece live is still overwhelming. The first time he recorded it, he had to leave the studio to compose himself. Some music you don't just hear – you feel it in your chest.

And perhaps that is the purest form of identity. Music not as a place you come from, but as proof of something – or someone – you never want to forget.

## Music as a Connector

Much of Mark's professional life is spent helping people feel connected – especially through choirs. He leads workplace choirs, community choirs, and one-off team-building sessions that use singing as a way of bringing people together.

He describes group singing as "the most naked you can get, other than getting naked."Your voice is who you are. There is no guitar to hide behind. No effects pedal. No filters. When you sing, you're exposed.

And yet, paradoxically, that vulnerability is what allows connection.

Most people are self-conscious about their speaking voice – never mind their singing voice – and he sees that nervous shuffle every time he starts a new choir session. But put them in a choir, surrounded by others, and something different happens. The edges of embarrassment soften. The need to "sound good" dissolves into something more important – *collective intention.*

Everyone wants the same outcome. Everyone is part of the same harmony. In that moment, hierarchy disappears. Senior leaders, junior staff, people who've sung for years, people who haven't sung since school – they all contribute equally.

And these days – when workplace belonging can feel a bit thin around the edges – choirs offer something rare. Togetherness that doesn't need explaining or permission.

Just voices. Just people finding their footing together.

## Music as a Well-Being Tool

When Mark speaks about music and well-being, he frames it in practical, accessible terms. He doesn't advocate for grand rituals or complicated systems. Instead, he encourages people to create just three simple playlists: one filled with songs that make you smile, another with music that helps you relax, and a third made up of tracks that remind you of someone you love.

"Everyone can make those," he says. "It takes minutes." When put on the spot, Mark gave us these three selections of tracks that make him smile: "The Evil That Men Do" by Iron Maiden, "Man in the Box" by Alice in Chains, and "Spoonman" by Soundgarden.

These playlists become emotional tools – resources that you can reach for when you need to shift your state. Whether it's to find comfort, energize yourself, or simply pause for a moment, intentional listening helps you choose how you want to feel.

That level of self-awareness becomes easier when you realize something important. Music doesn't need explanation to be effective. It bypasses the resistance we often have to well-being interventions.

Breathing exercises need teaching. Meditation needs guidance. Behavior change models need framing.

But ask someone what song makes them smile, and they can almost always answer immediately.

Music doesn't need warming up or explanation – it simply gets through. It goes straight to feeling. And in Mark's view, that's what makes it so powerful.

---

Scan the QR code for Mark's Music, Loss and Connection Playlist with some "Relaxing Metal."

---

## The Pressure Valve

One of the most striking ideas he shares is the notion of music as a pressure valve. Heavy metal – often dismissed as aggressive or chaotic – has always been his release.

He laughs as he explains that Iron Maiden is, for him, one of the most relaxing things he can listen to.

The drums, the guitars, the energy – it lifts something off his shoulders the way a long run might lift someone else's. Music can calm us not just through softness, but through intensity. Through familiarity. Through catharsis.

"Relaxation doesn't have to be gentle," he says. "Sometimes it's about letting something out."

This is a reminder that well-being isn't one-size-fits-all. Sometimes you restore your balance through quiet piano chords. Sometimes you restore it through a wall of sound.

Either way, music helps you steady yourself again – in whatever way makes sense to you.

## The Human Voice, the Human Story

By the end of my conversation with Mark, the themes were clear. Music slips into all the cracks of a life – shaping who we are, helping us remember what matters, giving us room to feel, and, at its best, pulling us closer to one another.

Mark's story is a reminder that music is not an accessory to life – it is a language for the moments we can't articulate.

Some of those moments are light – a crowd belting out the same chorus, a workplace choir hitting a chord that surprises them, a song that makes you dance in the kitchen without meaning to.

Sometimes those moments are shattering with grief, loss, fear, love and remembrance.

But in every case, music gives us a way through.

For Mark, music is both the map and the memory. It is how he connects to people, how he processes emotion, how he honors his daughter, and how he helps others find belonging.

And for him, it remains one of the most reliable ways back to feeling human.

# 23 Gabby – The Sound of Being Me

The world can feel loud when you hear everything. Every sound, every flicker, every heartbeat in the room. For some, that sensitivity feels like too much – but for my daughter Gabby, it's also her greatest gift. At 14, she's learning what it means to live in a body and brain that process the world in high definition. Music is where that intensity finally makes sense.

When the noise of the day becomes too sharp, she turns to sound that feels like her own language. Through melody, she finds calm; through rhythm, focus; through lyrics, meaning. Music doesn't just help her regulate – it helps her recognize herself.

Gabby's story isn't one of struggle, but of translation. It's about discovering that difference can be rhythmic, that emotion can be tuned, and that sometimes, the surest way to understand yourself is to listen closely to your own frequency – the sound of being you.

## Identity and Empowerment

Gabby identifies proudly as autistic and ADHD, and her understanding of these identities is mature beyond her 14 years – though she'd be the first to admit she's still figuring bits of it out as she goes. She speaks about her neurodivergence not as something to be managed or fixed, but as an essential part of who she is – the source of her creativity, empathy, and sensitivity. Through experience, she has learned that understanding her brain's unique rhythm is the key to navigating the world on her own terms.

Music is central to this understanding. It gives Gabby both language and permission to be herself – especially on days when words feel clumsy or too slow to keep up. When she listens to or plays music, she experiences a deep sense of alignment – as if the sound organizes her thoughts and feelings into something coherent. Music allows her to celebrate what makes her different, and to see her sensitivity not as a vulnerability but as a kind of emotional intelligence. She describes this feeling as "being in sync with myself," though she laughs when she says it, because it's less poetic in reality – more like everything finally stops buzzing for a minute.

Her story reminds us that identity and empowerment are inseparable from self-understanding. Music offers her both mirror and amplifier – a way to see herself clearly and to express things she says she'd "never get out properly if I tried to talk them."

Music helps neurodivergent individuals not just cope with difference, but celebrate it.

## School Overload and Burnout

For Gabby, school can feel like a marathon she didn't sign up for – and definitely didn't train for. Long days filled with back-to-back classes, shifting social expectations, and constant background noise leave her completely drained by the end of the day. The sensory and emotional demands of a typical school environment – bright lights, crowded hallways, overlapping conversations – can feel unrelenting. By the time she gets home, she has nothing left to give – her brain feels like it's been running on fumes since lunchtime.

This exhaustion isn't laziness or lack of interest – it's the cost of constant regulation. Gabby often finds herself needing long stretches of quiet time to recover. She describes these moments not as isolation, but as necessary repair. When she's finally able to put on her headphones and retreat into music, she feels her energy begin to return. The world narrows to something safe and predictable – the beat, the melody, the repetition – like finally shutting a door on a noisy room.

Her experience is a powerful reminder that burnout in neurodivergent young people often begins in environments designed for "average" brains.

The absence of sensory accommodations and recovery time transforms everyday learning into an endurance test.

Overwhelm isn't about effort or ability – it's the cumulative weight of sensory and emotional load.

## Sensory Overstimulation and Emotional Regulation

Gabby describes the world as both fascinating and overwhelming. She can notice things others might miss – the change in tone in someone's voice, the flicker of fluorescent lights, the hum of technology – but these same sensitivities can also be painful. When the noise and activity reach a certain threshold, her brain feels overloaded, as if too many tabs are open at once.

In these moments, she turns to music as her first line of defense. Plugging in her headphones, she creates a sensory bubble where she can filter the chaos into something familiar. Fleetwood Mac's "Dreams" or any rhythmically steady song offers her control. The predictability of the beat provides a sense of safety. The melody doesn't fight for her attention – it guides it.

Music, for Gabby, is not a distraction but a form of sensory design. It transforms her environment, giving her autonomy over what enters her awareness. This autonomy is crucial for regulation; it restores her ability to engage with the world on her own terms.

---

Scan the QR code for Gabby's Playlist.

---

## Music as Emotional Mirror

Gabby's emotional world is vivid and unapologetically intense – sometimes overwhelming, sometimes exhilarating, always unmistakably hers. She doesn't experience emotions halfway; they arrive in full color and volume. Music gives her a safe way to experience this intensity. When she's sad, she listens to tracks like "White Ferrari" by Frank Ocean – not to wallow, but to sit with what she feels long enough for it to loosen its grip a little. When she's joyful, she leans into that energy through lively, rhythmic songs that let her emotions expand rather than be contained.

This way of using music – meeting emotion exactly where it is – gives her a quiet sense of agency, a kind of emotional exhale. She explains that she doesn't use music to change her mood but to "match" it – her way of saying, "I need to feel this before I can move past it." It's a process of acknowledgment, not avoidance. Music becomes both validation and guidance, helping her recognize that no emotion is permanent.

For neurodivergent individuals, music doesn't just reflect emotion – it regulates and validates it.

## Repetition and Focus

Gabby has an instinctive, almost quirky understanding of how rhythm helps her brain focus. When working on long creative tasks like art projects, she gravitates toward repetitive, steady music – particularly electronic tracks with looping patterns and predictable beats. She describes this kind of sound as "something my brain can lean on." Songs like "Emotion" by Purple Disco Machine give her just enough structure to keep her attention from drifting off into the nearest daydream.

For someone with ADHD, maintaining attention can be a constant negotiation between stimulation and distraction. Repetitive, rhythm-based music provides just enough stimulation to keep her engaged, while reducing cognitive noise. The beat acts like scaffolding – steadying her focus without bossing her brain around. In this flow state, time becomes less linear – it bends and expands in rhythm with the music.

Repetition and rhythm provide structure when attention is fragmented.

## Choice Paralysis and Music as Reset

Decision-making can be exhausting for Gabby – not dramatic, just quietly draining in a way most people don't see. On difficult days, even small choices – what to eat, what task to start, what message to reply to – can feel overwhelming. She describes this as her brain being "too crowded to find a pathway through." When that happens, she turns to the piano.

Playing the piano is her way of clearing mental clutter – like shaking out a rug and letting the dust settle. It's not about performing or achieving anything; it's about creating sound in the moment. The physical act of playing – pressing keys, feeling vibration, hearing resonance – grounds her attention. As the music emerges, her thoughts begin to organize themselves again.

This process is a form of cognitive reset. Where language and logic fail, rhythm and movement take over. In minutes, she can move from paralysis to flow. The act of creating music frees her from the pressure of choosing – it allows her to simply be.

Musical play can help break cognitive loops and restore executive function.

## Music as Connection and Joy

Despite her need for solitude, Gabby's relationship with music is also deeply social – something that surprises people who only see the quiet parts of her. She loves sharing songs, curating playlists for friends, and creating the right atmosphere for group settings. In these spaces, her sensitivity becomes an asset – she can read a room faster than she can read a group chat, and she picks songs that pull people toward each other.

In social situations where verbal interaction might feel awkward, music bridges the gap. When others dance, sing, or laugh in response to a song she's chosen, she feels seen and included. The music becomes a shared emotional language, allowing connection without the need for words.

Gabby describes these moments of shared rhythm as pure joy – evidence that her neurodivergent sensitivity can unite rather than isolate her. The same traits that sometimes make social situations difficult – deep empathy, intense focus, emotional awareness – become sources of strength when channeled through sound.

Music transforms sensitivity into social connection – it's both communication and celebration.

## Philosophical Thinking and Deep Musical Analysis

Gabby's engagement with music goes far beyond listening – she dives into it the way some people dive into novels or rabbit-hole Wikipedia searches. She analyses songs the way a philosopher might unpack a text – listening for meaning, symbolism, emotional truth, and sometimes things she admits "probably aren't there but feel true anyway." When she talks about "Pink Matter" by Frank Ocean and André 3,000, she connects the lyrics to ideas about gender, perception, and human consciousness. Her reflections reveal a rare blend of intuition and intellect – an ability to see the world through sound.

For Gabby, music is a language for understanding existence. She isn't just hearing melodies; she's decoding emotional and conceptual systems. This deep pattern recognition reflects how her neurodivergent mind works – connecting ideas across layers, noticing nuance, finding coherence in complexity.

Her analytical listening is a quiet form of empathy – she steps into the emotional landscape of the artist and comes back with insights she didn't even know she was looking for. It's also a reminder that neurodivergent intelligence often manifests not in speed or conformity, but in depth, connection, and curiosity.

Neurodivergent thinkers often engage with art through depth, pattern, and meaning – finding layers that others might overlook.

## Reflection Prompt

Think about the songs or sounds that help you feel most like yourself. When do you use music to find calm, focus, or confidence? What might your own "sound of being me" look or feel like – and how could you use it more intentionally in your daily life?

## Chapter Takeaway

Gabby's story reminds us that music can become a map – a way back to balance, belonging, and self-belief. When she listens, she's not escaping the world but re-entering it on her own terms. Each track she chooses restores order to the noise and turns sensitivity into strength.

In the quiet between songs, she rediscovers what it means to be fully herself – not broken, not too much, but beautifully attuned. And in that moment of resonance, when sound and self align, she teaches us what harmony really means – the sound of being human, in all its vivid difference.

The key insight from the chat with Gabby is that music acts as a portable sensory boundary – it filters chaos into something manageable.

> ***Mantra:*** *You don't need to change your rhythm – You just need to find the music that moves with you.*

# 24

# Tim – The Dance Floor Alchemist: Finding Flow Through Sound

There's a particular kind of magic that happens on a dance floor. The lights shift, the bass hits, and suddenly a room full of strangers starts moving as if they'd planned it. If you've ever lost yourself in that shared moment – hands in the air, smile rising uninvited – you'll know exactly why I wanted to speak with Tim Cullen for this book. Some DJs play great music. Others somehow create a feeling in the room you can't quite put into words. Tim belongs firmly in the second camp. As a long-time Ministry of Sound resident, a respected music producer, and the founder of Mint DJs – an award-winning DJ collective known for bringing dance floor magic to private events and major celebrations – he's spent decades mastering the craft of shaping energy in a room.

We've been friends for years, and I've danced to his sets more times than I can count. But sitting down to talk about the *why* behind his craft opened up a deeper understanding of something I'd always felt instinctively – music doesn't just move our bodies. It stirs something older and deeper – something we often feel before we fully notice it.

## The Power of the Groove

Tim told me he knew from the age of 14 that music and DJing held a power he couldn't quite explain. What fascinated him wasn't just how a record sounded, but how it *landed* – how the right kick drum could ripple across a room and change the entire emotional temperature.

"It's amazing how one track can completely change the atmosphere," he said. "It can make people cry, laugh, feel connected. And as a DJ, you get to guide that."

That word – *guide* – is important. DJing, in Tim's world, isn't about showing off or controlling a crowd. It's about reading the room with the sensitivity of a therapist and the agility of an athlete. Long before a single person stands up, he's scanning for subtle cues. A tapping toe, a nodding head, an exhale that follows the beat.

"You can feel it even when no one's moving," he said. "There's just . . . something in the air."

We found ourselves returning to this idea throughout the conversation – that unspoken feeling between the DJ and the room. It's something classical musicians talk about too – the silent feedback loop between performer and audience, the sense of energy returning like a tide. Aldo, the first violinist I interviewed in Chapter 21, "Aldo – Music as a Language, a Lifeline, and a Lighthouse," described it in almost identical terms. Even in a quiet concert hall where applause is forbidden until the end, he feels the swell of emotion from the seats.

Whether it's Mozart or Ministry of Sound, the human nervous system recognizes when it's being moved.

## Building Trust, Beat by Beat

One idea kept resurfacing that I loved. That of *trust*. A great DJ doesn't walk on stage and immediately empty the bag of bangers. They earn their moment.

"You've got to get the dance floor on your side," Tim said. "Once they trust you, you can take them anywhere."

He talked about starting sets with groove – fun, funky, warm sounds that ease people in. Familiar but not obvious. Energetic but not overwhelming. Then he watches. Waits. Feels them leaning in.

Only then does he start turning the dial.

"If you peak too soon," he said, "you've got nowhere to go."

And this isn't just good DJing – it's understanding how to guide people's emotions gradually, not forcefully. We rarely cope well with intensity when it arrives out of nowhere – we need the build-up, the context. We need build-up, anticipation, narrative. We need a sense that the journey makes sense.

Tim described a set as a kind of musical story, full of rises and falls. Not unlike the shape of a film, with bursts of action followed by moments of stillness. You can't sprint for two hours straight. The body doesn't work like that. The mind doesn't either.

"I often compare DJ sets to James Bond films," he joked. "You need tension, drama, a big payoff – but not all at once."

## The Dance Floor as Human Biology

Tim's instincts line up beautifully with the science. When he talked about how 128 BPM feels "right" in the body, he was intuitively describing entrainment – the phenomenon where our internal rhythms sync with external sound.

Your resting heart rate might be around 70. When you're moving – socializing, dancing, energized – it rises closer to 120–130. A kick drum at that speed doesn't just sound good. Your body recognizes it. The beat becomes a biological signal to move, to connect, and to feel alive.

Music was also part of human communication long before language. We chanted, drummed, swayed, and sang together as early humans. Long before we spoke in sentences, we spoke in rhythm.

"Music came before language," I told Tim, referencing some of the research from earlier chapters. "That's why it taps into such ancient brain circuitry."

He nodded. "Makes sense. Babies respond to tune before they respond to words. And at the other end, people with dementia remember songs even when they don't remember loved ones. It's a different part of the brain."

He's right. Emotion, memory, rhythm – they converge in the same neural networks. Which is why hearing even a *millisecond* of a song can trigger recognition and feeling. Tim laughed as he described a radio game where contestants guessed songs from tiny fragments.

"It's crazy," he said. "There's millions of tracks out there, but you just *know*."

That instinct is precisely what makes him such an intuitive DJ. He can remember almost every tune he's ever played over 30 years – yet struggles to recall the name of someone he met at lunch. Music is stored differently. More deeply. More emotionally.

## The Joy and Stress of Creation

When we talked about music production, Tim revealed a side of the craft that people rarely see. Yes, it's creative and playful. But it can also be riddled with pressure.

"I'm a perfectionist," he admitted. "So sometimes producing is flow . . . and sometimes it's stress."

He described the bliss of the early creative phase, when ideas spill out freely and time dissolves. Hours go by in minutes. It makes sense when you think about what the brain does in flow – self-criticism quietens and ideas move more freely.

But then comes the technical stage – the mixdowns, the EQ tweaks, the countless versions.

"I've worked with people who listen to a snare drum for three hours," he said. "I can't do it. I lose all perspective."

This is where knowing himself really helps him stay grounded. When he feels himself slipping into the perfectionism spiral, he steps away. Makes tea. Moves on. Reminds himself who the track is for. Not the version of him obsessing over frequencies, but the people who'll dance to it.

He uses visualization too. Before a track even exists, he imagines where it's being played – beach bars, open-air terraces, cliff edges in Sardinia. He imagines a dancer hearing it for the first time.

"It takes you out of the computer mindset and back into the real world," he said. "It pulls you out of your head and back into feeling – which is where the best ideas tend to come from."

## The Need for Feedback

Something I found incredibly human was Tim's honesty about needing external validation – something most creative people feel but rarely admit.

"If everyone's loving it except one guy at the front shaking his head, that's all I can see," he said. "It gets in my head."

He told a story about his dad, who ran a restaurant and became addicted to checking reviews. Tim recognized the same pattern in himself. One moment of criticism can overshadow a hundred positives – something most creative people will recognize.

This need for feedback makes livestreaming and radio particularly brutal.

"When you don't get any reaction back," he said, "it just feels wrong. You're playing into a void."

During lockdown, he found digital DJ sets challenging. Without the loop of human energy, it didn't feel like music. It felt like work.

Neuroscience backs this up. We're wired for social reward–micro-expressions, movement, feedback. Remove them, and the brain's mirror systems quieten. We lose the sense of connection that makes music meaningful.

## Music as Self-Care

Toward the end of my conversation with Tim, we moved into more personal territory. Tim has struggled with his own mental health at times. Those experiences shape not just how he plays, but how he lives.

"There were moments I wasn't in a great place," he said. "And going through that makes you more aware of it in others. You see people getting sad or angry and not knowing why."

He supports local mental health charities in Tunbridge Wells and regularly uses his events to raise money for support hubs. But what struck me was how music helps *him*.

He keeps music playing through his home – not pounding club tracks, but mood-setters. Different genres for different days. A way to shift the emotional landscape gently.

But for deeper release, he needs something more physical.

"I've got to get on a dance floor," he said. "Even though I DJ all the time, I don't get to *dance*. And when I do – it's like something lifts off my shoulders."

Anyone who has danced themselves back to life after a stressful week will understand that feeling. Movement, music, being around other people – together they loosen something in you and help you feel more human. It soothes the brain in ways therapy sometimes can't.

## The Moments That Stay with You

Some of the most joyful parts of the interview were the stories – moments that reveal the emotional heartbeat of a DJ's life.

Like hearing his own track unexpectedly played by Bushwhacker at the Brighton Music Conference.

Or the night Carl Cox dropped one of his records at Space Ibiza.

And the time he was given 10 minutes' notice to follow Armin van Buuren at Ministry of Sound – the DJ who had just been crowned Mixmag's number one in the world.

"I remember thinking, *I've got to stay true to myself,*" he said. Instead of playing trance anthems, he stuck to rolling house – his sound, his identity. He went for "Domino's" by Chris Lake & Michael Woods. And it worked.

These stories do more than entertain – they reveal something important – Tim's relationship with music isn't theoretical. It's lived. It's felt. It's personal.

---

Scan the QR code for Tim's references and productions.

---

## Tracks That Change State

I ended by asking Tim to name a couple of tracks that reliably shift a room's mood – a small challenge for someone with thousands of records in his mental library. He chose "Move Your Body" by Xpansions for pure joy, explaining that the piano line "just lifts the whole room." For emotional resonance, he picked "Finished Symphony" by Hybrid, drawn to its strings, tension, release, and the inevitable goosebumps that follow. Together, the two tracks capture exactly what this book is about: the way music can transform our emotional state in a matter of seconds.

## What Tim Teaches Us

Speaking to Tim reminded me once again that music isn't just sound. It's connection and biology and storytelling – and sometimes it feels like a kind of emotional magic you can't fully explain.

He feels what many people sense but can't articulate – that the right track at the right moment can shift a room, a mindset, even a life.

Tim's craft is a reminder that intentional listening isn't about expertise. It's about tuning into how music makes you *feel*. Letting it guide you. Letting it move you closer to joy, to presence, to belonging.

When the beat kicks in and the room lifts with you, that isn't coincidence. It's human design.

And maybe there's a quiet truth beneath everything Tim shared. *We're not just listeners. We're participants. The dance floor happens because we make it together.*

# 25 Sarah – Music, Anxiety, and the Art of Being Human

Sarah Restall has spent her life helping people feel seen. She'd probably laugh at that, but it's true. Her career has carried her through classrooms, charities, corporate corridors, community projects, and the kind of backstage moments where someone finally shares how they're really doing. She is a strategist, an artist, a folk musician's daughter, and a woman who lives with anxiety – not as an idea, but as a force she's learned to understand, recognize, and navigate.

Before all of that, it's worth saying this plainly. Sarah is someone who feels the world intensely, and she has spent years working out how to live with that tenderness rather than against it.

This is her story of how music, creativity, and presence help her soften the sharp edges of anxiety – and how those same tools might help us too. It is also a reminder that the ways we cope are rarely neat or linear; they are shaped by memory, emotion, and the rituals we return to again and again.

## The Shape of Anxiety

For Sarah, anxiety rarely announces itself. It creeps – quiet, insistent, like a shadow shifting before you notice the light has changed.

"It's not a bang," she says. "It's an energy."

She imagines her mind as a room – spacious when calm, filled with ordinary thoughts – dinner plans, a conversation replayed, a worry for tomorrow. But when anxiety rises, that room collapses. Thoughts that normally spread out are suddenly forced through a cardboard toilet paper tube. What was wide becomes narrow. Thoughts rush, collide, cascade like a waterfall – too loud to separate, too fast to reason with.

Words disappear. Heat flares. Her glasses steam. Her heart picks up pace.

"It gets so loud it stops making sense."

It's not a single looping fear – more like fragments of many thoughts flaring at once. *Did I forget something? Am I late? Did I say the wrong thing? What happens if . . .?* It's thousands of overlapping ones – messy, irrational, impossible to untangle. Cognitive behavioral therapy can help, but only when someone else holds the threads. Anxiety, for her, isn't theoretical. It's physical.

## The Fastest Route Back to Herself

When the noise overwhelms, Sarah doesn't reach for logic. She reaches for art.

"Painting is the shortest line back to myself. Sometimes I sit down with shaking hands, paint the first stroke, and feel my breath return."

Art gives her what anxiety steals – structure, rhythm, boundaries. Whether abstract or figurative, making something offers her a pattern to follow – a safe system of color, movement, and intention.

"I think of art as building a bridge into another universe," she says. "We ache to communicate the worlds inside us. Art and music are how we do that."

Her current series, *Happy to Wait*, captures the liminal space most of us rush through. For example, waiting for a friend, a bus, a kettle. Instead of numbing the space with her phone, she pays attention. These moments, once irritations, became scenes she could actually see: steam rising from a takeaway cup, the shuffle of strangers' feet, the slow arrival of a bus in drizzle – have become gifts – small pockets of time to breathe, observe, and notice the beauty she used to rush past.

The link between her art and her anxiety tools is simple – presence, rhythm, containment, truth. But behind that simplicity lies years of trial, error, discovery, and the quiet realization that creativity can sometimes speak when words fail.

## Music – The Constant Companion

Music has never been background for Sarah. It is atmosphere.

Growing up in a folk family, she lived inside music – festivals, jam circles, harmonies drifting through the house. Her father even assigned soundtracks to life. Spicy gumbo demanded New Orleans jazz. Saturday cleaning required opera at full volume.

"I still can't hear opera without smelling cleaning products," she laughs.

Music carries her memories. It maps her inner world, often more accurately than language ever could. A single chord progression can transport her instantly to childhood kitchens filled with steam and chatter, festival fields where she danced barefoot, or long car rides through winding New Zealand landscapes.

And it's one of her most reliable tools for managing anxiety.

## Wide Open Spaces

When anxiety tightens around her, Sarah's instinct is immediate: get outside.

Headphones in. Music on. Step into sky.

The more compressed she feels internally, the more she seeks places that expand – beaches, plains, long open lines of horizon.

"It's not music *and* nature," she says. "It's one ritual."

Her soundtrack for these moments is tender with tracks from Bon Iver, Bonnie "Prince" Billy, Jeff Buckley, Tracy Chapman, Mazzy Star, and more. Songs that feel like a hand on the shoulder.

Sometimes she cries while walking. Not in despair, but in release. The rhythm of her footsteps and the swell of a lyric often meet in a way that feels like being understood. The music gives her permission to feel everything fully, without needing to explain or justify it.

When she needs a different shift, she drives. Windows down, playlist chosen, road humming beneath her. Driving steadies her. Sometimes she stays in the car longer than the journey requires, letting the last 30 seconds of a song finish before she re-enters the world.

---

Scan the QR code for Sarah's Being Human Playlist.

---

### The MRI Lesson

A therapist once told Sarah, "You can't feel anxious while you're singing. Even in your head."

She didn't believe it until she was inside an MRI machine – metallic air, the thud of magnets, the strange pressure of heat on her skin. Enclosed, hot, vision blurred without her glasses.

"I panicked. I had to get out."

She stepped out, breathed, remembered the advice.

Then she went back in and sang – not aloud, but silently. A children's round from school. Five looping lines. Something steady.

For 25 minutes she repeated it. A tiny rhythmic lifeline. Later, she realized it had given her something her anxious mind rarely offers on its own – a sense of sequence, a place to move next, a path out.

"It was the only thing that worked," she says.

Singing shifted her brain out of panic and into pattern. Rhythm replaced chaos. The spiral stopped.

## The Love Letters We Keep

When Sarah left New Zealand, a university friend, also a DJ, promised to send her 100 mix CDs. He titled the first playlist 99 More to Go.

They weren't just mixes. They were love letters.

She kept every one. Some are scratched now, some smudged, but she refuses to part with them. They remind her of a time, a feeling, a friendship – like the afternoon she rediscovered a CD while clearing out a drawer and sat on the floor, listening, smiling without meaning to – moments she might have forgotten if the music hadn't held them safely for her.

"Here are the songs that make me think of you," they seemed to say. "Here's the feeling I want to share."

For Sarah, music has always carried affection more honestly than words.

## Vibes, Cake, and How We Hear

Sarah and her partner, a classical composer, hear music differently.

He listens in layers – snare timbre, harmonic structure, the architecture of sound.

Sarah hears the whole thing at once.

"I don't hear the ingredients," she says. "I hear cake."

One emotional flavor.

In vision, they're reversed, where Sarah sees every detail. Like the keys on the table, the angle of shadow, the exact placement of objects. Her partner perceives atmosphere.

Two sensory maps. Two ways of experiencing the world, both valid, both revealing how differently human beings interpret the same moment.

This is why music affects people differently – and why any well-being tool built around music must be personal, not prescriptive.

## Music as Emotional Environment

Sarah lives inside music. It shapes her days. It softens silence. It helps her work, move, reflect, and rest.

For focus, she leans toward ambient, instrumental sound – often Sigur Rós – music that guides concentration without stealing attention.

For joy, she turns to funk. For momentum, 1990s New York rap. For sadness, she returns to her heartbreak playlist, the one titled For Human Emotions.

Some days she chooses deliberately, selecting a song with the care of someone choosing the right key for a lock. Others, music simply holds her together in the background – like emotional scaffolding she doesn't have to think about but would feel instantly if it disappeared.

## The Workplace: A Future for Music

After two decades supporting workplaces with mental health and culture, Sarah is clear in her view that music belongs at work.

"It supports focus, calms anxiety, creates emotional continuity," she says.

The barrier isn't usefulness – it's taste.

She once worked somewhere that banned headphones during focus work.

"It was bananas," she laughs. "I was twice as productive with music."

Hybrid working has shown people the impact of curating their own environment – light, sound, space, rhythm. Music can be part of that. She once worked with a team who started Friday mornings with a gentle group playlist – three songs chosen by three different colleagues, a tiny ritual that changed the feel of the day, whether through quiet zones, playlists, or simply permission to wear headphones without apology.

## The Aesthetic of Attention

Sarah's story is about attention, how anxiety fractures it and how music gathers it back.

Whether she's painting in morning light, walking with Bon Iver in her ears, singing silently inside a metal tube, or sorting through old mix CDs she can't bear to throw away, music widens the room inside her mind. Some days the shift is subtle – a softening. Other days it feels like someone quietly opening a window.

Not every time – but often enough.

It reminds her she's not powerless. She's in relationship with her mind, not at its mercy.

Intentional listening doesn't change who we are. It helps us return to ourselves, especially in moments when anxiety makes that return feel distant or impossible.

And for Sarah, that return is grounded in rhythm, memory, creativity, and compassion.

*Music isn't just something we listen to. It's something we can live inside of, if we choose.*

# 26 Russ – Tuning Technology to the Human Heart

Russ Newell's life has always moved to a rhythm – from photographing artists in 1970s Peckham to building digital platforms that shape how people experience sound. It's always been there, that pulse he follows instinctively. That creative thread eventually led him to co-found Isofi, an app that merges music, AI, and mental health. "Our aim," Russ explains, "is simple – to help people engage with their mental health through music."

## From Vinyl to Algorithms

Russ's journey began behind the camera, shooting musicians long before the internet existed. He carried that same creative energy into the digital revolution of the 1990s, working with record labels like Sony and artists across genres – from Goldie and Metalheadz to Jamiroquai and Des'ree. He'll tell you it wasn't glamorous, just graft and curiosity. "I brought these guys to the internet," he says with a smile. "It was about connecting creativity with technology – long before tech became cool."

That connection deepened when Russ noticed how his teenage son – and his business partner's son – were both turning to music as a coping mechanism for anxiety and low mood. "We could see how vital music was for them, but also how it could sometimes reinforce rumination. We wanted to find a way to help people use music better – more intentionally."

From that seed, Isofi was born. An app designed to help people *journal their emotions through music*, linking with Spotify to categorize tracks by mood and provide AI-generated reflections and therapeutic guidance.

---

Scan the QR code for Russ's Music and Technology Playlist.

---

## A Life Scored by Sound

Russ's relationship with music runs deep and wide. Growing up in a Jamaican household filled with soul, Bob Marley, rare groove, rock, and punk, his musical education came through family. "My stepdad was a huge music fan – there was always something playing. My uncle was into punk and The Police. So, I grew up with this eclectic mix – I think that's why music touches me so profoundly."

That emotional connection is still vivid today. "There are songs I can't play without crying," he admits. "Music connects me straight back to childhood, to certain places, certain people." He pauses. "At my daughter's mother's funeral earlier this year, music was everything – choosing the songs, listening together, it gave me continuity in grief. It's how I remember her."

Then he adds quietly, "I don't mind feeling sad. Music lets me sit with it," he says, almost in a whisper, like he's stating something he's known for decades.

## The Science and the Soul

Russ speaks fluently about the brain's response to music – the chemistry, the vibrations, the dopamine and endorphins. "We're processing sound on multiple levels at once – physical, emotional, neurological. It's incredible. I'm not a neuroscientist, but I've worked with music therapists who are. They can show how certain keys and frequencies help with pain management or mood regulation. There's real science behind what we feel."

He describes music therapy as "music in action" – a clinical practice rooted in active music-making and emotional expression. But he also believes that everyday listening can have similar benefits. "If you ask someone how they feel, they might struggle to explain. But if you ask them to play a song that matches how they feel, they can do it instantly. Music helps people unpack emotions that words can't reach."

## The Power of Intention

I particularly enjoyed our discussion on *intentional listening* – choosing music with purpose. "Intentional listening's simply having a goal," Russ says, shrugging as if it's the most obvious thing in the world. "You listen to lift your mood, to focus, to dance, to rest. Most people do it without realizing." He believes that giving this habit a name helps people recognize it as a valid mental-health tool.

"Music is as powerful as going for a run or taking a cold shower. It can change how you feel in minutes. The key is awareness – knowing what helps you and using it on purpose."

Russ recalls his love of jazz and classical music – "Haydn, Mozart, chamber pieces . . . intimate, soothing, like a five-piece band in your living room." Music, he says, has always been his way of resetting – "my version of taking a breath," as he puts it. "It's the closest thing I know to meditation."

## When Technology Learns to Feel

Isofi sits at the intersection of that emotional and scientific world. The app helps users decode what they listen to – analyzing songs through AI to explore mood, themes, and emotional tone. Rob tested it with "Electric Feel (Justice Remix)" by MGMT. The AI interpreted it as a song about energy, connection, and emotional release – and Rob agreed completely. "It's like having a music journalist built into your phone," Russ laughs, shaking his head as if he still can't quite believe the tech works. "But with empathy."

Under the hood, Isofi blends AI models with therapeutic frameworks. Weekly summaries reflect a user's mood and listening themes, encouraging small well-being goals. The app even includes writing from accredited music therapists, offering safe guidance and signposting to further support.

Russ is quick to clarify, "We're not trying to replace therapy. We're creating a bridge – helping people engage with how they feel, through music," he explains, hands open, as if offering the idea gently.

## Redefining Personalization

Isofi also challenges the way big streaming platforms work. "Spotify says, 'You liked that, so you'll like this.' But music isn't just about taste – it's about emotion and memory. One person's happy song might be someone else's heartbreak. We want to give people back *agency* – to help them curate their own emotional soundtracks."

In a world dominated by algorithms, Isofi is trying to humanize technology. "AI can either flatten us or help us grow – depends how we use it," Russ says, in that matter-of-fact way of his. "We use AI not to predict you, but to help you know yourself."

## Music as a Mirror, Not a Mask

Russ's most moving insight comes near the end of his conversation with me. "People say 'music is my therapy,' but real music therapy is about using sound to express what you can't say. That's what Isofi is built on – the ISO principle – meeting you where you are emotionally, then gently guiding you toward where you need to be."

It's a principle that echoes the heart of *Music Is the Answer.* That music isn't just a distraction, it's a dialogue – a mirror reflecting our emotional truth. As Russ puts it, "If even one person listens, reflects, and decides to reach out for help because of something they felt through a song – then we've done our job."

## Chapter Takeaway

Music connects technology and humanity in the same breath. Through intentional listening and creative tools like Isofi, we can reclaim agency over our emotional landscape – using sound not to escape ourselves, but to reconnect.

> ***Mantra:*** *Let music meet you where you are – and gently guide you toward where you need to be.*

# 27 Dr. Hazel and Phillipa – How Music Holds Us in Grief

There are moments in grief when language simply falls apart. You reach for a sentence and find nothing there – just a thud in the chest, a hollowing of breath, a feeling too sharp or too shapeless to name. And then a song plays. A familiar chord, a voice, a melody that shouldn't know you at all – and suddenly it does. It carries the weight you cannot hold. It speaks the feeling you cannot form. Music becomes the translator of your heart at the very moment it most refuses to speak.

This is the quiet power of music in grief – it gives shape to the unsayable.

Music to Die For is a project built around a single, disarmingly simple invitation: "Tell us about a piece of music and how it connects you to someone you've lost." What follows from that question is rarely simple at all. People share memories, moments, emotions, and the songs that have become anchors in their grief. The project has become a compassionate archive of stories about love, loss, and the music that helps us hold on.

The two Founders behind the project bring both professional expertise and deep personal insight. Dr. Hazel Harrison is a clinical psychologist and writer whose work explores how we make sense of emotion, memory, and meaning – especially in times of loss. Phillipa Anders spent her career leading community music programs across schools, care homes, prisons, and orchestras, always with a focus on how music can be genuinely useful in people's lives. Together, they created Music to Die For as a space where grief could be spoken about – not through clinical language, but through the songs that carry our stories.

I had the privilege of speaking with Hazel and Phillipa for this chapter. Their perspectives, experiences and the generosity with which they shared them underpin much of what follows.

## Why Music Matters in Grief – The Emotional Logic of Sound

Music's ability to articulate indescribable emotion is one of the reasons it becomes so central in grief. When someone we love dies (or experience deep loss), the system we normally rely on to make sense of experience – thoughts, words, narrative – can stall. Music can step in where language falters. A lyric articulates longing before you've named it; a single sustained note mirrors the ache in your chest.

People often describe this as "being understood" by a piece of music. It is not intellectual – it is embodied. Music bypasses the thinking brain and meets the emotional one with accuracy and gentleness.

At the same time, grief pulls us into emotional states that can feel either overwhelming or strangely muted. Music supports both. It can hold you safely in sadness, providing a frame around an otherwise uncontained feeling. It can also help you move – lifting you slightly, giving you momentum, offering light where there was only heaviness. This natural oscillation between immersion and restoration is central to healthy grieving, and music supports that oscillation in ways words often can't.

Grief is not linear. It pulls you under, releases you, sweeps you sideways, then drops you without warning. Music becomes a steadying companion through this unpredictability. It can hold you safely in sadness or move you gently toward relief when you feel ready. It meets you where you are and stays without pressure or judgment.

## The Disruption of Grief – When Music Disappears

This emotional unpredictability helps explain why, for some people, the early weeks or months after a loss are marked by silence – not just emotional silence, but musical silence. This can be frightening. Music that once soothed now stings. Songs that were woven into daily life suddenly become unbearable.

Phillipa describes this vividly. After her husband died, she couldn't listen to music at all – not in the car, not in the house, not in passing. It wasn't one song that hurt. It was *the whole world* music belonged to: the life she had shared, the identity she had built, the safe place that no longer existed.

This loss of music is a secondary loss – a sign of how deeply grief rearranges the self.

In time, as Phillipa rebuilt her life, her musical identity rebuilt itself too. The songs she returned to weren't always the same as before; her tastes widened, deepened, shifted. Her Spotify "age" may be 22, she jokes, but this playfulness masks a deeper truth in that music becomes part of the story of who you are becoming after loss.

Over time, the music you return to becomes a quiet map of how your inner world is changing.

## Control and Agency – Music as Predictable Ground

All of this sits alongside the truth that grief is disorienting. Your routines fracture, your emotions ricochet, your sense of reality can feel thin and unstable. Amid all this turbulence, music offers a small but meaningful pocket of control.

You can choose what to play, when to play it, how loud it is, and whether it fills the room or sits quietly in your ears.

That tiny moment of agency matters. It reminds the grieving brain that some choices still belong to you.

Many people intuitively craft emotional arcs through music. A playlist may begin at the bottom – slow, sparse, melancholic – and gently lift toward something rhythmic or hopeful. This isn't accidental. It is the psychology of music meeting the psychology of grief.

My own experience of mixing a set that began in deep melancholy and ended in celebration mirrors this natural movement. Music didn't "fix" the pain of depression, but it offered momentum – like a hand on the back, helping you stand again.

---

Scan the QR code for Rob's Uplifter Mix.

---

## Music as Memory – Time Travel, Storytelling, and the Continuing Bond

One of music's most astonishing qualities is its ability to collapse time. A single opening note can lift you out of the present and return you to a teenage bedroom, a first holiday with someone you loved, a wedding dance or a moment you thought you would never revisit.

This time travel can be painful, but it can also be profound. It is a reminder that grief is not forgetting; grief is learning to carry memory differently.

And it isn't only events we remember – we remember feelings. Songs become containers for the emotional texture of a relationship. They hold private jokes, shared journeys, small rituals, and defining moments – those tiny but defining textures of a relationship that music can bring back into the room in an instant.

A song becomes a doorway, not to the death, but to the life.

In the early stages, a shared song may feel unbearable. Later, it might bring warmth, gratitude, or even joy. Over years, the meaning of a song shifts. This evolution is not a sign of "moving on," but of integrating loss into a new way of living.

Music becomes a barometer of where we are – and where we are heading.

## Connection and Community – When Music Holds Us Together

Beyond the personal, music is rarely a solitary phenomenon. Even when we listen alone, we are often singing along with thousands of others who have sung those same notes before. At concerts, funerals, vigils, even spontaneous gatherings on balconies during lockdown, music synchronizes breath, rhythm, and emotion.

This collective energy – what psychologists call "collective effervescence" – reduces isolation. It reminds us we are part of something larger than our loss.

This kind of shared experience echoes what happens across cultures, where music is central to grief rituals. Sometimes solemn, sometimes celebratory, sometimes both, these practices help communities honor the dead, comfort the living, and express what words cannot.

Shared sound becomes shared meaning.

## Serendipity, Signs, and Meaning-Making

Many people describe uncanny musical moments – a song appearing in a supermarket, a radio, an airport, a club – precisely when they needed it. Some call these signs; others call them coincidences. What matters is what the moment *means* to the person experiencing it.

The "disco ball story," where Rachel heard "Everywhere" by Fleetwood Mac at the exact moment she needed a sense of permission and presence, illustrates how music can feel like a message from the person we've lost.

For Rachel, this moment marked a turning point – a feeling that her late husband was blessing the next chapter of her life. Used intentionally, music can hold this symbolic power because it is so deeply entwined with memory and identity. It gives us a way to feel accompanied – even in profound transition.

Meaning-making is not a flaw of grief. It is a function of it.

## The Music to Die For Approach – A New Lens on Grief

This is why the heart of the Music to Die For project is one simple but powerful question:

> "Tell us about a piece of music and how it connects you to someone you've lost."

It opens a door. It gives people a safe starting point – a single song, a single story – from which deeper truths naturally emerge.

To honor this invitation, Hazel and Phillipa read every submission slowly. They listen to the chosen song, take time to reflect, and then write a thoughtful, personal response. Many contributors say it is the first time they have felt truly heard in their grief.

This human witnessing is part of the healing.

And it isn't only the contributors who feel the impact. Readers often describe a quiet shift as these stories open up their perspective – *if they found a way through, maybe I can too.*

One contributor, Jo, realized that reading others' stories gave her a sense of emotional preparedness when her own mother died. The stories had quietly taught her that survival was possible.

## Why We Struggle to Talk About Grief – And How Music Can Help

Despite grief being a universal experience, in many cultures – especially in the United Kingdom – people avoid talking about death or grief for fear of "making it worse." This leads to silence – precisely when grieving people need connection.

Music can offer a gentle, safe way into these conversations. Instead of "Tell me about your grief," we can ask, "Tell me about the song."

"What does this track mean to you?"

This allows the person to share at a level that feels manageable, grounded, and held.

## Practice – Using Music to Support Grieving

Music can match your mood when you need validation, soften it when you need relief, and give shape to feelings that are still forming.

The key is listening *on purpose*, not just letting sound happen to you.

A grief playlist might weave together songs of memory – tracks that belonged to the person you've lost – with pieces that help you cry safely, pieces that gently lift you when you're ready, and songs that connect you back to others.

Families, communities, and even workplaces can use the Music to Die For question as a way to open conversation. It creates bridges between isolation and connection.

---

Scan the QR code for Hazel's Music To Die For Playlist.

---

## Reflection Prompt

*What song connects you to someone you've lost?*

What memory does it hold, and how does it help you feel now? Does its meaning change over time? What might it be inviting you to remember, honor, or release?

Ultimately, grief does not disappear. We grow around it.

Music helps us do that growing. It holds us when we cannot yet hold ourselves and carries parts of love forward in ways words never quite can.

# 28 DJ Paulette – Music as a Lifeline

DJ Paulette has been a defining presence in British dance music for more than three decades. She is known for her longevity, her cultural impact, and her refusal to disappear in an industry that rarely made space for a Black woman to last – let alone lead – on her own terms. Publicly, she is visible, authoritative, and admired. But this is not where her story with music begins.

It begins at home.

The vacuum cleaner is already humming when the music comes on. It's ordinary, domestic, unglamorous – the kind of moment that never makes it into documentaries or press profiles. There is family pressure in the background, the low-grade weight of responsibility and worry that never quite leaves. Her mind is noisy. Heavy. Tired.

Then an 80s track cuts through the room.

Without any conscious decision, her body starts to move. The vacuum becomes a prop, then a partner. There's no choreography, no audience, no intention to perform. She just starts dancing. Not to feel better – just to move. The shift comes later.

Paulette talks about depression not as something that arrives once and leaves forever, but as a long-term companion. "It never goes away," she says. "It just gets less." Over the years, she has learned to recognize its weight, its signals, the way it settles in the body before it announces itself in thought. What she has also learned is that thinking her way out of it works well.

Music, though, does something else.

In moments like this, music isn't entertainment or escapism. It's not about taste, identity, or even pleasure. It is a first line of support – something that reaches the body before the mind has a chance to argue back. The movement loosens something. The noise in her head softens. Not dramatically. Not permanently. Just enough.

This is the role music has played throughout Paulette's life. Not just as a backdrop to success, but as a constant companion through anxiety, burnout, care, recovery, and reinvention. Long before conversations about well-being entered the language of the music industry, music itself was doing quiet, invisible work – regulating, holding, and releasing.

The story of DJ Paulette is often told through clubs, cities, and cultural milestones. But underneath all of that is a simpler truth: when things start to tip, when the pressure builds and the mind spirals, music is where she turns first. Not to fix anything. Just to stay human and wait for that moment to pass.

## The Lost Art of Learning in Public

Paulette didn't learn to DJ in a bedroom, carefully rehearsing transitions until they were flawless. She learned in public.

At the Hacienda, one of the most scrutinized dance floors in the country, she was handed a set of decks and expected to work it out live. Paulette didn't own a set of decks. There were no hours of private practice beforehand, no safety net, no chance to perfect the craft away from other people's ears. The learning happened in real time, with bodies moving – or not – in front of her.

The mixes weren't always clean. Beats galloped. Genres rubbed awkwardly against each other. Sometimes the records didn't behave the way she expected them to. But the room stayed with her. Not because everything sounded right, but because something *felt* right.

What Paulette was learning, without naming it at the time, was that DJing wasn't about technical purity. It was about connection. About reading energy. About staying present enough to recover when things went wrong and carrying on anyway.

Seen through today's lens, this way of learning feels almost radical. In a culture obsessed with optimization, perfection, and pre-validation – where creative work is often hidden until it is polished, filtered, and approved – Paulette's education was the opposite. Mistakes weren't something to be avoided; they were part of the language. You didn't wait until you were ready. You became ready by doing.

That experience shaped more than her DJing. It laid down a pattern she would return to again and again: growth happens inside the moment, not before it. Confidence is not something you acquire and then act on; it is something that emerges *through* action.

This stands in sharp contrast to the perfectionist culture many of us now swim in – one that encourages endless preparation, comparison, and self-editing before we ever show up. Paulette's early years remind us of something quietly important: when creativity is lived in real time, it leaves room for humanity. And that humanity is often what people connect to most.

## Resilience Without Romance

Resilience is often spoken about as something admirable – even noble. In Paulette's life, it was something far more practical.

Growing up, resilience wasn't framed as a quality you cultivated; it was simply how people around her lived. You got on with things. You adapted. You didn't wait for permission. As a Black woman entering a music industry overwhelmingly dominated by white men, that instinct followed her in.

Paulette didn't always notice the barriers at the time. Doors closed, rooms unwelcoming, expectations quietly lowered – much of it only became clear in hindsight. In the moment, she was too busy doing the work. Playing records. Showing up. Staying visible.

That stubborn forward motion mattered. Not because it was heroic, but because it was protective. Pausing to analyze every slight or exclusion would have made it harder to continue. Resilience, in this sense, wasn't about strength as a badge of honor. It was a strategy for survival.

Only later did the pattern reveal itself: resilience as refusal. Refusal to disappear. Refusal to be diminished. Refusal to accept that certain spaces simply weren't meant for her.

But resilience like this is not free. It never is.

## The Cost of Staying

What kept Paulette in the room also came at a price.

DJing, from the outside, is often imagined as instinctive and effortless – a person selecting records while a crowd dances. From the inside, Paulette describes something far more demanding. Every set requires constant processing: reading the room, sensing shifts in energy, managing equipment, shaping narrative, holding confidence steady while remaining emotionally open.

Alongside that cognitive load sits a quieter strain. Gestures from the crowd. Comments shouted mid-set. A look of disapproval caught in the corner of the eye. Each one small, easily dismissed – until they accumulate.

Over time, Paulette began to recognize the effect of that accumulation. The heightened vigilance. The internal scanning for threat or rejection. The way certain moments could pull her out of flow and into self-doubt in seconds. She has likened it to a form of low-level trauma – not dramatic enough to name in the moment, but persistent enough to shape how the body and mind respond.

This is the part of DJing that rarely gets acknowledged: the emotional labor of staying present while being judged, sometimes aggressively, in real time. Resilience kept her working. But it also meant carrying far more than the music itself.

Understanding that cost didn't make her weaker. It gave her language. And, eventually, it opened the door to different ways of caring for herself – ways that didn't rely solely on pushing through.

## When the Body Leads the Way

There is a moment, Paulette explains, when the body knows what to do before the mind can intervene.

In periods of depression, she doesn't reach first for analysis or explanation. She reaches for music, often a classical or jazz piece in the car. Sometimes deliberately, sometimes almost by accident. A track comes on and, without planning it, her body responds. A foot taps. A shoulder rolls. Then movement takes over.

This isn't performance. It's regulation, plain and simple.

The act of dancing – alone, unobserved, unjudged – moves something that words cannot. Energy that feels stuck begins to circulate. The heaviness doesn't vanish, but it loosens. Ten or fifteen minutes can be enough to shift the emotional weather just slightly, creating space where there was none.

Paulette talks about this instinctively, but it aligns with what many somatic practices have long understood: the body can lead the mind out of distress. Music becomes the cue. Movement becomes the release. Thought follows later, if at all.

In those moments, music is not asking anything of her. It isn't demanding productivity, insight, or optimism. It simply invites motion and incites joy. And that invitation, repeated over years, has become one of her most reliable forms of self-care.

## Memory, Identity, and Emotional Time Travel

Some music doesn't just move the body. It moves time.

When Paulette puts on tracks she loved at 16, something remarkable happens. She doesn't just remember that version of herself – she *re-enters* her. She asks, *how did I used to dance to this*? The posture changes. The expression softens. Joy arrives, not as nostalgia, but as a physical presence.

This is not escapism. It's continuity – the difference matters.

In periods when depression threatens to flatten identity into something narrow and colorless, music restores dimension. It reminds her that she has been many things before – curious, playful, hopeful, alive. That those versions are not lost. They are stored, waiting, in sound.

Music, in this sense, becomes a bridge across time. It collapses distance between who she was, who she is, and who she might still become. When life feels fractured or heavy, that continuity matters. It offers perspective without argument.

For Paulette, this is one of music's quiet powers. It doesn't just change how she feels in the moment; it reconnects her with herself across decades. Movement leads to memory. Memory leads to identity. And identity, once restored, makes it easier to keep going.

## Sobriety, Clarity, and Honest Self-Work

For Paulette, the shift toward sobriety was never about reinvention or self-improvement. It was about clarity.

For years, alcohol was woven into the fabric of nightlife and creativity. Drinking was normalized, expected, even encouraged – a way to come down after sets, to cope with travel, to soften the edges of pressure. But over time, Paulette began to notice something unsettling. The days after drinking felt indistinguishable from depression. The fog, the heaviness, the emotional volatility – it all blurred together.

"I couldn't tell where the hangover ended and the depression began," she mentioned.

That realization mattered. If she couldn't accurately read her own emotional state, she couldn't respond to it honestly. Therapy, reflection, self-work – none of it could land properly while alcohol was distorting the signal. Sobriety, then, became less a decision about abstinence and more a decision about truth.

Paulette is clear about this, and unapologetic. In her experience, therapy does not work without sobriety. Not because alcohol is immoral or forbidden, but because it interferes. It numbs, masks, and muddies what needs to be felt and understood.

Removing alcohol didn't make life easier overnight. It made it clearer. Feelings arrived without disguise. Low moods could no longer be written off as chemical aftermath. Anxiety had to be met directly. That honesty was uncomfortable – but it was also freeing.

Sobriety, in this sense, became a foundation rather than a fix. A way of establishing a reliable baseline from which everything else could be addressed. It allowed Paulette to distinguish between what was situational, what was emotional, and what required deeper attention.

This is not presented as a rule or a prescription. It is simply her lived reality. For Paulette, clarity came first. Everything else followed.

## Therapy as Practice, Not Cure

Therapy, for Paulette, was never about being fixed or made "better" but about accepting and integrating all of "what is."

There was no single breakthrough moment, no clean before-and-after line. Instead, it unfolded as a long, uneven practice – something returned to again and again, sometimes with hope, sometimes with resistance, sometimes simply because there was no other honest option.

Over the years, she tried different approaches, not in search of a miracle cure, but in search of understanding. Some things helped a little. Some helped for a while. Others didn't land at all. What mattered was not the method, but the willingness to stay with the process.

One form of therapy did stand out later in life: EMDR (Eye Movement Desensitization and Reprocessing). Not because it erased the past, but because it shifted her relationship to it. Experiences that once carried a sharp emotional charge softened. The memories were still there, but they no longer hijacked the present in the same way.

That distinction matters. For Paulette, mental health has never been about eliminating pain or difficulty. It has been about reducing its grip. About creating enough internal space to respond, rather than react.

Therapy worked best when it was paired with the clarity sobriety brought. Without alcohol blurring the signal, sessions became more honest. Feelings arrived cleanly. Patterns could be recognized without distortion. The work became quieter, but deeper.

Seen this way, therapy isn't a destination. It's a practice – imperfect, cumulative, and personal. Something you engage with over time, adjusting as life changes. For Paulette, that ongoing commitment to understanding herself has been as important as any single intervention.

## Designing for Longevity

If resilience kept Paulette going, longevity required something different.

Years of touring, late nights, early travel, and constant transitions take a quiet toll. Airports blur into clubs. Sleep becomes irregular. The body absorbs more than it has time to process. For a long time, Paulette did what many people in creative industries do – she endured it.

Eventually, that approach stopped working.

Designing for longevity didn't mean doing less of what she loved. It meant learning to respect her own limits. Planning became an act of care rather than control – a way of protecting energy instead of extracting from it. Rest days were no longer indulgent. They were necessary. Recovery was treated as part of the work, not something separate from it.

This wasn't about productivity or optimization. It was about sustainability. About recognizing that creative work draws from emotional and physical reserves, and that those reserves need deliberate replenishment.

Paulette began to think more intentionally about how she moved through her year, not just her week. When to say yes. When to step back. When to leave space between commitments so that music could remain something she *gave* from, rather than something that depleted her.

Longevity, she realized, isn't built through endurance alone. Endurance only gets you so far. It's built through self-respect – through choices that allow you to stay present, engaged, and well enough to keep doing the work you care about over the long term.

## Music, Community, and Shared Survival

Music has never worked only at an individual level for Paulette. It never really could.

During the pandemic, when clubs went quiet and the usual structures of nightlife collapsed, she began livestreaming sets from home. At the time, it felt simple – a way of staying connected, of keeping music moving when everything else had stopped.

The impact became clear much later.

Years on, people still approach her to talk about those streams. Not about track selections or mixing, but about how they felt. Alone in their kitchens or living rooms. Frightened, isolated, unsure how long the world would remain closed. The music gave shape to time. It marked evenings. It offered rhythm when days blurred into one another.

Paulette didn't set out to provide comfort or therapy. But music did what it has always done best – it regulated collectively. It reminded people they were not alone, even when physically separated. That someone else was there, listening too.

This is one of the quiet truths of music: it works across scales. It can meet you privately, through headphones, in moments of distress or reflection. And it can gather people together, creating shared emotional space where meaning emerges between listeners.

For Paulette, those two functions have always been intertwined. Music holds the individual, but it also binds communities. It becomes a shared language for feeling – one that doesn't require explanation, only presence.

## Presence, Listening, and the Fragility of the Moment

There is one shift Paulette has noticed more than most over the years: how rarely people now allow themselves to be fully present with music.

In clubs, phones rise instinctively. Moments are documented before they are felt. A set becomes something to capture rather than something to inhabit. Paulette doesn't say this with judgment – she understands the impulse. But she has seen what gets lost in the exchange.

Recording a moment changes your relationship to it. Attention moves outward. The body leaves first, even if you're still standing on the dance floor. Music that once passed directly through you becomes something you hold at arm's length.

She often contrasts this with spaces where deep listening still exists – concert halls, orchestras, places where the expectation is not to record but to receive. The silence between notes matters. So does the stillness of the audience. Presence becomes collective.

For Paulette, intentional listening is not about rules or nostalgia. It's about allowing music to do its work. To move the body. To shift emotion. To create memory that lives inside you rather than on a screen.

In a culture that encourages constant capture, choosing presence is a small but meaningful act of care. One that brings the listener back into relationship – with the music, with the moment, and with themselves.

## Music as a Friend for Life

Toward the end of our conversation, Paulette returns to a simple truth about DJing – one that feels earned. At its best, she says, it isn't about technical skill or flawless transitions. It's about storytelling.

A DJ, in her eyes, is someone who reads a room and tells the story with sound – shaping emotional arcs, holding attention, knowing when to build and when to let things breathe. It's a form of communication that doesn't rely on words, but on feeling. And it's one she has been practicing, refining, and living inside for most of her adult life.

That idea lands with particular weight here. This is the final story chapter of *Music Is the Answer*, before the book turns toward its conclusion. And Paulette's story offers something quietly fitting as a way to close this part of the journey.

Across this chapter, music has appeared not as performance or product, but as companion. As something that regulates the body when the mind is overwhelmed. That reconnects us to who we've been when the present feels narrow and who we are if the future feels dark. That allows truth to surface, clarity to form, and community to gather – sometimes in clubs, sometimes in kitchens, sometimes alone with a vacuum cleaner humming in the background.

Storytelling, in this sense, isn't only what DJs do behind the decks. It's what music does for all of us. It helps us make sense of our inner worlds, not by explaining them, but by giving them shape and movement.

Paulette's relationship with music reminds us that you don't need expertise, confidence, or a perfect setup to begin. You don't need to optimize or perform your listening. You simply need to let music meet you where you are – and allow it to stay with you, as it has with her, across a lifetime.

---

Scan the QR code for DJ Paulette's Global Residency Mix – Ep 12.

---

# 29 Conclusion – An Invitation

This final chapter is not here to summarize what you've read so far. It's here to help you feel it.

What follows brings together the science, the stories, and the practices you've encountered in these pages but shifts the emphasis away from explanation and toward lived experience – away from what music *can* do and toward how it shows up in real life.

Rather than offering you answers or prescriptions, this chapter stays with experience. It reflects on what music can offer when things are difficult, unsettled, or unresolved – not as a cure, but as a companion. The intention is that you feel met and supported as you read, not instructed; invited into your own relationship with music, rather than told how to use it.

## Music Is Not a Talent – It's a Human Capacity

For many of us, music has been quietly placed behind a rope. We are encouraged to listen, to admire, to consume – but not to participate. Somewhere along the way, we absorbed the idea that music belongs to the talented, the trained, or the confident, and that unless we can do it *well*, it isn't really for us.

But music was never meant to be a performance reserved for the few. It is a human capacity, not a specialist skill. Long before concert halls, streaming platforms, or music lessons, we sang to soothe babies, to coordinate work, to grieve, to celebrate, and to connect. Making music was not about ability or outcome – it was about participation.

This was a theme in my conversations with Mark Deeks. Again and again, he made the point – when we strip music of expectation and judgment, we discover that almost everyone can benefit from making it. Not to impress, not to perfect, but simply to express. To feel. To be present.

Making music doesn't have to look like learning an instrument or standing on a stage. It can be humming under your breath, tapping a rhythm on the table, singing badly in the car, loading up a simple beat, or playing with sound for a few minutes at the end of the day. What matters is not how it sounds to others, but how it feels to you.

When we reframe music in this way, something loosens. The pressure to be good falls away, and in its place comes permission – permission to explore, to play, and to connect. The goal is no longer to produce something impressive, but to inhabit the moment you are in.

Music, in this sense, is not something you earn through talent. It is something you return to through presence.

## When the Body Sings, the Mind Softens

When we are anxious, panicked, or overwhelmed, our instinct is often to think our way out. We try to reason with our thoughts, analyze what's happening, or search for reassurance. But in those moments, the mind is rarely the place where relief begins.

The body gets there first.

One of the most striking observations shared by Sarah is that it is extremely difficult – if not impossible – to experience a full panic attack while singing. This isn't because singing magically removes fear, but because it changes what the body is doing. Breath slows and deepens. The voice vibrates through the chest and throat. Attention shifts from threat to sensation.

In other words, singing interrupts the physiological pattern that panic depends on.

That is what makes music so powerful in moments of acute anxiety or overwhelm. It works from the bottom up, engaging breath, rhythm, and sensation before the thinking mind has a chance to spiral. Often, before we can make sense of what we're feeling, the body has already begun to respond.

You don't need to sing well for this to work. You don't even need words. Humming, chanting, or quietly vocalizing along to a melody can be enough to soften the nervous system and create a sense of steadiness. What matters is not performance, but participation.

This is also why music can feel more accessible than other well-being tools when things are intense. When thinking feels unreliable or exhausting, the body still knows how to breathe, move, and resonate. Music gives it something to work with.

In moments when the mind feels loud or unmanageable, letting the body lead – through sound, rhythm, or voice – can be the gentlest way back to safety.

## Before We Listen to Music, We Have to Listen to Ourselves

One of the most important shifts I've learned through this work is that music is rarely the starting point. We are.

It can be tempting to treat music as a quick solution – something we put on to change how we feel, distract ourselves, or push through what's difficult. And sometimes, that's exactly what we need. But without a moment of awareness, music can just as easily become background noise, or another way of avoiding what's really going on.

Aldo, a world-class musician, put this far more simply. If we want music to genuinely support our well-being, we first need a basic understanding of ourselves – our moods, our patterns, our inner state. Music is most effective when it meets a need we've taken the time to notice.

That doesn't require deep introspection or analysis. It can be as simple as pausing before pressing play and asking a gentle question. *What do I need right now?* Comfort, energy, focus, release, reassurance? The answer doesn't have to be precise. The act of noticing is often enough.

When we listen to ourselves first, music stops being something we use to override our experience and becomes something that reflects it. It can mirror how we're feeling, help us process it, or gently guide us somewhere else – but only if we're honest about where we're starting from.

In this way, music becomes less of a mask and more of a mirror. Not something to drown things out, but something that helps us tune in.

The paradox is that by taking a moment to listen inwardly, we often find that music meets us more fully. Not because we chose the "right" track, but because we chose to pay attention.

## Holding the Unsayable – Music, Grief, and Emotional Pain

There are moments in life when words stop working.

Grief, loss, and emotional pain don't arrive neatly packaged or easily explained. They are often heavy, confusing, and contradictory. We can want to talk and yet have nothing to say. We can feel everything at once or feel nothing at all. In those moments, language can feel inadequate, even intrusive.

Music offers something different. It doesn't ask us to explain or resolve what we're feeling. It doesn't demand progress or clarity. Instead, it creates a space where emotion can exist without needing to be fixed.

For many people, music becomes a companion in grief rather than a solution to it. A song can sit alongside sadness, hold it, give it shape, or simply acknowledge its presence. It can allow tears to come or provide a moment of steadiness when everything else feels unmoored.

This is one of music's quiet strengths. It gives us permission to feel deeply and slowly, without rushing toward acceptance or closure. It allows pain to move at its own pace. In doing so, it reminds us that experiencing emotion is not a problem to be solved, but a human process to be honored.

Sometimes music mirrors what we are carrying. At other times, it offers contrast – a small reminder of beauty, connection, or continuity when those things feel distant. Neither is better than the other. What matters is that we are not alone with what we feel.

In grief and emotional pain, music doesn't heal by erasing the hurt. It heals, if it heals at all, by staying with us. By holding the unsayable when words fall short, and by offering presence when everything else feels fragile.

## Finding Focus When the Mind Won't Settle

For many of us, difficulty focusing isn't a lack of discipline or motivation. It's a sign that the mind is overloaded, restless, or pulled in too many directions at once. The harder we try to force concentration, the more it seems to slip away.

Music offers a different route in. Rather than demanding focus, it invites it.

When the right music is playing, attention often gathers naturally. A rhythm provides structure. A melody offers continuity. Instead of battling distraction, the mind has something to rest on, something to move with. Focus emerges not through effort, but through absorption.

For this reason, music can be a powerful support for work, study, or any task that requires sustained attention. It helps narrow the field of awareness without shutting it down. External noise fades, internal chatter softens, and the mind becomes more available to what is in front of it.

This can be especially true for neurodivergent people, where focus and regulation are often closely linked. In conversations with Gabby and Catherine, this came through clearly. Music wasn't just helpful in getting things done – it was a lifeline. A way of creating structure, predictability, and emotional safety in environments that might otherwise feel overwhelming or chaotic.

The key, as ever, is fit. Music that supports focus for one person may distract another. Lyrics might help some people and overwhelm others. Tempo, familiarity, and emotional tone all matter. Finding what works is less about following rules and more about noticing how different sounds affect your attention.

When focus is difficult, music doesn't act as a switch that suddenly makes everything easy. But it can act as an anchor – something steady to return to when the mind wanders. In that sense, it doesn't force concentration. It makes it possible.

For a restless mind, that gentle support can be the difference between pushing through and settling in.

## Curiosity Is the Missing Ingredient

If there is one habit that consistently gets in the way of using music well, it is the urge to get it right.

We look for the perfect playlist, the optimal tempo, the track that will finally calm us down, lift us up, or sharpen our focus. Sometimes it works, and it can feel like a small victory. Other times it doesn't, and it's easy to assume we've chosen badly, or that music simply isn't helping.

But music doesn't respond well to optimization. It responds to curiosity.

What supports your well-being today may not support it tomorrow. The song that steadied you once might irritate you another time. Your nervous system changes, your circumstances change, and your relationship with music changes too. This isn't inconsistency – it's information.

Approaching music with curiosity means experimenting rather than judging. Noticing rather than evaluating. Asking simple questions: *What happens if I listen to this? How does my body respond? Does this bring me closer to what I need, or push me further away?*

Over time, this way of listening builds trust. Not just in music, but in yourself. You begin to recognize patterns, preferences, and responses that are uniquely yours. You stop searching for universal answers and start developing a personal language with sound.

Curiosity removes pressure. It turns music from a test you can pass or fail into a conversation you can return to. And in doing so, it keeps the door open – allowing music to keep meeting you, again and again, wherever you happen to be.

## Music as a Practice, Not a Prescription

One of the quiet shifts that happens when we begin to relate to music differently is that it stops being something we reach for only when things are falling apart.

It becomes part of the rhythm of everyday life.

Music tends to support us best when it is woven into our days in small, repeatable ways – not held back as a last resort or brought out only in moments of crisis. This might look like a familiar track on the morning walk, a playlist that signals the end of the working day, a song you return to before sleep, or a few minutes of making sound simply because it helps you arrive where you are.

None of these practices are dramatic. They don't need to be. What matters is their consistency. Returning to music again and again, even when it feels ordinary, messy, or unremarkable, builds a relationship that can be relied on when things are harder.

Seen this way, music isn't a prescription to be followed or a technique to be deployed. It's a practice – something that evolves alongside you, responding to different seasons of your life rather than fixing them.

Some days that practice will feel supportive and steady. Other days it may feel flat, irritating, or out of reach. That doesn't mean it has stopped working. It simply means you're human, and that your needs are shifting.

When we allow music to meet us where we are – rather than where we think we should be – it becomes less about managing ourselves and more about accompanying ourselves. And that, over time, is what gives it its quiet power.

## When It Was Dark, Music Became the Light

I am writing this at a time when I am living through the most difficult episode of depression I have experienced in many years. My thoughts have been dark. My mind restless and hard to settle. Even in moments of quiet, there has been a constant sense of unease – a feeling of being unable to fully land anywhere.

In the middle of this, I made a simple decision. I decided to make some music again.

It wasn't a grand plan or a therapeutic intervention. It was something I used to do regularly but had quietly slipped away in recent months as life filled the available space. I found the time on two long train journeys to visit my mum in Wales. Hours of track, movement, and enforced stillness – the kind of space where thoughts usually spiral.

Instead, I opened my laptop and began to produce.

I became so absorbed in the process that I missed my stop. By the time I realized, the train was already pulling away, and what should have been a straightforward journey had gained another two hours. Ordinarily, that would have been frustrating. On this occasion, it barely registered. I was locked into the creative process, fully present in what I was making.

What struck me afterwards was not just how focused I had been, but how I had felt while doing it. The familiar weight of depression – the heaviness, the looping thoughts – simply wasn't there. Much like Sarah's observation that it is almost impossible to experience a panic attack while singing, I realized that while I was producing, I wasn't experiencing depression. I was engaged, absorbed, alive in the moment.

The track itself reflects that emotional space. It is melancholic, built on emotive chords that carry a sense of sadness and longing. But woven through it is a more uplifting synth line – something lighter, more hopeful, refusing to let the piece sink entirely into darkness. As the track took shape, I came across a spoken-word sample: "Tell me when it's dark, I will be your light." The line landed immediately. It felt like the right words for the music, and for where I was.

---

Scan the QR code to listen to "I will be your light."

---

My track isn't perfect or polished and it doesn't need to be heard. But it is real. It is a record of a moment when music didn't solve anything, didn't fix my life or erase the difficulty but did something just as important. It held me. It gave my mind somewhere to rest. It reminded me that feeling and focus were still available to me, even in the midst of darkness.

*For me, music was – and remains – the answer.*

## An Invitation, Not an Instruction

If there is one thing I hope you take from this book, it is not a method, a playlist, or a set of rules. It is an invitation.

Music doesn't ask us to get it right. It asks us to show up.

Intentional listening is often misunderstood as another thing to do well – another lever to pull in the hope of feeling better. But at its heart, it is much simpler than that. It is the practice of noticing. Noticing how a piece of music lands in your body. Noticing what it stirs, what it settles, what it brings closer and what it allows to soften.

Sometimes intentional listening means choosing a song because you know, from experience, that it helps. At other times, it's about letting a track find you unexpectedly. And sometimes it means turning the music off altogether and sitting in the quiet, allowing whatever is there to be there.

There will be days when music lifts you, days when it holds you, and days when it simply keeps you company. None of these are failures. They are different forms of the same relationship.

Your needs will change. The music that works for you now may not work next week, or next year. That isn't a problem to be solved – it's a sign that you're paying attention.

So, take what you need from these pages, and leave the rest. Sing if you feel like singing. Make music if you feel the pull to create. Build playlists, dismantle them, return to the same song on repeat, or sit in silence. There is no correct way to use music in your life.

Whatever shape that relationship takes, and however often you return to it, you don't have to rush, perform, or get it right.

> *Music will be there. Waiting for you.*

# References

## Chapter 1: Music and the Brain

Levitin, Daniel J. 2006. *This Is Your Brain on Music: The Science of a Human Obsession*. New York: Dutton.

Varèse, Edgard and Chou Wen-Chung. 1966. "The Liberation of Sound." *Perspectives of New Music* 5: 18. https://doi.org/10.2307/832385.

## Chapter 3: Intentional Listening and Building Playlists

Chanda, Mona Lisa and Daniel J., Levitin. 2013. "The Neurochemistry of Music." *Trends in Cognitive Sciences* 17 (4): 179–193. https://doi.org/10.1016/j.tics.2013.02.007.

Ferguson, Yuna L. and Kennon M. Sheldon. 2013. "Trying to Be Happier Really Can Work: Two Experimental Studies." *The Journal of Positive Psychology* 8 (1): 23–33. https://doi.org/10.1080/17439760.2012.747000.

Krause, Amanda E., Jane W. Davidson, and Sandra Garrido. 2020. "The Social and Emotional Uses of Music in Mental Health Contexts." *Musicae Scientiae*. Advance online publication. https://doi.org/10.1177/10298649231203628.

Saarikallio, Suvi and Jukka Erkkilä. 2007. "The Role of Music in Adolescents' Mood Regulation." *Psychology of Music* 35 (1): 88–109. https://doi.org/10.1177/0305735607068889.

Thoma, Myriam V., Roberto La Marca, Rebecca Brönnimann, Linda Finkel, Ulrike Ehlert, and Urs M. Nater. 2013. "The Effect of Music on the Human Stress Response." *PLoS ONE* 8 (8): e70156. https://doi.org/10.1371/journal.pone.0070156.

## Chapter 4: Stress, Recovery, and Rhythm

Bernardi, Luciano, Carolina Porta, and Peter Sleight. 2006. "Cardiovascular, Cerebrovascular, and Respiratory Changes Induced by Different Types of Music in Musicians and Non-Musicians: The Importance of Silence." *Heart* 92 (4): 445–452. https://doi.org/10.1136/hrt.2005.064600.

Koelsch, Stefan. 2014. "Brain Correlates of Music-Evoked Emotions." *Nature Reviews Neuroscience* 15 (3): 170–180. https://doi.org/10.1038/nrn3666.

Mental Health UK. 2025. "Burnout Report 2025 Reveals Generational Divide in Levels of Stress and Work Absence." *Mental Health UK Blog*, February. https://mentalhealth-uk.org/blog/burnout-report-2025-reveals-generational-divide-in-levels-of-stress-and-work-absence/.

Onieva-Zafra, María Dolores, Adelaida María Castro-Sánchez, Guillermo A. Matarán-Peñarrocha, and Carmen Moreno-Lorenzo. 2013. "Effect of Music as Nursing Intervention for People Diagnosed with Fibromyalgia." *Pain Management Nursing* 11 (4): 233–238. https://doi.org/10.1016/j.pmn.2010.09.004.

Robinson, Bryan. 2025. "Job Burnout at 66% In 2025, New Study Shows." *Forbes*, February 8. https://www.forbes.com/sites/bryanrobinson/2025/02/08/job-burnout-at-66-in-2025-new-study-shows/.

World Health Organization. 2024a. "Mental Health at Work: Fact Sheet." *WHO News Room*. https://www.who.int/news-room/fact-sheets/detail/mental-health-at-work.

Yerkes, Robert M. and John D. Dodson. 1908. "The Relation of Strength of Stimulus to Rapidity of Habit-Formation." *Journal of Comparative Neurology and Psychology* 18 (5): 459–482. https://www.yorku.ca/pclassic/Yerkes/Law/.

## Chapter 5: Music, Sleep, and Restoration

Abeln, Vera, Jürgen Kleinert, Hans-Christian Strüder, and Sabine Schneider. 2014. "Brainwave Entrainment for Better Sleep and Post-Sleep State of Young Elite Soccer Players – A Pilot Study." *European Journal of Sport Science* 14 (5): 393–402. https://pubmed.ncbi.nlm.nih.gov/23862643/.

Calamassi, Davide and Giuseppe Pomponi. 2019. "Music Tuned to 440 Hz Versus 432 Hz and the Health Effects: A Pilot Observational Study." *Explore* 15 (4): 283–290. https://pubmed.ncbi.nlm.nih.gov/31031095/.

Institute of Medicine. 2006. *Sleep Disorders and Sleep Deprivation: An Unmet Public Health Problem*. Washington, DC: The National Academies Press. https://nap.nationalacademies.org/catalog/11617/sleep-disorders-and-sleep-deprivation-an-unmet-public-health-problem.

Kumar, Anil M., Frances Tims, Douglas G. Cruess, Margaret J. Mintzer, Gail Ironson, David Loewenstein, and Mahendra Kumar. 1999. "Music Therapy Increases Serum Melatonin Levels in Patients with Alzheimer's Disease." *Alternative Therapies in Health and Medicine* 5 (6): 49–57. https://pubmed.ncbi.nlm.nih.gov/10550905/.

National Sleep Foundation. 2005. "2005 Sleep in America Poll." WB&A Market Research. https://www.thensf.org/wp-content/uploads/2021/03/2005_summary_of_findings.pdf.

Roehrs, Thomas and Timothy Roth. 2001. "Alcohol Use as a Sleep Aid: Concerns and Consequences." *Alcohol Research & Health* 25 (5): 493–497. https://pubmed.ncbi.nlm.nih.gov/11584549/.

Thoma, Myriam V., Roberto La Marca, Rebecca Brönnimann, Linda Finkel, Ulrike Ehlert, and Urs M. Nater. 2013. "The Effect of Music on the Human Stress Response." *PLoS ONE* 8 (8): e70156. https://doi.org/10.1371/journal.pone.0070156.

## Chapter 6: Music, Focus, Work, and Learning

Ferreri, Laura, Emmanuel Bigand, and Aude Bugaiska. 2013. "The Influence of Music on Memory: Emotionally Valenced Music Enhances Memory." *Frontiers in Psychology* 4:541. https://doi.org/10.3389/fpsyg.2013.00541.

Gallup. 2023. *State of the Global Workplace*. Gallup Report. https://www.gallup.com/workplace/349484/state-of-the-global-workplace.aspx.

Gold, Benjamin P., Michael J. Frank, Brigitte Bogert, and Elvira Brattico. 2019. "Pleasurable Music Affects Reinforcement Learning According to the Listener." *Frontiers in Psychology* 10: 1505. https://doi.org/10.3389/fpsyg.2019.01505.

Kahneman, Daniel. 1973. *Attention and Effort*. Englewood Cliffs, NJ: Prentice Hall.

Karageorghis, Costas I. and David-Lee Priest. 2012. "Music in the Exercise Domain: A Review and Synthesis." *International Review of Sport and Exercise Psychology* 5 (1): 44–66. https://pmc.ncbi.nlm.nih.gov/articles/PMC3339578/.

King's College London. 2022. *How People Focus and Live in the Modern Information Environment*. Policy Institute Report. https://www.kcl.ac.uk/policy-institute/assets/how-people-focus-and-live-in-the-modern-information-environment.pdf.

Ludke, Karen M., Fernanda Ferreira, and Katie Overy. 2014. "Singing Can Facilitate Foreign Language Learning." *Memory & Cognition* 42 (1): 41–52. https://doi.org/10.3758/s13421-013-0342-5.

Mark, Gloria, Victor M. Gonzalez, and Jean Harris. 2005. "No Task Left Behind? Examining the Nature of Fragmented Work." *Proceedings of the SIGCHI Conference on Human Factors in Computing Systems*, 321–330. https://www.ics.uci.edu/~gmark/chi08-mark.pdf.

Mark, Gloria, Daniela Gudith, and Ulrich Klocke. 2008. "The Cost of Interrupted Work: More Speed and Stress." *Proceedings of the SIGCHI Conference on Human Factors in Computing Systems*, 107–110. https://doi.org/10.1145/1357054.1357072.

Posner, Michael I. and Steven E. Petersen. 1990. "The Attention System of the Human Brain." *Annual Review of Neuroscience* 13: 25–42. https://doi.org/10.1146/annurev.ne.13.030190.000325.

Rainey, David W. and Janet D. Larsen. 2002. Improved Memory for Proper Names When They Are Learned Through Song. Memory & Cognition, https://doi.org/10.1525/mp.20.2.20.2.173.

Ritter, Simone M., Sam Ferguson, and Rick B. van Baaren. 2012. "Music and Creativity: The Effects of Background Music on Divergent

Thinking." *Psychology of Music* 42 (3): 347–354. https://pmc.ncbi.nlm.nih.gov/articles/PMC5587106/.

Salimpoor, Valorie N., Mitchel Benovoy, Kevin Larcher, Alain Dagher, and Robert J. Zatorre. 2011. "Anatomically Distinct Dopamine Release During Anticipation and Experience of Peak Emotion to Music." *Nature Neuroscience* 14 (2): 257–262. https://doi.org/10.1038/nn.2726.

Udemy. 2018. *Workplace Distraction Report*. Udemy for Business Research. https://research.udemy.com/wp-content/uploads/2018/03/Workplace-Distraction-Report-2018-2021-Rebrand-v3-gs.pdf.

World Health Organization. 2019a. *Burn-Out: An Occupational Phenomenon–International Classification of Diseases*. https://www.who.int/news/item/28-05-2019-burn-out-an-occupational-phenomenon-international-classification-of-diseases.

## Chapter 7: Music, Energy, Movement, and Motivation

Ferreri, Laura and Laura Verga. 2016. "Benefits of Music on Verbal Learning and Memory." *Music Perception* 34 (2): 167–182. https://doi.org/10.1525/mp.2.16.34.2.167.

Haake, A. Brett. 2011. "Individual Music Listening in Workplace Settings: An Exploratory Survey of Offices in the UK." *Musicae Scientiae* 15 (1): 107–129. https://doi.org/10.1177/1029864911398065.

Karageorghis, Costas I. and Lee Jones. 2009. "Effects of Music Tempo upon Submaximal Cycling Performance." *Scandinavian Journal of Medicine & Science in Sports* 19 (5): 664–673. https://doi.org/10.1111/j.1600-0838.2009.00948.x.

Lesiuk, Teresa. 2005. "The Effect of Music Listening on Work Performance." *Psychology of Music* 33 (2): 173–191. https://doi.org/10.1177/0305735605050650.

Moessinger, Michele, Ralf Stürmer, and Markus Mühlensiep. 2021. "Acoustic Brain Entrainment as a Countermeasure Against Fatigue." *Frontiers in Human Neuroscience* 14: 779980. https://pmc.ncbi.nlm.nih.gov/articles/PMC7799808/.

Snyder, Kristine L., Mark Snaterse, and J. Maxwell Donelan. 2012. "Running Perturbations Reveal General Strategies for Step Frequency Selection." *Journal of Applied Physiology* 112 (3): 435–445. https://journals.physiology.org/doi/full/10.1152/japplphysiol.01156.2011.

Tian, Shanshan, Qianwen Wang, Tingfang Wu, Suhua Chang, Wenwen Dun, Ling Zhang, Anning Li, and Gang Wang. 2025. "Healthy Lifestyle and Risk of Incidence, Mortality and Life Expectancy of Mental Disorders." *Journal of Affective Disorders* 388: 119592. https://doi.org/10.1016/j.jad.2025.119592.

World Health Organization. 2024b. "Physical Activity: Fact Sheet." Accessed 2025. https://www.who.int/news-room/fact-sheets/detail/physical-activity.

## Chapter 8: Music, Pain, and Physical Healing

Bantick, Stephen J., Richard G. Wise, Alexander Ploghaus, Sarah Clare, Stephen M. Smith, and Irene Tracey. 2002. "Imaging How Attention Modulates Pain in Humans Using Functional MRI." *Brain* 125 (2): 310–319. https://doi.org/10.1093/brain/awf022.

Bradt, Joke, Cheryl Dileo, and Nicholas Potvin. 2021. "Music Interventions for Pain in Adults." *Cochrane Database of Systematic Reviews* (8): CD004843. https://doi.org/10.1002/14651858.CD004843.pub4.

Breivik, Harald, Berit Collett, Vittorio Ventafridda, Richard Cohen, and Derek Gallacher. 2006. "Survey of Chronic Pain in Europe: Prevalence, Impact on Daily Life, and Treatment." *European Journal of Pain* 10 (4): 287–333. https://doi.org/10.1016/j.ejpain.2005.06.009.

Cleveland Clinic. 2021. "Endorphins: Your Body's Natural Pain Relievers." https://my.clevelandclinic.org/health/body/23040-endorphins.

Dahlhamer, James, Jon Lucas, Carla Zelaya, Richard Nahin, Sean Mackey, Lynn DeBar, Robert Kerns, Michael Von Korff, Laura Porter, and Charles Helmick. 2018. "Prevalence of Chronic Pain and High-Impact Chronic Pain Among Adults – United States, 2016." *MMWR* 67 (36): 1001–1006. https://doi.org/10.15585/mmwr.mm6736a2.

Gutgsell, Kelly J., Maria Schluchter, Susan Margevicius, Paul A. DeGolia, Beth McLaughlin, Melissa Harris, and John Mecklenburg. 2013. "Music Therapy Reduces Pain in Palliative Care Patients: A Randomized Controlled Trial." *Journal of Pain and Symptom Management* 45 (5): 822–831. https://doi.org/10.1016/j.jpainsymman.2012.05.008.

Health and Safety Executive. 2021. *Work-Related Musculoskeletal Disorders Statistics in Great Britain 2021*. https://www.hse.gov.uk/statistics/causdis/musculoskeletal.pdf.

Hilliard, Russel E. 2005. "Music Therapy in Hospice and Palliative Care: A Review of the Empirical Data." *Evidence-Based Complementary and Alternative Medicine* 2 (2): 173–178. https://doi.org/10.1093/ecam/neh076.

Hole, Jenny, Martin Hirsch, Elizabeth Ball, and Catherine Meads. 2015. "Music as an Aid for Postoperative Recovery in Adults: A Systematic Review and Meta-Analysis." *The Lancet* 386 (10004): 1659–1671. https://doi.org/10.1016/S0140-6736(15)60169-6.

Institute for Health Metrics and Evaluation. 2023. The Global Burden of Disease Study. https://ghdx.healthdata.org/gbd-2023.

Institute of Medicine. 2011. *Relieving Pain in America: A Blueprint for Transforming Prevention, Care, Education, and Research*. Washington, DC: National Academies Press. https://doi.org/10.17226/13172.

International Federation of the Phonographic Industry (IFPI). 2023. *Engaging with Music 2023*. London: IFPI.

Janata, Petr. 2009. "The Neural Architecture of Music-Evoked Autobiographical Memories." *Cerebral Cortex* 19 (11): 2579–2594. https://doi.org/10.1093/cercor/bhp008.

Martin-Saavedra, Juan S., Laura D. Vergara-Mendez, and Claudia Talero-Gutierrez. 2018. "Music Is an Effective Intervention for the Management of Pain: An Umbrella Review." *Complementary Therapies in Clinical Practice* 32: 103–114. https://doi.org/10.1016/j.ctcp.2018.06.003.

McEwen, Bruce S. 2007. "Physiology and Neurobiology of Stress and Adaptation: Central Role of the Brain." *Physiological Reviews* 87 (3): 873–904. https://doi.org/10.1152/physrev.00041.2006.

Nguyen, Thanh Nhan, Stefan Nilsson, Anna-Lena Hellström, and Ann Bengtson. 2010. "Music Therapy to Reduce Pain and Anxiety in Children with Cancer Undergoing Lumbar Puncture: A Randomized Clinical Trial." *Journal of Pediatric Oncology Nursing* 27 (3): 146–155. https://doi.org/10.1177/1043454209355983.

NorthShore University HealthSystem. 2020. "9 Health Benefits of Music." https://www.northshore.org/healthy-you/9-health-benefits-of-music.

Uggla, Lena, Lars Ole Bonde, Britt-Marie Svahn, Mattias Remberger, Björn Wrangsjö, and Britt Gustafsson. 2016. "Music Therapy Can Lower the Heart Rates of Severely Sick Children." *Acta Paediatrica* 105 (10): 1225–1230. https://doi.org/10.1111/apa.13452.

Volkow, Nora D. and A. Thomas McLellan. 2016. "The Evolving Opioid Epidemic: A Public Health Challenge." *New England Journal of Medicine* 375 (9): 810–813. https://doi.org/10.1056/NEJMp1604412.

## Chapter 9: Music, Sadness, and Emotional Healing

Baker, Felicity A., Olivia Metcalf, Tracey Varker, and Meaghan O'Donnell. 2018. "A Systematic Review of the Effectiveness of Creative Arts Interventions for Adults with PTSD." *Psychological Trauma: Theory, Research, Practice, and Policy* 10 (6): 643–651. https://doi.org/10.1037/tra0000353.

Butler, Emily A., Boris Egloff, Frank H. Wilhelm, Neal C. Smith, Elizabeth A. Erickson, and James J. Gross. 2003. "The Social Consequences of Expressive Suppression." *Emotion* 3 (1): 48–67. https://doi.org/10.1037/1528-3542.3.1.48.

Ferreri, Laura, Ernest Mas-Herrero, Robert J. Zatorre, Pablo Ripollés, Jordi Gomez-Andres, Eva Alicart, Joan Serra-Grabulosa, and Josep Marco-Pallarés. 2019. "Dopamine Modulates the Reward Experiences Elicited by Music." *Proceedings of the National Academy of Sciences* 116 (9): 3793–3798.

Gross, James J. and Robert W. Levenson. 1997. "Hiding Feelings: The Acute Effects of Inhibiting Negative and Positive Emotion." *Journal of Abnormal Psychology* 106 (1): 95–103. https://doi.org/10.1037/0021-843X.106.1.95.

Lazarus, Richard S., and Susan Folkman. 1984. *Stress, Appraisal, and Coping.* New York: Springer.

Sachs, Matthew E., Assal Habibi, and Antonio Damasio. 2020. "Sad Music as a Means for Emotional Expression and Regulation." *Frontiers in Psychology* 11: 555.

## Chapter 10: Music and Memory


AARP and Global Council on Brain Health. 2023. *The Brain Health and Music Report*. Washington, DC: AARP Research Center. https://www.aarp.org/health/brain-health/global-council-on-brain-health/music/.

Altenmüller, Eckart and Gottfried Schlaug. 2015. "Apollo's Gift: New Aspects of Neurologic Music Therapy." *Progress in Brain Research* 217: 237–252. https://doi.org/10.1016/bs.pbr.2014.11.029.

Baddeley, Alan D. 2003. "Working Memory: Looking Back and Looking Forward." *Nature Reviews Neuroscience* 4 (10): 829–839. https://doi.org/10.1038/nrn1201.

Juslin, Patrik N. and Daniel Västfjäll. 2008. "Emotional Responses to Music: The Need to Consider Underlying Mechanisms." *Behavioral and Brain Sciences* 31 (5):559–621.https://doi.org/10.1017/S0140525X08005293.

Levitin, Daniel J. 2024. *Music as Medicine: The Science and Secrets of Healing with Sound*. New York: Penguin Random House.

Sacks, Oliver. 2007. *Musicophilia: Tales of Music and the Brain*. New York: Alfred A. Knopf.

Särkämö, Teppo, Mari Tervaniemi, and Minna Huotilainen. 2014. "Music-Based Interventions in Neurological Rehabilitation: From Clinical Practice to Scientific Evidence." *Annals of the New York Academy of Sciences* 1337 (1): 252–261. https://doi.org/10.1016/s1474-4422(17)30168-0.

Thompson, Grace, Bonnie McKenzie, and Josephine Tomlinson. 2024. "How and Why Music Therapy Reduces Distress and Improves Well-Being in Advanced Dementia Care: A Realist Review." *Nature Mental Health* 2 (4): 342–355. https://doi.org/10.1038/s44220-024-00342-x.

Wan, Catherine Y. and Gottfried Schlaug. 2010. "Music Making as a Tool for Promoting Brain Plasticity Across the Life Span." *The Neuroscientist* 16 (5): 566–577. https://doi.org/10.1177/1073858410377805.

World Health Organization. 2019. *What Is the Evidence on the Role of the Arts in Improving Health and Well-Being? A Scoping Review*. Copenhagen: WHO Regional Office for Europe. https://www.who.int/publications/i/item/what-is-the-evidence-on-the-role-of-the-arts-in-improving-health-and-well-being-a-scoping-review.

Zatorre, Robert J. and Valorie N. Salimpoor. 2013. "From Perception to Pleasure: Music and Its Neural Substrates." *Proceedings of the National Academy of Sciences* 110 (Supplement 2): 10430–10437. https://www.pnas.org/doi/abs/10.1073/pnas.1301228110.

## Chapter 11: Music and Neurodivergence

British Dyslexia Association. 2024. *Adult ADHD: Not Just a Trend.* https://www.bda.uk.com/resource/adult-adhd-not-just-a-trend.html.

EurekAlert. 2024. "New Study Reveals 90% of Autistic Adults over 40 Remain Undiagnosed." https://www.eurekalert.org/news-releases/1096116.

Grahn, Jessica A. and Matthew Brett. 2007. "Rhythm and Beat Perception in Motor Areas of the Brain." *Journal of Cognitive Neuroscience* 19 (5): 893–906. https://doi.org/10.1162/jocn.2007.19.5.893.

NHS Digital. 2025. *MI ADHD: Monthly Statistics – May 2025.* https://digital.nhs.uk/data-and-information/publications/statistical/mi-adhd/may-2025.

NPR. 2014. "Interview: Pharrell Williams on Synaesthesia and Creativity." *NPR Music.* https://www.npr.org/sections/allsongs/2014/11/12/pharrell-williams-on-synesthesia.

Russell, Ginny, Sally Stapley, Tamsin Newlove-Delgado, Andrew Salmon, Rhianna White, Fiona Warren, Anita Pearson, and Tamsin Ford. 2021. "Time Trends in Autism Diagnosis over 20 Years: Population-Based Cohort Study in the UK." *BMJ Open* 11: e045387. https://pubmed.ncbi.nlm.nih.gov/34414570.

Thaut, Michael H. and Volker Hoemberg, eds. 2014. *Handbook of Neurologic Music Therapy.* Oxford: Oxford University Press.

University College London (UCL). 2023. "Significant Rise in ADHD Diagnoses in the UK over 20 Years." https://www.ucl.ac.uk/news/2023/jul/significant-rise-adhd-diagnoses-uk.

## Chapter 12: Music and Anxiety

National Health Service Digital. 2023. *Adult Psychiatric Morbidity Survey: Mental Health, Wellbeing, and Anxiety Prevalence in England.* London: NHS Digital. https://digital.nhs.uk/data-and-information/publications/statistical/adult-psychiatric-morbidity-survey/survey-of-mental-health-and-wellbeing-england-2023-24.

Soroka, Stuart, Patrick Fournier, and Lilach Nir. 2019. "Cross-National Evidence of a Negativity Bias in Psychophysiological Reactions to News." *Proceedings of the National Academy of Sciences* 116 (38): 18888–18892. https://doi.org/10.1073/pnas.1908369116.

World Health Organization. 2023. *Mental Health and Substance Use: Anxiety Disorders Fact Sheet*. Geneva: WHO. https://www.who.int/news-room/fact-sheets/detail/anxiety-disorders.

## Chapter 16: Music in Community: Culture, Connection, and Collective Healing

Cross, Ian. 2003. "Music, Cognition, Culture, and Evolution." In *The Cognitive Neuroscience of Music*, edited by Isabelle Peretz and Robert J. Zatorre, 42–56. Oxford: Oxford University Press.

Mithen, Steven. 2005. *The Singing Neanderthals: The Origins of Music, Language, Mind, and Body*. London: Weidenfeld & Nicolson.

## Chapter 18: Music Therapy and Clinical Insight

Aalbers, Sonja, Laura Fusar-Poli, Ruth E. Freeman, Marinus Spreen, Johannes Cf Ket, Annemiek C. Vink, Anna Maratos, Mike Crawford, Xi-Jing Chen, and Christian Gold. 2017. "Music Therapy for Depression." *Cochrane Database of Systematic Reviews* 11: CD004517.

Baird, Amee and Séverine Samson. 2015. "Music and Dementia." *Progress in Brain Research* 217: 207–235.

Thaut, Michael H., Gerald C. McIntosh, Robert R. Rice, Ronald A. Miller, Joseph Rathbun, and James M. Brault. 1996. "Rhythmic Auditory Stimulation in Gait Training for Parkinson's Disease Patients." *Movement Disorders* 11 (2): 193–200. https://doi.org/10.1002/mds.870110.13.

# Acknowledgments

This book would exist, but it would not be as human without the generosity, openness, and time of the many guests who contributed through interviews in Part III. These conversations were one of the most enjoyable and meaningful parts of writing *Music Is the Answer*, and I am deeply grateful to everyone who trusted me with their stories, reflections, and experiences of music. My thanks to Catherine (The Autistic Raver), Aldo, Mark, Gabby, Tim, Sarah, Russell, Dr. Hazel, Phillipa, and DJ Paulette for the honesty, insight, and humanity they brought to this book.

Deep thanks go to my wife, Mary, for giving me the time and space to write this book. Thank you to Craig and Smithy for their ongoing support and belief in this project, especially during the moments when belief mattered most.

I am also grateful to my therapist, Lucy, whose work with me helped me find the self-belief to call myself an author and see this book through to completion.

Thank you to everyone who has ever booked me to perform at their event or venue. Playing music for others to enjoy is my happy place, and those shared moments on dance floors, in rooms, and across sound systems have shaped both this book and the person who wrote it.

Finally, my thanks to the team at Wiley – Brian, Michael, Pinky, and my developmental editor, Kelly – for their guidance, care, and support in bringing this book into the world.

I also want to acknowledge the musicians and producers whose work enriches our lives every day. Their craft carries feeling across time, place, and circumstance, often without recognition. This book exists – and so does the opportunity for all of us to improve our well-being – because of the power of music and the people who create it.

# About the Author

**Rob Stephenson** is a well-being practitioner and working DJ who believes that music may be the most powerful thing humans have ever invented. Acknowledging his own ongoing mental health challenges, he writes and works from the perspective of someone who is thriving most of the time, not because life is optimized, but because it is intentionally supported.

Professionally, Rob works with leaders and organizations across corporate, public, and creative sectors to improve workplace well-being and sustainable performance through keynote talks, workshops, and music-led experiences that bridge science, storytelling, and lived experience. He is the founder of Wellbeing Foundations, a practical framework that helps individuals and teams build small, high-impact well-being habits into everyday working life.

Alongside his consultancy and speaking work, Rob is an active DJ and music curator, performing live as Robbie J and integrating music into his well-being practice as both a tool for regulation and a source of connection and meaning. His work sits at the intersection of leadership, mental health, and music, with a focus on helping people reconnect with feeling in a world that often prioritises productivity over humanity.

Rob is a TEDx speaker and previously authored *Be More Human: Practical Steps to Improve Your Wellbeing* (self-published, 2021). *Music Is the Answer* is his first major trade book.

# Index